Journeys That Opened up the World

I am so glad that
our journey intersected.

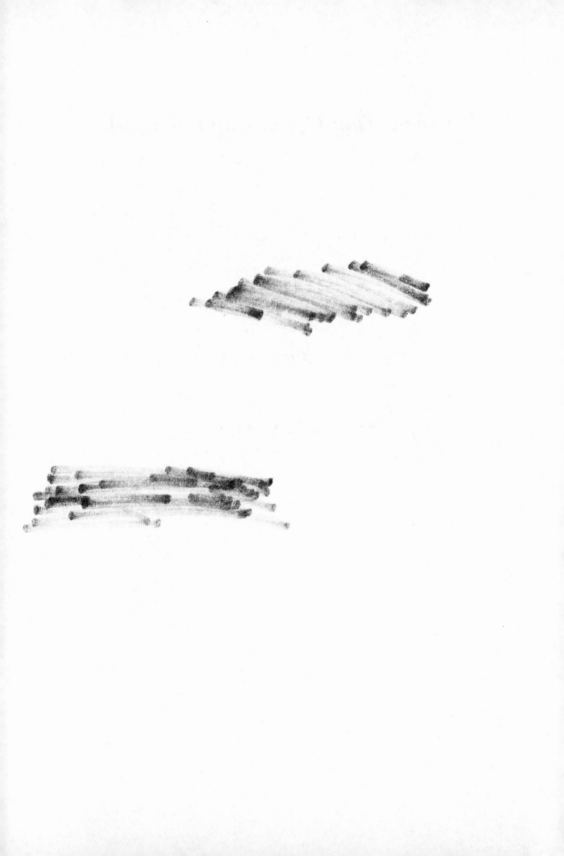

Journeys That Opened up the World

WOMEN, STUDENT CHRISTIAN MOVEMENTS, AND SOCIAL JUSTICE, 1955–1975

EDITED BY SARA M. EVANS

Rutgers University Press

New Brunswick, New Jersey, and London

Library of Congress Cataloging-in-Publication Data

Journeys that opened up the world : women, student Christian movements, and social justice, 1955–1975 / edited by Sara M. Evans.
    p. cm.
Includes bibliographical references and index.
    ISBN 0–8135–3313–9 (alk. paper) — ISBN 0–8135–3314–7 (pbk. : alk. paper)
1. Christian college students—United States—Societies, etc.—History—20th century.
2. Women social reformers—Religious life—United States—History—20th century.
3. Christianity and justice—United States—History—20th century. I. Evans, Sara M. (Sara Margaret), 1943–
    BV970.A1J68 2003
    267'.61—dc21

                                                     2003000308

British Cataloging-in-Publication information is available from the British Library

Manufactured in the United States of America

To Ruth Harris,
whose inspiration and dedication made all our stories possible

CONTENTS

ACKNOWLEDGMENTS

Journeys That Opened up the World has been a labor of love for many years. We are especially grateful to the World Student Christian Foundation Board of Trustees for their financial support and administrative and fiscal assistance in the course of this project. Through them we received grants from Campus Ministry Women, the Sister Fund, the United Church Board for Homeland Ministry, Women's Division of the United Methodist Board of Global Ministries, and United Ministries in Higher Education. We also received support from the University of Minnesota Graduate School and the Center for Women's Global Leadership at Rutgers. These made it possible for us to meet in person and by conference call, and to have access to editorial and staff support that made it much easier to bring this project to fruition. Ruth Harris's role as organizer and cheerleader made this happen. The core group—Ruth, elmira Kendricks Nazombe, Jan Griesinger, Charlotte Bunch, and Jill Hultin—has consulted regularly, met several times, and collectively framed our approach to the project. Helen Ewer and Karen Bloomquist, both leaders in Campus Ministry Women in the 1970s, attended the initial consultation that formed the spirit of this project. They played an important role in helping us to recall these stories.

In 1998–99, Katherine Meerse served as a research assistant through a grant from the University of Minnesota. She devoted hours to correspondence and editing, becoming deeply attached to the project in the process. In the final phase of gathering manuscripts and communicating with authors, Jill Hultin generously served as a key node in our communications network. Cheri Register's contribution is imbedded in every chapter. Drawing on her skills as a memoirist, writing teacher, and freelance editor, her editing made each contribution clearer and smoother while respecting the individuality of each voice.

Two of the women in this book are no longer with us. Valerie Russell was too ill to attend the initial consultation, though she sent words of support and encouragement. To our great sorrow, she died in 1997. Because of her centrality to the events in these chapters, we asked her dear friend and colleague Letty Russell to evoke her spirit for this volume. Rebecca Owen died in 2002 but not before completing her chapter with the assistance of her daughter, Melinda van Dalen. Their loss reinforces our awareness that memory can be ephemeral unless the heritage is passed on. Though each of us has discovered in this process that our own stories take on new meaning now that they are in conversation with all of the others, this book can only hint at the hundreds of stories still waiting to be told. With gratitude and love we now send these memoirs out in the hope that the storytelling will go on and on.

Journeys That Opened up the World

Introduction

Sara M. Evans

*F*or thousands of young women in the
1950s and 1960s, involvement with the student Christian movement (SCM)—
comprising denominational campus ministries, the Student YM and YWCA,
and national and international associations such as the World Student Christian Federation—changed their world and their worldview. It took them out
of the context in which they were raised and introduced them to radically
different perspectives in other parts of the country and around the globe. It
also opened them up to their own capacities. As leaders, as thinkers, as organizers, they came face to face with social realities like racial prejudice, poverty, and oppression and with the possibility of action. A primary site of civil
rights and student activism in the 1960s, the SCM trained a remarkable generation of leaders who moved directly into the civil rights movement, the student antiwar movement, and women's liberation.[1] For women in particular,
the SCM was a unique training ground that offered both female mentors and
a greater openness to female leadership than its secular counterparts in the
student new left. This collection of memoirs brings to life the experience of
a critical generation of young women and a dimension of the social justice
activism of the 1960s and 1970s that has been almost invisible until now, despite its deep roots in American history and the large numbers of American
youth that it engaged from the early years of the cold war.

*T*hat religious engagement offered American women an unusually free space
in which to develop leadership skills and a broad vision of their potential to
shape history in the cold war era should not surprise us. Historically, women's
rights in the United States have deep roots in evangelical reform movements.

1

In the nineteenth century, evangelical Protestantism in the Second Great Awakening made it possible for women to forge new public spaces and to develop the skills of civic participation even at a time when they were formally barred from most aspects of public life, including voting, serving on juries, and practicing most professions. Religion, as an arena for emotion, nurture, and conscience—and like the women who were culturally defined by these same qualities—was forced to the margins of an aggressively competitive economic system and an emerging scientific worldview. Within the feminized spaces of evangelical reform, women and their male allies developed a moral critique of the cruelty of human slavery and the crushing injustices of nineteenth-century capitalism.

In the 1830s, for example, Sarah and Angelina Grimke, Quakers raised in a South Carolina slaveholding family, began to make public presentations exposing the brutality and inhumanity of human slavery. The women to whom they spoke were already accustomed to working for evangelical reforms such as temperance, peace, and abolition. But as the Grimkes discovered, in order to speak out against the "sin of slavery," they had to defend their right to participate in public discourse against those—including many clergy—who claimed that women belonged only in the home. Schooled in a biblical idiom and accustomed to inspiring women to activity by drawing on strong female figures from the Scriptures, they refused to cede any religious sanction for male domination. Responding to clerical criticism, Sarah Grimke cited chapter and verse to prove that Jesus never set different moral standards for men and women. Rather "Men and women were CREATED EQUAL; they are both moral and accountable beings and whatever is *right* for a man to do, is *right* for a woman to do." For several decades, thousands of women followed in the Grimkes' footsteps to work actively for the end of slavery and for the cause of temperance. As they did so, they developed critical public skills—speaking, organizing door-to-door petition campaigns, raising funds, and lobbying legislatures. With new skills and a deep sense of mission, they began to claim the rights of citizenship and civic participation for themselves.

The first women's rights convention in 1848 shifted Sarah Grimke's assertion of moral equality to the civic realm, revising the Declaration of Independence to read, "We hold these truths to be self-evident that all men and women are created equal." The growth of the movement for woman suffrage in the late nineteenth century drew heavily on the organizing experiences of women in the Women's Christian Temperance Union and the settlement house movement. Thus the movement for woman suffrage was the daughter of evangelical reform.[2]

By the middle of the twentieth century American women faced a reassertion of "separate spheres" ideology. Cold war culture assumed that adult women's most appropriate roles were entirely domestic, though women had extended their familial responsibilities into an extensive range of volunteer activities and a growing involvement in feminized sectors of the labor force. Young women coming of age in the 1950s—especially the thousands who flooded into colleges and universities—received contradictory messages about their own potential. On the one hand, as students they learned professional skills. On the other, popular culture surrounded them with injunctions to subordinate their future aspirations. There were jokes about "senior panic" among fourth-year female students who lacked marital prospects and about the graduate degree especially for women, the "PHT" (putting hubby through).

Thus there are strong historical parallels to the role of the student Christian movement in the 1950s and 1960s as it provided women with opportunities to develop leadership skills and a vision of justice. Although the SCM—with the striking exception of the YWCA—was, like its church sponsors, male dominated, it nonetheless harbored an array of talented women in key leadership positions. They were frequently behind the scenes in staff positions: Ruth Harris (chapter 1) with the Student Volunteer Movement (SVM) and the Methodist Student Movement; Margaret Flory in the Presbyterian Church organizing travel seminars and the Frontier Intern program; Peggy Billings, secretary for race relations of the Methodist Church's Women's Division; Margaret (Peg) Rigg, art editor of *motive* magazine; Jeanne Audrey Powers (chapter 2), Nancy Richardson (chapter 12), and Jan Griesinger (chapter 10) staffing local campus ministries and YWCAs; Valerie Russell (chapter 13) and Dorothy Height in the YWCA, where they mentored young militants and worked to place the issue of race at the center of the Y's mission. Feminists before their time, they reached out to young women, offering new experiences and pushing them to take responsibility and lead. These women had access to institutional resources, which they used actively and consciously to open new possibilities for young people and nourish their leadership capabilities. Their mentoring enabled untold numbers to respond to the sudden emergence of women's liberation with "of course."

And yet those not in the all-female environment of the YWCA experienced years of marginalization and silencing. Ruth describes her shock in the 1970s when she looked back at the all-male programs of the huge conferences she helped to organize in the 1950s. Jeanne Audrey's lesbianism remained a closeted secret with the potential to cost her not only her job but also her ordination until she made a public announcement in 1994 shortly before retiring. Alice Hageman (chapter 9) and Sheila McCurdy (chapter 8) attended seminary but did not seek ordination for many years because the very idea of a "female minister" was an oxymoron. Once the thought was there, however, they led the way not only in ministry but also in articulating feminist theological perspectives. In many ways they retraced a twentieth-century version of their foremothers in the abolition movement and the Women's Christian temperance movement; most especially they walked in the footsteps of suffrage leader Elizabeth Cady Stanton, whose *Woman's Bible* so scandalized her contemporaries in the 1890s.

The Protestant student movement had its roots in the late nineteenth century with the creation of the Young Men's and Young Women's Christian Associations (YMCA and YWCA). The YWCA set out to serve the needs of young working women (providing housing and "wholesome" recreation) and with the YMCA created an array of collegiate student services ranging from housing to freshman orientation. In the years after World War I, many denominations—including not only mainline Protestant denominations but also Roman Catholics (Newman Centers) and Jews (Hillel)—began to invest in campus-based ministries, sometimes providing physical facilities and staff to organize student worship services, reading groups, service projects, and travel seminars. This infrastructure provided resources, mentors, and leadership opportunities to several generations of college students in the United States. For Protestants, it was linked to the World Student Christian Federation (WSCF), with its many national student organizations and its connections to the World Council of Churches headquartered in Geneva, Switzerland. Participants in all of the groups with links to the WSCF, and especially their leaders, referred to themselves as the student Christian movement, though most entered it through the doors of a particular denomination. This loosely defined "movement" became more coherent in the early years of the cold war (1950s and 1960s) before dissipating in the 1970s, but its legacy remains a powerful part of the story of the many movements for social justice that emerged in those same years.

In the decades after World War II, the SCM became a vehicle for the postwar generation's search for meaning and authenticity. Students avidly read theologians like Dietrich Bonhoeffer, whose courageous resistance to the evil of fascism led to imprisonment and hanging by the Nazis. Gripped by the need to find a language for religion in a world torn by cold war and the threat of nuclear annihilation, students devoured both secular existentialists like Jean-Paul Sartre and Albert Camus and Christian existentialists like Søren

Kierkegaard and Paul Tillich. Tillich offered new ways of imagining God as the "ground of being," and challenged Christians to overcome the estrangement from God and the anxiety characteristic of modern life by having—as one of his book titles said—*The Courage to Be*. A life of religious commitment and action in solidarity with those who suffer was a deeply compelling vision for youth in the SCM.

Beginning in the late 1930s, each year thousands of students gathered somewhere in the Midwest for several days after Christmas at national conferences under the auspices (on a rotating basis) of the Student Volunteer Movement, various Protestant denominations, and the Student YW and YMCA. With the international student meeting in 1955 in Athens, Ohio, which challenged American cold war culture head-on, these conferences became huge, life-changing events. At these events the SCM became visible to itself as a movement intensely focused on faith and action in a world fraught with economic and racial injustice. Barely noticed in the mainstream press, these gatherings live on in the memories of participants as turning points in their lives. A few key examples illustrate how this was so.

At the height of the cold war, 3,500 students from eighty nations gathered on December 28, 1955, in Athens, Ohio, for the seventeenth quadrennial conference of the Student Volunteer Movement. Primarily Protestant Christians, the sixty religious groups represented also included Roman Catholics, Buddhists, Hindus, and Muslims. Whereas American leaders emphasized the importance of opposing communism throughout the third world, students in Athens spent six days of intense discussion on the conference theme, "Revolution and Reconciliation." Indeed, they learned that revolutionary ferment in the world was caused less by communist agitation than by a negative response to the imposition of American culture. They wrestled with the failure of American society to live up to its own democratic ideals and moved quickly to hold churches responsible for change: "A primary task of the church in the modern world is to smash the barriers of racial segregation and prejudice everywhere" read the lead sentence in one report in the *New York Times*.[3] Ruth Harris, as field program director of the Student Volunteer Movement, was a key organizer of this conference. Ruth had witnessed the Chinese Revolution in 1949 as a missionary and deeply appreciated the yearnings for liberation of colonized people around the world. Forced to leave China, she joined the staff of the Student Volunteer Movement, where she bent the resources of her office to make it possible for thousands of American youth to have experiences that could bypass the stereotypes of the cold war and open them up to new realities. The Athens conference reflected her vision.

From that point on, the social justice issue that gripped participants in the SCM was civil rights, and virtually every quadrennial conference in the late fifties and early sixties featured speakers like Martin Luther King, Jr., James Lawson, and Fannie Lou Hamer from the civil rights movement. The meetings boiled with urgency about the necessity of addressing racism and supporting the movement in the South. For example, students at University of Texas returned from the National Student Assembly of the YM-YWCA quadrennial gathering in 1958 at the University of Illinois at Urbana and initiated a series of sit-ins in downtown Austin, almost a year before the famous sit-ins in Greensboro that are seen as the spark to the civil rights movement of the 1960s.[4]

Even more striking was the impact of the 1959 Eighteenth Ecumenical Student Conference at Athens, Ohio. Ruth, again, was one of the planners of the gathering, organized around the theme of "Inquiry and Involvement on Strategic Frontiers," and she worked hard to ensure not only international diversity but also racial diversity among the American students. Anticolonialism and race wove through the frontiers identified as conference subthemes: new nationalisms in Africa and Asia, race relations, militant non-Christian faiths. The implicit self-critique of the church became explicit in a session that advocated a new approach to missions in which "the missionary must atone for his own sins and for centuries of exploitation and injustice wrought by the West." Prominent speakers, including Martin Luther King, Jr., addressed 3,609 students, 1,010 of whom were from seventy-seven countries outside the United States (including 397 from Asia, 109 from Africa). Forums followed these lectures on topics such as international politics, industrialization, exploding populations and birth control, education, and Christian faith. Evening firesides continued these discussions into the night. Throughout the conference there was a strong emphasis on action. The conference newspaper editorialized, "Each of us must create for himself the bridge whereby his faith can lead to works."[5] When the sit-in movement erupted just a month later, students who had attended the Athens conference could be found participating across the country.

A New England campus minister wrote later, "each time there was a large national conference, we would organize buses and trains from New England, picking up people along the way from Maine to Boston, and then travel out to the Midwest, sometimes with as many as two train coaches full of students and local staff and advisors. Those were great experiences for all of us. . . . These involvements and relationships were with all kinds of students over these years: black, white, Asian American, Latin American, Native

American and others. We were all persons of faith in search of common answers and a quality of liberated life that was faithful before God. We sought
social justice, growth, and affirmation for all persons."[6]

Campus SCM groups soon worked closely with civil rights groups to
provide support and volunteers. The YWCA sponsored a dozen voter registration projects in the South. An ecumenical group in New England initiated
the Northern Student Movement that launched activist and volunteer projects
in minority communities across the country.[7]

Out of the 1959 Athens conference also came an idea for a new form
of overseas mission, Frontier Interns, who would go to live, work, and share
the struggle with people on strategic frontiers. Under the direction of Margaret Flory, Student World Relations staff of the United Presbyterian Ecumenical Commission, Frontier Interns were commissioned to work and study,
living at a subsistence level, where they could best come to understand the
underlying issues of race relations, new nationalisms, militant non-Christian
faiths, and technology. Three contributors to this volume served as Frontier
Interns: Tamela (Tami) Hultman (chapter 7), Alice Hageman, and elmira
Kendricks Nazombe (chapter 4). There were short-term experiences as well.
Local Ys and campus ministries offered hundreds of travel seminars to major cities. The national office of the Methodist Student Movement organized
annual weeklong Christian Citizenship Seminars, which brought students first
to the United Nations to learn about international issues like apartheid in
South Africa and then to Washington, D.C., where they talked with and lobbied policy leaders and legislators. Seminars on South Africa and Latin
America sparked organized study/travel seminars to those parts of the world.
Ruth Harris, Jill Foreman Hultin (chapter 5), and elmira Kendricks Nazombe
describe their powerful experience in 1964 when they visited a number of
Latin American countries to learn about their social realities, the causes of
injustice, and the role of the church.

By the late sixties, the student Christian movement suffered from the
same disintegrative forces that were undermining most activist organizations.
In the firestorm of radical activism, the SCM tried to create its own utopian,
activist, ecumenical structure, the University Christian Movement (UCM), of
which Charlotte Bunch (chapter 6) was the first president. UCM sought to
realize the ecumenical dream by abolishing denominational distinctions and
supporting a radical, social justice activism on campuses and beyond. By
1969, however, the UCM had self-destructed, torn from within by compet-
ing radicalisms and from without by diminishing institutional support. The
late sixties were an apocalyptic time for most activists. The massive antiwar

movement grew from demonstration to demonstration and yet the war continued. The civil rights movement shifted from a religiously rooted non-violent struggle for integration to a separatist, black power movement that flirted with violence and envisioned imminent revolution. Churches previously willing to support their own institutional campus outreach and to tolerate the youthful agitation it unleashed were increasingly reluctant to support an ecumenical effort with such radical overtones. And, like other organizations of the time, UCM found it impossible to sustain itself as an interracial movement. It died at about the same time that other national new left organizations like Students for a Democratic Society (SDS) and the Student Nonviolent Coordinating Committee (SNCC) were also disintegrating.

Yet even as those in the UCM agonized over the loss of a part of their dream, young women in the YWCA were able to engage in genuine interracial coalition building. Renetia Martin (chapter 14), Margarita Mendoza de Sugiyama (chapter 16), and Frances Kendall (chapter 15) were a couple of student generations younger than the founders of the UCM. They came of age in a time of extreme racial polarization and found in the YWCA an environment that encouraged their leadership, offered them a powerful interracial group of mentors, and allowed them to place the struggle against racism at the forefront of an all-women's organization. Black women in the YWCA, under the leadership of Dorothy Height and Valerie Russell, were already wrestling with the meaning of black power, and they organized a separate meeting prior to the YWCA National Convention in Houston in April 1970. Young women also held a separate meeting, and Renetia—chair of the National Student YWCA and therefore a leader in both—became a pivotal figure in pushing adult blacks toward militance while winning the active support of young women of all colors. When the formal conference opened, 2,700 women of "all kinds, all ages, all shapes, all sizes" met in a hall hung with banners "for peace, for justice, for freedom, for dignity." Young women (aged 17–35) declared their activism and their discomfort with religious labels, naming themselves Young Women Committed to Action. All five hundred black delegates stood as their report was read demanding that the fight against racism become the singular focus of the YWCA. In response the convention adopted the One Imperative: "To thrust our collective power toward the elimination of racism wherever it exists and by any means necessary." Everyone present still remembers slender, militant young Renetia Martin pronouncing her benediction: "In the name of Malcolm, Martin, and Jesus—Power to the struggle."[8]

The driving force behind the telling of these stories is Ruth Harris, the former missionary to China in the 1940s who served as national staff for the Student Volunteer Movement for Christian Mission from 1954 to 1959 and secretary for student work of the Woman's Division of Christian Service of the Methodist Board of Missions in the 1960s. Ruth mentored generations of students, exposing them to international perspectives, liberation theology, and struggles for justice both at home and around the world. Just as she was settling into a well-deserved retirement, she became alarmed that the histories of the WSCF ignored the presence and achievements of women. Encouraged by the WSCF Trustees, Ruth went into action. She raised a bit of money, and called together a core planning group of women who had been student leaders in the 1960s (Charlotte Bunch, Jan Griesinger, Jill Hultin, and elmira Kendricks Nazombe) who then convened a consultation of fifteen women on May 3–5, 1996.

For three days we told each other our stories. We drew a timeline on which we marked major national and international events, SCM conferences, seminars, and activities, and events in our own lives. Then we paired up and interviewed each other to probe the life histories that brought us into this stream of activism. Among us were former presidents of the Methodist Student Movement, the Student YWCA, the National Student Christian Federation (a confederation of denominational student organizations), and the University Christian Movement. We also had key staff people in campus ministries at both the local and the national level. Our intersecting and overlapping stories brought gales of laughter, tears of remembrance, and gasps of surprise as we realized not only how much we had forgotten but how much we never knew—each in her own niche.

Together these stories underlined the importance of a subversive thread within mainstream Protestantism that nourished activism and leadership—for some from early childhood, for all in college, and for a few throughout their lives. Most of us arrived on college campuses in the 1950s and 1960s to find an energetic, intellectually lively student Christian movement. We didn't think about the institutional investment involved in providing campus-based staff, national and international seminars and work camps, and massive conferences involving thousands of students from many nations as well as many denominations. We ignored the fact that most public leaders were men even as we took for granted the presence of numerous women in positions of institutional power who pushed and prodded and challenged us. Some of us found that the challenges shook us to our roots, forcing a confrontation between deeply held values of our Christian heritage and the realities of social injustice. Others were thrilled finally to have a language (existential theology, for the most part) that released us from attention to dogma and focused instead on action, on living a life in response to the injunction to "love thy neighbor."

The generational differences were striking. Ruth Harris (b. 1920) and Jeanne Audrey Powers (b. 1932) found professional employment in the church at a time when there were few other opportunities for ambitious women who wanted to make a difference in the world. They were a critical generation for those who followed. In their footsteps came Nancy Richardson, Jan Griesinger, Valerie Russell, and Eleanor Scott Meyers (chapter 11), who staffed campus ministries, taught at seminaries, and organized women inside and outside the church through the 1970s and beyond. Overlapping with the latter was a group of women for whom the SCM served as a training ground for leadership and activism on civil rights, women's rights, and global injustice. Rebecca Owen (chapter 3), Charlotte Bunch, elmira Nazombe, Jill Hultin, Tami Hultman, and Alice Hageman have each devoted their lives to the cause of social justice, and the roots of their commitment as well as their leadership lie in the SCM. Finally Renetia Martin, Frances Kendall, and Margarita Mendoza de Sugiyama describe the transformative community of students in the YWCA in the late 1960s and 1970s, where the difficult, painful, and exhilarating struggle to communicate across racial lines never ceased.

The group was amazed by the power of memory and by the grief of forgetting. In many instances we did not know each other's stories. No one had the larger picture that exists only when they are all told together. In an impromptu homily, Rebecca Owen reminded us that the word "remembering" relates to a Greek god whose body parts spread out across the whole earth. Literally, remembering is bringing scattered parts back together. We needed to do this for ourselves, for our own wholeness. But we also thought about future generations—whether literal or virtual daughters—and lamented the loss of the knowledge about the shoulders on which they stand. And so we committed ourselves to write a book.

Ultimately we came to believe that these stories teach important lessons about how a confluence of factors—family background, actions of religious institutions, political and social events in the broader society—combine to forge women leaders. It is time to break the cycle of silence that prevents new generations of women from learning from and building on the accomplishment as well as the frustrations and mistakes of those who preceded them. The community represented in this book offers a range of experiences by generation, by race, and by region. It is just a beginning, however, as these authors are here as the result of an overlapping set of personal networks rather than as a systematic collection of "representative" stories. Many of the linkages suggested here deserve further exploration and, it is our hope, many more memoirs to fill in the picture.

*A*s editor and historian, I am also a part of the "we" in this storytelling project, someone whose history intersects directly with some of these memoirs and indirectly with all the rest. Although my activism in the SCM was at the local, not the national and international, level, it had everything to do with my subsequent activism on race, labor, and feminist issues, and my work as a feminist historian. Virtually all of our stories begin with family and religion, and for those of us who grew up in the South, with race. Mine begins the year before my birth.

In July 1942 my father, Rev. J. Claude Evans, preached a sermon on race at the Washington Street Methodist Church in downtown Columbia, South Carolina. He was just twenty-five years old, in his first appointment as an associate pastor, and that Sunday he was filling in for the main minister who was on vacation. The gist of the sermon was based on Paul's admonition that "God has made all men [*sic*] of one blood to dwell on the face of the earth together in peace." Thinking he had found a biblically based solution to the "race problem," Daddy set out to show the congregation that a biological definition of race made no sense. After all, we are all literally "of one blood." There are no separate blood types for different races. He went on to challenge racially based ideas of intellectual or physical inferiority and to call for the United States—already at war with fascism—to live up to its democratic ideals by abolishing the white primary in southern states and admitting African Americans to full civic participation.

Daddy was naive, but not ignorant. He had grown up in Anderson, South Carolina, where his father managed a textile mill and ran a pharmacy. He was taught that segregation was right and natural but that "good people" did not use racial epithets or personally treat African Americans with disrespect. His sermon had been incubating for years, ever since as a seminary student he had been assigned to preach on the "colored ward" at Duke Hospital and had found, to his delight, that they "help you preach" with their "amens."

The morning Daddy preached happened to be the monthly "radio Sunday." Across the state, most white listeners were enraged at such a frontal assault on the ideological underpinnings of segregation. Liberals, of course, thrilled at the breaking of the taboo. When one of the dorm counselors at the

University of South Carolina, where Daddy had been doing outreach with college students, heard his voice and his topic, she raced up and down the hall knocking on doors and hollering, "turn on your radio." Within twenty-four hours the head minister had been called back from vacation; Daddy was interrogated by the board of the church, and they voted to bar him from the pulpit and to request that the South Carolina Conference reassign him to another church at its November meeting. Their mistake was not to suspend him from his youth work, for the college students spent the next four months in a running seminar on the issue of race. Then Daddy was sent to a remote church in a town that hadn't had a young preacher in so long they didn't care what he had done to get sent there. And that is why I was born in a Methodist parsonage in McCormick, South Carolina, late in 1943.

I discovered existential theology in high school as I hung out with my father (by then the campus chaplain at Southern Methodist University) when he attended gatherings of the Methodist Student Movement. For the first time I was not alone (the only kid on my South Carolina playground, for example, who thought the North *should* have won "the War," and the only one whose mother had warned me not to believe it when my schoolbooks said slavery was not the cause of the Civil War). When I arrived at Duke University in the fall of 1962, I found that the most stimulating groups on campus were the YWCA and a group called Lay Scholars at the Methodist Student Center. Both were suffused with an urgent search for meaning and for meaningful action. Because the Methodist Student Center was the organizing center for civil rights activism on campus, Sunday worship services were filled with joys and concerns about recent sit-in activity.

My story at Duke intertwines with those of Charlotte Bunch, Tami Hultman, and Nancy Richardson, who have also written for this volume. With Charlotte, my first demonstration was a "pray-in" at the First Baptist Church in Durham, and we each spent the summer of 1964 abroad—Africa in my case, laying bricks with Operation Crossroads Africa—returning fired with new zeal to work against imperialism and the war in Vietnam from our leadership positions in the campus YWCA. I did not become active at the state and national levels in the student Christian movement, but when Charlotte, Jill Hultin, and elmira Nazombe as members of the Methodist Student Movement National Council headed for Montgomery in March 1965 to work on preparations for the arrival of marchers from Selma, I hooked a ride with nine other Duke students who drove through the night to participate in the march.

Our stories do not all continue to run parallel. The contradiction between the lumbering institutional conservatism of the church, with its deeply imbedded sexism and racism, and the passion for justice it had awakened had very different consequences for the women in this book as for the thousands who shared similar experiences. Some, especially in the late 1960s, experienced a crisis of faith. Others continued the battle on the inside. The latter include people like Ruth and Jeanne Audrey, whose lives and livelihoods were imbedded in the work of the church; elmira Nazombe, for whom spirituality and church community are inseparable from her life as an African American woman; and Jan Griesinger and Sheila McCurdy, who fought for and found new opportunities for institutional leadership. For Charlotte Bunch and Jill Hultin, the demise of the University Christian Movement removed the structures through which they had worked for many years. They shared the despair of a generation whose idealism was shattered by the brutality of war, ongoing racial polarization, the assassinations of Martin Luther King and Robert Kennedy, and the unresponsiveness of government. Charlotte, however, was already assuming leadership in the emerging women's liberation movement and stepped easily from one arena to another.

It is no surprise that a substantial number of these women became feminist leaders both inside and outside the church in the 1970s. Sheila McCurdy went from her Frontier Internship to activism in New York Radical Women and then to working with women in ministry to challenge the sexism as well as racism of the Methodist Church. Jan Griesinger, campus minister at Ohio State, joined the women's liberation movement in Dayton and then set out to organize women campus ministers. In the sisterhood of Women in Campus Ministry, Jan crossed paths with Eleanor Scott Meyers, who was working on issues of domestic violence through the YWCA at the University of Kansas. Meyers went on to become a leading voice of Christian feminism and the first woman president of the Pacific School of Religion in Berkeley.

Alice Hageman was a founder of the Committee of Returned Volunteers (CRV), which brought together Frontier Interns with returned Peace Corps volunteers for activism against the war in Vietnam and toward a broader understanding of the role of the United States in the world. Through the CRV she was active in the Columbia University uprising in 1968 and traveled to Cuba in 1969. Active in campus ministry in the 1970s, she offered an early feminist critique in her book *Sexist Religion and Women in the Church: No More Silence.*[9]

Perhaps the best-known activist in this collection outside church circles is Charlotte Bunch, who had honed her organizational skills through leadership in the Duke YWCA, the Methodist Student Movement, the University Christian Movement, and the WSCF. She continued that work as an early theorist of lesbian feminism and through the 1980s and 1990s as a key leader in the international movement for women's human and civic rights. Director of the Center for Women's Global Leadership at Rutgers (where she also works with elmira Nazombe), Charlotte is one of the most important leaders of American feminism today.

Notes

1. See Doug Rossinow, *The Politics of Authenticity* (New York: Columbia University Press, 1998). In a close study of the student new left in Texas, Rossinow documents the religious roots of the new left, which, he argues, can best be understood as a generational search for authenticity. My own research traced the religious motivations of southern whites involved in civil rights who subsequently became "founding mothers" of the women's liberation movement. See Sara Evans, *Personal Politics: The Roots of Women's Liberation in the Civil Rights Movement and the New Left* (New York: Knopf, 1979).
2. See Sara M. Evans, *Born for Liberty: A History of Women in America* (New York: Free Press, 1997), chaps. 4–6, quotes on pp. 80, 95. On the Grimke sisters, see the powerful biography by Gerda Lerner, *The Grimke Sisters from South Carolina: Pioneers for Women's Rights and Abolition* (New York: Schocken, 1966).
3. See Stanley Rowland, Jr., "End Racial Bars, Church Is Urged," *New York Times*, December 31, 1955, 6; See Stanley Rowland, Jr., "Apartheid Issue Put to Students," *New York Times*, December 30, 1955, 12; "West Held a Seed of Global Revolt," *New York Times*, December 29, 1955, 4; T.A.G., "Revolution at Athens," *Christian Century* 73:3 (January 18, 1956): 70–72.
4. Doug Rossinow, "'The Break-through to New Life': Christianity and the Emergence of the New Left in Austin, Texas, 1956–1964," *American Quarterly* 46:3 (September 1994): 309–340, esp. 315–318.
5. Finley Eversole, "The Witness of Jonah," *Christian Century*, 77:3 (January 20, 1960): 70–71, quote on 71.
6. Samuel Slie, "A Reflection on Race Relations in the Student Christian Movement," *Journal of Ecumenical Studies* 32:4 (fall 1995): 527.
7. Ibid., 529.
8. Ida Sloan Snyder, "Convention 1970: A Gentle Revolution," *YWCA Magazine* 64 (June 1970): 5–7, quote on 5; Snyder, "One Imperative for All," *YWCA Magazine* 64 (June 1970), 8–11, quote on 8.
9. Association Press, 1974.

CHAPTER 1

Ruth Harris

〜〜〜⌒

On December 27, 1959, more than four thousand college and university students made a pilgrimage to Athens, Ohio, for what was to be one of the most significant ecumenical encounters ever of Christian students in the United States. Busload after busload came from every part of the country, from the eight provinces of Canada, from Puerto Rico, the British West Indies, and Mexico. More than a thousand were international students from all over the world studying in the United States. The Eighteenth Ecumenical Student Conference on Christian World Mission was history engaging and history making. It inspired a generation of students to become active Christians for social change.

I was a member of the international ecumenical team that planned and organized the conference. Our team included Bola Ige, Anglican barrister from Nigeria, and C. I. Itty, a Methodist theological student from India. It was led by Newton Thurber, who had worked as a Presbyterian missionary in Japan for four years. Students from Yale, Princeton, and Union seminaries were also involved in the planning. Our plan was innovative and ambitious. We drew heavily on our experiences with an earlier ground-breaking conference, the 1955 quadrennial of the Student Volunteer Movement (SVM), of which I was also a national staff member. Several important worldwide phenomena had helped shape the SVM quadrennial: The first was "the revolt of the disinherited" that was taking place in many parts of the world against colonialism, racial discrimination, hunger, disease, and illiteracy. Another was the concept of "one world," the idea that all nations are intimately bound together and that we must see the problems causing social revolution everywhere as *our* problems. The third phenomenon was the intensified struggle for justice and the urgent need for reconciliation. Yet another was the large number of foreign students coming to the United States to study. Our primary study text for the SVM conference had been *Encounter with Revolution* by Richard

Schaull, a professor of theology and Presbyterian missionary who had spent twelve years in hot spots of the revolution in Latin America. Dick's book had a broad influence on Christian students and campus ministers.

The SVM quadrennial had provided a unique opportunity for American students to learn about social revolution directly from fellow Christian students from other parts of the world. Although half the participants were international students studying in the United States, we realized, in planning the 1959 conference, that the number of African American students and other ethnic or racial minorities had been low by comparison. We were determined to be very intentional in recruiting and setting quotas for African American and other minority students, especially since the social revolution had by now come to the United States. At the same time, we kept the strong recruitment of international participants, the centrality of a conference study book, and a third feature of the earlier conference: each participant was required to be a member of an ecumenical and international study/involvement group on a local campus. This requirement became a significant catalyst for the development of local ecumenical work.

The year 1959 was a critical historical moment for students to come together. The civil rights movement was growing in the southern states. New directions in mission were emerging. The theme of the Eighteenth Ecumenical Student Conference was "Inquiry and Involvement on Strategic Frontiers." Nine strategic frontiers in mission had been identified: racial tensions, new nationalisms, communism, militant non-Christian faiths, modern secularism, technological upheaval, responsibility for statesmanship, universities and students, and displaced, uprooted, and rejected peoples. All were clear departures from the geographical frontiers that had defined mission in years past. The conference plan developed around these frontiers, with subgroups led by people actively involved in each of the strategic areas.

The keynote speaker was Martin Luther King, Jr. He spoke about the frontier of racial tensions, holding forth the hope of a society built on justice and reconciliation and calling Christian students to join him in the struggle to build it. Another conference leader was James Lawson, who had spent three years as a Methodist short-term missionary in India, where he studied Mohandas Gandhi's principles of nonviolence. Dr. King had met Jim at Oberlin College and persuaded him to come south and help build a movement using Gandhian techniques to protest racial discrimination. Jim moved to Nashville, enrolled at Vanderbilt Seminary, and began conducting workshops on nonviolence for African American students in the Nashville area. Throughout the conference I noticed Jim huddled with little clusters of students, and only later realized that he had been conducting "workshops" in the hallways.

There were signs throughout the nation of a generation at the ready mark. Many students returned from Athens to their campuses on integrated buses, serious about putting their faith into action. They were seeking to break the barriers between north and south, black and white. There was a new spirit, a sense of urgency, a new strategy that would change America.

One month later, on February 1, the student lunch counter sit-ins began in Greensboro, North Carolina. Over the next few months, there were sit-ins in Tallahassee, Florida; Portsmouth, Virginia; Nashville, Tennessee; Orangeburg, South Carolina; and Baton Rouge, Louisiana. An article in the *New York Times* headlined "Campuses in North Back Southern Students" stated, "The present campus generation has been accused of self-concern and a pallid indifference to social and political questions. This issue appears to have aroused it as have few others."

Sit-ins were reported at such leading colleges as Yale, Harvard, Princeton, and Columbia, as well as at Skidmore in Saratoga Springs, New York. There were lunch counter demonstrations not only in the South but also in the North, Midwest, and West. Between February 1 and June 1, 1960, more than two thousand students were arrested, mostly African Americans. A study done later revealed that every lunch counter demonstration included at least one student who had attended the 1959 conference in Athens, Ohio.

$\mathcal{M}$y personal journey began in Emmet, Nebraska, a tiny town on the edge of the sandhills with a population of eighty-eight. My uncle's hay company advertised Emmet as "The Hay Capital of the World." I was born in 1920, the first year that women in the United States had the right to vote.

Three women were important influences in my early life: my grandmother, my mother, and my good friend Merj. My grandmother, Clara Brion Cole, had pioneered with my grandfather, Rev. George Cole, to the Nebraska plains after the Civil War. They were active, devout Methodists. There were many hardships in the early days on the Nebraska plains, especially for ministers, who got very little pay. It was at my grandmother's apron strings that I learned of her faith. She often sang softly as she worked, and the songs she sang and what they represented in my life were important to me as a small child. In my memory I hear her singing, "God will take care of you, through all the day, o'er the way," and "Leaning on the Everlasting Arms." They were expressions of her complete reliance on God's love through all hardships.

I watched my grandmother tithe every tenth egg when she had nothing else to give to the work of the church. I grew up with stories of her vigorous participation in the Women's Christian Temperance Union, when she and her friends went into saloons to urge the men to go home and save the money they spent on liquor so that their children and wives would have enough to eat. As my grandmother's friends gathered in her parlor around the quilting frame, I listened to their tales of Frances Willard and the long-fought battles for women's suffrage. Every Sunday in Emmet I attended "Grandma's little church," which she helped build. Throughout my life I carried with me her songs, her assurance that we can rely on God's steadfast love.

My mother, Esther, was Clara's youngest daughter. When I was nine years old, the nationwide financial crash of 1929 destroyed my father's grocery store and my father left, abandoning my mother with five children and almost no means of support. Fortunately, my mother found a job the following year taking the U.S. census in Holt County. She traveled from farm to farm in my uncle's car, and thus became known throughout the area. On the strength of her census taking, her work at the bank, and a sympathy vote, Esther Cole Harris, a Republican, was elected as the Holt County Register of Deeds in 1932, the year of the Democratic landslide that elected Franklin Delano Roosevelt president. Even then I knew that this was a remarkable achievement for a woman. Thus began my lifelong interest in politics.

Every four years we faced the sobering possibility that our mother might not be reelected. She supported her five children on a monthly salary of $125. Although we had very few resources, for the rest of her life she provided for us, parented us, loved us, and held us together as a family. We all loved to sing and often sang together—in church, Christmas caroling, or just for the enjoyment of it. To our mother, we were her "precious jewels." Week after week, year after year, through thick and thin, by the example of her life, she taught us about faithfulness and the importance of family.

These two women, my grandmother Clara, a tiny, soft-spoken matriarch staunchly undergirded by her Christian faith and her Methodist tradition of moral influence in society and personal life, and my mother Esther, the strong provider and defender of her children, have made me feel proud and given me a sense of dignity and direction and rootedness. At the 1993 Re-Imagining Gathering in Minneapolis, I learned a song that immediately became my own:

> From my mother's womb and grandmother's tongue,
> I have heard my name, been given my song.
> With their blood and their beauty I have grown strong.
> With the fire of love and rage I will sing on!

Another important influence in my life was growing up as a Protestant in a predominantly Catholic town with my best friend, Merj, who was a Catholic. At that time there was still a large gulf between Catholics and Protestants. Although Merj attended a Catholic school and I the public school, we became friends during high school. When we went off to college—she to a Catholic women's college in Omaha and I to a Methodist college in Sioux City, Iowa—our friendship deepened through correspondence and during visits home.

During these formative years, our conversations inevitably turned toward the future and how we would spend our lives. Pearl Harbor and President Roosevelt's announcement, in 1941, that our country was at war came just six months after our graduation from college. History, too, was challenging us to make our lives count. I was planning to become a teacher, and she became more and more serious about becoming a nun. She would explain to me the reasons she was about to join the Sisters of the Sacred Heart, an order that would not allow her ever to return home. Although her not coming home shocked me, I came to be deeply impressed by her commitment to her faith. After she became a novice, I went to visit her in the Sacred Heart school in Chicago and later visited her at other Sacred Heart schools. I have since realized that our friendship was my first experience of ecumenism. I had begun to see how God reaches us in many different ways. Later, as my own plans developed, I wondered if my life work was somehow parallel to hers.

World War II made us all much more aware of the suffering of people in many parts of the world. One day in church, a Scripture passage came alive to me in a very intense way. It was Jesus' response to the young lawyer's question, "What shall I do to live?" Jesus said, "You shall love the Lord your God with all your heart, and with all your soul, and with all your strength, and with all your mind, and your neighbor as yourself. Do this and you will live." In response to the next question, "Who is my neighbor?" Jesus told the parable of the Good Samaritan. Questions were forming in my mind that wouldn't go away: Who is my neighbor? Is there anywhere out there in the world where I can use my skills and training as a teacher to help bind up the wounds of war? The answer came from a wise woman, Rachel Low, who led my young adult Sunday school class during my last year of teaching in Nebraska. "The women of the Methodist Church have schools in Asia and Africa and Latin America that are very much in need of teachers like you," she said to me. So it was that in the summer of 1945 I applied to the Woman's Division of the Methodist Board of Missions for service as a missionary teacher. I was soon on my way to Scarritt College, a graduate school in Nashville founded by Methodist women to prepare women for Christian service at home and abroad.

My apprehension about what Scarritt would be like was strong, because my stereotypes about missionaries were very vivid. I was considerably relieved to find my experience at the college exciting and sometimes exhilarating. It was my first encounter with courses in Old Testament, New Testament, and anthropology, and my fellow students, my professors, my classes were all very stimulating and important to me. I was grateful to God for what was happening in my life.

That year in Nashville was filled with new experiences and important decisions. Living in Tennessee brought me my first opportunity to live in an interracial society. I regularly worshiped at Fisk University, reveling in the incredible music making of the Fisk Jubilee Singers. I participated in discussions on race relations and was exposed to "southern living." At Scarritt in 1945–46, African Americans were the "servants," cooking, cleaning, and doing yard work. My friend and fellow student Doris Caldwell took me to the nearby Appalachian Mountains to visit in the homes of southern mountain folks. For the first time, I saw Americans living in deplorable conditions of poverty. She called on me to pray with those people, and I had my first experience of praying in public—not an easy one. In the months ahead, I heard about conditions in China and the need for teachers, had consultations with Mission Board personnel, and by the end of my year at Scarritt had made the decision to go to China as a Christian teacher.

During that summer, I attended a weeklong ecumenical conference for a large group of young missionaries who, as World War II came to an end, were preparing to depart for overseas assignments. I was so taken with the quality of ideas, the diversity of perspectives, the depth of dialogue, that I began to sense within myself a profound commitment to the ecumenical movement. This passion has never gone away. That fall I began studying Chinese language and history at the Yale School of Asian Studies in New Haven, Connecticut. It was a relief to find that my ear for music was an important asset in learning a tonal language. Learning to speak Chinese was hard work, but great fun, too. Soon I would be speaking Chinese with Chinese people, though I wondered if I ever could learn to read and write!

By Christmas, the exciting news reached us that the Chinese Language School in Peking was ready to open. Hundreds of us headed for Asia in mid-January, leaving from San Francisco on the *Marine Lynx III*, a converted troop ship that carried us on a three-week journey across the Pacific to Shanghai. On board ship, I had a most jarring experience when I learned that some of the missionaries were staying up all night "praying for the souls" of the other missionaries on board. This was my initial experience with conservative Christian zealots and their certainty that those who didn't express their faith in quite the same way as they did were doomed.

I will never forget my first two sights of China. When I awoke on that February morning in 1947, I realized that the vibrations of the ship's engines had stopped. We had arrived. I ran up on deck. The ship was anchored. All I could see was mist and fog in total silence. Slowly, in the distance, a Chinese junk appeared. It was an indescribably beautiful moment—a Chinese painting. I learned then that our ship had been quarantined, and we were anchored at the mouth of the Hwangpu River for two days.

Then came my second sight of China, as we docked at the Bund in Shanghai. I will always remember looking down from the ship as dozens of small boats raced from the shore, crowding as close to our ship as possible. They were filled with Chinese people begging with outstretched arms for the rich foreigners to toss overboard food, clothing, money, anything. As we disembarked, a solid mass of humanity pushed toward us, falling over each other as they clamored to handle our baggage, provide us with transportation, or perform any service that would get them a few coins.

Had I not seen it myself, I could never have imagined the human suffering and degradation in Shanghai at the end of interminable years of war. Everywhere, malnourished people picked through muddy garbage for any scrap of leftover food. Men pushed and pulled immense wagonloads that I had seen only animals tow before. Along the sides of the streets lay bundles neatly wrapped in straw mats—dead babies, placed there by their families to be picked up and taken away. In China at that time, three out of four babies died in their first year.

Our pedicab made its way through the crowded streets with miserable beggar children hanging along the sides. It took us to the McTyeire School, where I would eventually teach choral music. I was not prepared for the contrast that awaited me as I went through the gates. The high walls had broken shards of glass cemented on top to keep out thieves. Inside were handsome buildings, delightful gardens with a dragon wall, an arched bridge and willow trees by a pond, and spacious, comfortable rooms at the missionary faculty house.

The McTyeire School for Girls had been founded by the women of the Methodist Church South to provide daughters of Chinese elites the opportunity for an excellent education. Since China placed so little value on girls, there was almost no opportunity for them to go to school. The American

Methodist women sought to fill this void by providing education that would fully prepare young women to go directly to the best women's colleges in the United States. Their goal was to prepare Chinese women leaders to serve the people of their own country. McTyeire was an outstanding school by any measure, yet I was shocked at the great economic difference inside and outside its walls, and I felt very uneasy about it.

After two weeks in Shanghai, I sailed up the coast to Tientsin in a small Chinese ship and then went overland to Peking. Peking in 1947 was out of this world. It was surrounded by great walls, with huge gateways on all four sides of the city. Homes were built around courtyards and behind high walls and connected by very narrow alleyways. In the center of Peking was the Forbidden City, a walled city within the walled city, the home of the former imperial families. Only bicycles, rickshaws, and pedicabs provided transportation. Incredible surprises awaited the foreigner: occasional lines of camels from the Gobi Desert walking slowly and with great dignity down the main thoroughfare, the Chinese opera house outside the South Gate, the endless gourmet delights of Chinese restaurants. I was filled with the anticipation of exploring China, and with two hundred other language students from all over the Western world, I worked hard to learn to speak Chinese.

The conditions of the Chinese people were unbearable. China had to have a revolution! Shanghai had shocked me with its sights of misery, and when I got to Peking, I began to see and feel the signs of the revolution already coming. One of the early clues was music. The Peking Language School had a mix of students from English-speaking countries who had come to China to work in embassies, businesses, churches, schools, hospitals, and YM/YWCAs. I was asked to be in charge of a one-hour weekly introduction to Chinese music. A group of young Chinese language school teachers were assigned to work with me. I soon realized that most of the songs they were providing were "liberation songs," songs increasingly popular throughout China with texts describing the people's suffering and calling all to rise up and bring about change. The songs were set to delightful folk melodies from China's western provinces. Our whole student body sang them with gusto.

My first introduction to the student Christian movement was in Peking. During the summer of 1947, I went on a YMCA-YWCA work camp with a group of Peking National University students. I participated with other work campers in hard physical labor in the villages and in educational performances we put on for the villagers in the evenings. This experience brought me intimate exposure to the revolutionary thinking of Chinese young people. As corruption increased, Chinese students had become the conscience of the nation, protesting against the fascist tendencies of the Chiang Kai-shek regime. As we sat each morning and each night in a circle of "criticism–self-criticism" meetings, the students spoke one by one of their deepest feelings about the poverty of the villagers and the future of their country. I heard their intense anger against the Western countries that had so oppressed and humiliated the Chinese people. The young people passionately despised imperialism and denounced the United States as imperialist. Hearing them, I was ashamed. I deeply regretted my meager knowledge of the history of my own country's international affairs and my shallow understanding of Chinese history, and I resolved to make up for my ignorance. My college education, which was almost totally tied to music education, had left me completely unprepared for what would happen to my life in China in the next four years. By the end of the summer I was reaching the conviction that the most important place to start my learning in China would be to ground myself in the realities of those suffering oppression.

Just after Christmas, I received word that I had to leave the language school to begin teaching in Shanghai. Leaving my studies more than a year early was very upsetting, because language was so essential to communication. But after eleven months in Peking, as I went to my assignment in Shanghai, important questions were forming within me: What were my convictions about the way God works in history? What is God saying to us in the events of our times? How was I to understand my nation as an imperial power? How did my role as missionary fit into all this?

$\mathcal{B}$y early summer 1949, the Communist army had taken the north and was drawing near to Shanghai. Some of us would gather on the flat roof of McTyeire School and watch the "fireworks" on the outskirts of Shanghai, where the Liberation Army, the Communist army, battled the Kuomintang army, which was trying to defend the city. It seemed unreal to me, vaguely reminding me of Fourth of July celebrations at home. I don't know why, but I didn't feel afraid. It must have been because I had never experienced war up close.

Early one morning, weeks after the fighting and shelling began, I was walking across the McTyeire campus to breakfast, whistling as I went, when a student poked her head out of the dorm window and called to me, "Shanghai is liberated!" The Liberation Army had entered Shanghai during the night and come down Yu Yuen Road, just a couple of blocks from the school. And I had slept through it! There had been gunfire, enough that some faculty and students hid in closets behind mattresses, but no one in the school was hurt.

Chiang Kai-shek and his government and military, and almost everyone else who could afford a ticket, had already left for Taiwan.

Overnight, we in Shanghai had become part of a new world, of New China! There were soldiers on every street corner, and their deportment was exemplary: disciplined, helpful, the very opposite of the propaganda that had preceded them. Shanghai was the showcase for the way New China was to be. Still, we could not foresee the incredible changes that would come. As the school began its reorganization process, it became clear that certain students and teachers had long been preparing for this day. Within a few days, everyone in the school community—students, faculty, administration, servants—was organized into study groups that met daily to discuss books prepared for this purpose. The books included Marxist philosophy, Chinese history, and the goals of the program of New China. As a part of each meeting, we carried on criticism and self-criticism to raise our consciousness. It seemed to me that within a week, every person in Shanghai was part of such a group. It was astonishing how soon changes came to our elite student body. Very soon, everyone was wearing plain, blue cotton clothing, no jewelry or makeup, and simple hairdos. Anything that symbolized identification with "the people" was in; everything that suggested separation from the people was out.

Our study books told of foreign imperialism and colonialism. They dealt with the hundred years of unequal treaties in the late eighteenth and early nineteenth centuries. They described the Opium War in 1839–1842, when the British forced China to continue receiving shipments of opium and China was forced to cede Hong Kong to Great Britain. They detailed the many unequal treaties with other European countries and finally with the United States, too. China had been forced to give foreign powers control over treaty ports and rights to navigate inland waters, until it actually became a colony of many nations.

The books explained the New China program's commitment to the people to restructure economic distribution by means of land reform, industrialization, and improvement of farming techniques. The program also promised innovations in sanitation, massive campaigns to combat disease, and expanded rights for women and ethnic and tribal minorities. A major emphasis was on literacy, as more than 80 percent of the Chinese people were illiterate and formal education was the privilege of the elite. The books discussed freedom of religion and freedom to oppose religion, with the Communist Party taking the position that religion was superstition.

Every student at McTyeire was now required to take the course on political thought. Previously a weekly chapel service had been required, but this could no longer be held. In these circumstances, however, a new church was born, made up of those students and teachers and neighborhood people who were Christians. Of the 1,800 students, fewer than 100 attended church. A wholly new situation developed as these students asked one another for prayer, and each phrase of the hymns we sang had real meaning for our lives. The church began to come remarkably alive when it was standing up to *be* the church.

The Youth Fellowship of the new church, influenced by a new awareness of the people and their suffering, began to see the gospel in a new light. Young people became interested in their neighbors and questioned, for the first time, why there were glass shards on the tops of the walls surrounding the school. They went outside the walls to see for themselves the working conditions of women who labored in nearby factories, to get acquainted with shopkeepers, and to teach in the nearby nursery schools.

We made plans to organize a summer work camp with women and children in the countryside near Soochow, a smaller city northeast of Shanghai where my friend Doris lived and worked. Our plans were threatened, however, because the government refused to allow travel outside of Shanghai. I vividly remember going to the office of a government official and urging him to give us travel permits. I explained that our goals for the work camp were the same as the goals of New China: to serve the people, to learn about the living conditions of poor rural folk, and to work for their liberation from poverty. To everyone's amazement, including mine, we were granted travel permits. We had not heard of anyone else being allowed to leave Shanghai at that time.

That summer experience proved to be a highlight of my three years in Shanghai. It was marked by a remarkable depth of sharing and worship among students and advisors. We deepened our knowledge of the Christian faith and our understanding of the lives of people living under the oppression of poverty. We came to care about the rural people we knew. We listened and learned. The bonds among our own community grew strong and lasting. Later, an American friend from Nanking asked me with much concern, "How are you?" I answered with complete conviction, "I'm great! I never realized the church could be like this." That expressed my amazement and excitement at my first experience of the church alive in that small, faithful community in Shanghai.

And then came the Korean War. When communism is mentioned as the power that changed China, I always add, "and nationalism." I was astonished at the sight in Shanghai as the call went out for recruits to fight at the

Yalu River. Lines of young men at the recruitment centers stretched for miles. Hundreds, thousands of China's youth—the most outstanding, the best scholastically—stood in line for hours and days to volunteer, hoping that they would be chosen to help defend their country against the invading foreigners, who this time were from my own country. There was no way to anticipate the far-reaching effects of the Korean War on the Christian community in China. Often over the previous two years, I had marveled at the fact that I was still there, an American teaching Chinese young people. I thought of the ways Germans and Japanese had been treated in my country during World War II. How could the Chinese be so accepting and trusting? But now the time had come when no American could make a positive contribution. Now I was a liability to my Chinese friends and colleagues.

Writing some years later in a student Christian movement study book, Katharine Hockin, a Canadian, summed up this final dilemma of alienation: "It was a salutory experience to find oneself something of an outcast, a category about which one could do nothing at all—it was just one's national origin and the color of one's skin that were to blame." It was time to leave China. If I stayed, I could do more harm than good, mostly in bringing suspicion on my friends and students. Signs of friendship to me might be difficult for them, perhaps even dangerous.

The whole incredible situation came home to me during my last Christmas in China, in 1950, at a concert of Handel's "Messiah." I was the only Western person in the chorus of a hundred Chinese singers. The large church was completely packed. I had to leave this country and people whom I had come to love, and my heart was yearning for reconciliation. Handel's powerful music still sings in my heart, "Wonderful, Counselor, the Mighty God, the Everlasting Father, the Prince of Peace." Somehow I knew that God was in this. But how were we to live on the real frontiers of reconciliation?

Doris Caldwell and Mary Mitchell, my two friends from Scarritt, had recently "evacuated to Shanghai" from their inland locations. We planned to leave China together. As we went by train to Canton and walked across the border to Hong Kong, my heart felt deep pain. Yet I was grateful for the desperately needed changes that New China's revolution was bringing to the Chinese people and for the church that had come alive in a time of trial. I prayed for God's reconciliation between my people and the Chinese people.

For the next three months, the three of us made our way home. We traveled by ship and plane and overland, from Hong Kong through Asia, stopping at Singapore, Malaysia, Burma, India, and then on to Lebanon, Jordan,

Jerusalem, and finally to Europe. In Geneva, Switzerland, I learned that the United Nations Commission on Human Rights was in session at the UN headquarters. For a week, I sat glued to the UN observers' section. I listened intently to every word of the proceedings as Eleanor Roosevelt, the Lebanese Christian diplomat Charles Malik, and other members of the commission worked on the implementation of the Declaration of Human Rights. The Declaration had been born on December 10, 1948, while I was still in China. It was intended to set minimum standards for the treatment of individuals everywhere in the world. Eleanor Roosevelt and Frederick Nolde of the International Affairs Commission of the World Council of Churches are the two people usually credited with conceiving the idea of the Universal Declaration.

That time in Geneva was, for me, a significant time of listening and reflection. It was music to my ears to find this representative international group of men and women working creatively and knowledgeably, with great dedication, on matters pertaining to the rights of all human beings. My soul was hungry for their words. It was the first time I had observed the UN in action. I knew that peace and reconciliation would come only through such an effort as this, and I knew I wanted to be a part of it. Here was common ground, a way for all nations to work together for the good of all people. Here people were laying the groundwork for the covenants yet to come with international codes of political, civil, economic, and social rights that would serve all people. Was this, I wondered, a way for China and America to live and work together?

When I reached the United States, one of my first acts was to go to the United Nations to see if I could work there, but there was no place for me. Hundreds of other people had applied before me. I was disappointed. I had not only hoped to work for the goals of the UN, but I felt that working with an international group on justice and peace issues could help me work through some of the confusion I was feeling after my experience in China. And it would deepen my grasp of what was going on in the world.

Just at that juncture, an extraordinary coincidence occurred. I was invited by Thelma Stevens to work as a missionary associate in the Department of Christian Social Relations of the Methodist Church's Woman's Division, headquartered in New York. My assignment was to strengthen the support of Methodists, especially women and young people, for the United Nations. I was to organize seminars for groups coming from across the United States to the new UN headquarters on the East River. My work was to help them learn what the UN stood for and to assist them in organizing for supportive action.

In 1951 the United States was in the midst of McCarthyism, and the United Nations was a major target. The House of Representatives had created the Committee on Un-American Activities in the 1940s to uncover and fight "subversives." Richard Nixon was among the most active members of the committee. Patriotic and religious zealots spread fear—fear of communism taking over the world. I was stunned as they pointed fingers at those who had "lost China." Fear and rumors led to witch hunts. Accusations came not only from official groups but from extremist citizens' groups such as the White Citizens Council and the John Birch Society. Along with the UN, the main targets were Jews, African Americans, and other racial and ethnic groups.

Our department was doing everything it could to bring an informed, intelligent perspective to American citizens. Two concepts guided our work: first, the importance of action, both individual and group; and second, the importance of preparation and training. Our slogan was "All action is local." In the two years I worked with Thelma Stevens and the Department of Christian Social Relations, I learned a great deal about working for social change. I learned that change is not built on passion alone, but on organization, training, and education for the long haul. I learned the importance of doing my homework: social change comes from carefully defining principles and then being faithful to them. I learned the essential tasks of making connections between issues and linking the past to the present to create a future of justice and peace. I learned the importance of building strong trust and team relationships, and of working cooperatively and systematically to analyze issues and bring about change. We who worked with Thelma knew her as a leader—forceful, visionary, courageous, a Christian fighter for justice. She was also my friend and my hero.

Another hero was Eleanor Roosevelt. To my great joy and inspiration, I now had the opportunity to see and hear her in action. When I started my new work, she was about to leave her position as a delegate to the UN. With the change of administration from Truman to Eisenhower, she moved across First Avenue to lead the American Association for the United Nations. One of the most rewarding aspects of my work was that I could call on her to speak to the seminars that I organized. Eleanor Roosevelt was a great human being—intelligent, compassionate, courageous. What struck me especially, as my seminar group sat around the table in those small UN briefing rooms, was how humble she was. She was completely at ease, graciously responding to each of our queries, no matter how uninformed or unsophisticated. In my mind's eye, I could see her talking with miners, Appalachian folk, wounded soldiers, women factory workers. It was one of the high privileges of my life to experience for myself her deep caring and total dedication to human rights for all people.

After two years in the Department of Christian Social Relations, I became field program director of the Student Volunteer Movement. From 1954 to 1959, I was the coordinator of campus visitation, small conferences, and seminars. Experienced and ready, I jumped into a vast ocean of organizing responsibilities. The Student Volunteer Movement for Christian Mission had long been one of the most dynamic student Christian movements in the country. It boldly called on college and university students to volunteer for missionary service in order "to evangelize the world in this generation." Throughout its long history, the SVM held a quadrennial conference for each generation of students. It continued to have the confidence and financial support of the powerful mission boards of U.S. Protestant churches. Now, at a dramatic moment in student history, it was this aging organization that planned and carried out the groundbreaking Ecumenical Student Conferences on Christian World Mission in Athens, Ohio, in 1955, 1959, and 1963.

*I*n mid–1959 I received an invitation to become the secretary of student work of the Woman's Division of Christian Service of the Methodist Board of Missions. For me, the timing couldn't have been better. I would begin the new work as soon as the Athens conference ended, on January 1, 1960. My assignment was twofold: to work with Methodist students and to be an advocate for students with the Woman's Division and the Board of Missions. I had seen what remarkable work my colleague Margaret Flory was doing in the United Presbyterian Church. In some ways I was "coming home," as I would be working again with Thelma Stevens and her department, this time as a staff colleague.

It was an important historical moment. John F. Kennedy was running for president. Martin Luther King, Jr., was giving outstanding leadership to end racial discrimination. Students were beginning to respond to the call for social change. I was challenged and thrilled with this new opportunity to help students become involved, and I felt that my experience had prepared me for the tasks ahead.

History moved very fast. On March 3, 1960, just two months after the Athens conference and scarcely a month after the Greensboro sit-in, Jim Lawson was expelled from Vanderbilt Divinity School for his role in nonviolent sit-in demonstrations in Nashville. The grounds were that there must be respect for the law. The day after his expulsion, he was arrested in church by the Nashville police, handcuffed, and taken to jail. I knew that in order to do advocacy work on behalf of students involved in controversial actions, we faced a major task of education and interpretation among Methodist women. We had to move immediately. Under the leadership of Nettie Alice Green, an African American from Kentucky, the Standing Committee on Student Work drew up a resolution on "The Student Sit-In Movement." The purpose was not only to support Jim Lawson but to provide the legal basis for the racial justice work that lay ahead. Working in consultation with Thelma and the Department of Christian Social Relations, we brought the resolution to the Woman's Division for consideration.

Our resolution was strong. It described the sit-in demonstrations, already in twenty-seven different colleges and eleven states, involving both African American and white students. It stated that these nonviolent demonstrations were part of the worldwide revolution and went on to say that people sensitive to the earth-shaking disturbances of our social order would sympathize with these students and understand why they were doing what they were doing. It gave solid endorsement to the methods of nonviolence and expressed profound regret that law enforcement authorities had in some cases permitted violence against demonstrators and made unfair arrests.

The resolution objected strongly to Jim Lawson's expulsion for following his Christian conscience and called on the Vanderbilt Seminary administration to reinstate him. The resolution also called on Methodist women to study the facts and participate in each local church "in the context of the Gospel to clarify its position on the race issue." Furthermore, they were urged to cooperate with like-minded community groups to contact local law enforcement authorities and urge that the rights of students be protected, to communicate with public eating places, and to support students who were involved in the civil rights struggle. Fortunately, Jim Lawson was well known to many of the division and staff members, as he had been a short-term missionary in India. The Woman's Division adopted the resolution on March 23, 1960, less than three months after I began as secretary of student work. I was profoundly grateful for this action.

The fervor of student involvement in the lunch counter sit-ins grew. The Woman's Division was ready to move ahead with our support for students working for racial justice. Sometimes this took the form of bail money for students who had been arrested, such as Rebecca Owen, an honors student at Randolph Macon Women's College, a Methodist college in Lynchburg, Virginia (see chapter 3). A few months before the lunch counter demonstration, Rebecca had checked with me to see if bail money would be available, and I had assured her that it would. Rebecca, a national leader in the Methodist Student Movement (MSM), was, however, one of the first white students to choose "jail, not bail." Later, in a time of crisis when Rebecca was not supported by her college and was forced out of her state because of her involvement in the civil rights movement, her support came from fellow students in the MSM and from her church—not her local church, but her church at the national level. Many other Christian students who followed their consciences in acting for racial justice, inspired by their faith, found themselves rejected by their local churches.

Our program also supported organized antiracism projects of the MSM. Campus ministry was in its heyday, highly organized on campuses around the country. The MSM was strong, organized in forty states. The state MSM presidents met together each summer with national staff as the National Council (NCMSM) to elect national officers and make plans for the coming year. As student work secretary, I was automatically on the national staff of the Methodist Student Movement. The National Council adopted a project to form a biracial team which would be available to state MSMs to visit campuses and help promote interracial understanding through interracial study groups. George McClain, a white graduate of Union Theological Seminary in New York City, and Howard Spencer, an African American sophomore at Rust College in Mississippi, were invited by NCMSM to be the biracial team. My office joined the Methodist Board of Education in providing financial support to the project. By 1964 tensions were running very high, especially in the southern states. It was critical that students who took courageous stands had support from a national church agency. Sheila McCurdy, president of the Alabama MSM, was a case in point (see chapter 8).

For Methodist women to stand by the students in this tense time, it was essential to close the growing gap between students and their churches. Every local Woman's Society had an officer elected to be the secretary of student work. Her responsibility was to be a contact and an advocate for students in the local church. The Standing Committee on Student Work and I were responsible for the training and preparation for action of these thirty thousand secretaries. This became one of the primary challenges of my job. Besides special training events and days on campus, we tried to share information in a number of ways. When possible, we arranged for students to speak for themselves, often by inviting international and interracial teams to visit board meetings, schools of mission, and campuses. But I also often spoke and taught about what was happening with students, and I wrote interpretive articles, including a monthly page in *Response* magazine.

One of our most successful ventures in helping students learn through involvement had been our participation in the March on Washington for Jobs and Freedom, led by Martin Luther King, Jr., on August 28, 1963. During that same week, six MSM Regional Leadership Training Conferences were taking place across the United States on the theme "Reconciliation and Revolution." I was the educational director of the Northeast Regional Conference in central New York State, the nearest to Washington, D.C. Along with Mae Gautier, a friend and campus minister who was working with me at the time, I knew that this was an excellent opportunity for students to be exposed to the growing civil rights movement and to experience the reality of the conference theme in their own country. We arranged for two buses to take students from the Northeast Region to the march.

Because the march would fit so naturally with the conference theme, we went ahead and arranged transportation without consulting the campus minister who served as dean of the Northeast Regional Conference. The buses were to leave very early in the morning on the day of the march and return late that night. The next day, we would report back to the rest of the conference. I was unprepared for the dean's anxiety and fear. He seemed to feel that studying the Bible and "Revolution and Reconciliation" was one thing, but participating in a demonstration for racial justice led by Dr. King was quite another. We talked for a long time and finally negotiated that the students who wanted to go should phone their parents and get permission. I stood by the students during the calls, ready to speak with anxious parents.

Mae and I began to realize that the march provided an excellent opportunity to network with the other five MSM regional conferences and multiply firsthand exposure for students. Phone calls were made inviting each of the regions to send a student and a state director to march with us and then return and report to their conferences. It worked. Each conference raised its own money to pay for their representatives' transportation.

Early in the morning of August 28, a large group of students and campus ministers from the Northeast Regional Conference was ready to go. With large Methodist Student Movement banners that they had made, they joined additional MSM members and three hundred thousand others in a huge outpouring of people concerned for racial justice. It turned out to be, as we all know now, a great historic event, an unforgettable experience. It was a beautiful day in every way. In that early time in the civil rights struggle, blacks and whites still marched arm in arm. Everyone seemed excited and happy to be there together. In the end, representatives of every MSM Regional returned with firsthand reports of that historic moment: the other marchers, the glorious weather, the friendly multitudes filling the lawn from the Lincoln Memorial to the Washington Monument, sharing their sandwiches in a Sunday school picnic atmosphere. Most memorable of all, of course, was the dramatic delivery of Dr. King's "I Have a Dream" speech.

Memories of that march have never left my mind. Through all the hardship that was to follow—Dr. King's assassination, so much hatred, so much suffering and death—the warm camaraderie of "blacks and whites together" and Dr. King's ringing declaration of his dream remain an indelible experience of the early ideals of the civil rights movement. And I felt a deep sense of satisfaction that our planning had made it possible for a number of students to have that experience, too.

I approached the task of building international awareness and solidarity with gusto. Grateful for what had happened to me in China, I wanted American students to have the opportunity to understand what was happening in two-thirds of the world, much of it caught in a life and death struggle to liberate itself from colonialism and imperialism. I inherited from my predecessor, Dorothy Nyland, an excellent vehicle for the task ahead: a national, week-long program called the Christian Citizenship Seminar. It was already accepted as an important part of the MSM's annual calendar. Sixty students and several campus ministers representing each state's MSM came to the United Nations headquarters for three or four days and then went on to the Capitol in Washington, D.C., for the other half of the week. The seminar became a valuable annual training event for building international awareness in the MSM, a focal point of some of the most important work I did.

My convictions about learning by involvement led me to turn over most of the responsibility for planning the seminar to the National Council of MSM. Each year they appointed a student chairperson and a committee to work with me on this. The 1961 chairperson was Wayne Proudfoot, a student at Harvard Divinity School and national president of MSM. What a joy it was to work with these students! As we became more and more deeply involved in our venture together and their excitement grew, I knew we were on the right track. Our first task was to determine the focus of the seminar, usually a particular hot spot somewhere in the world.

The focus for 1961 was the Portuguese colonies in Southern Africa—Mozambique and Angola—which were in deep crisis in their revolt against Portuguese oppression. The student committee developed study papers, a reading list, and eventually a National MSM solidarity campaign outlining a course of action. They worked hard to inform themselves, using their access to university libraries to research relevant information and sharing it with their fellow students. A sample from the April 1969 *MSM Bulletin*: "40,000 Africans and 1,500 whites were massacred in Angola in the first three months of 1961. 99.6% of the Angolan population is illiterate. There are only 25,000 students in secondary schools, and no universities exist in any of the Portuguese colonies."

An essential ingredient of solidarity work is direct contact with people involved in the struggles you are supporting. As a staff member of the Board of Missions, I had access to worldwide contacts and networks. There was a continual flow of firsthand information from African leaders and missionaries. Emilio DeCarvalho, a dynamic young leader of the Angolan Methodist Church, had been imprisoned. Fred Brancel and three other missionaries had been arrested and held without charge in Portugal. Rose Thomas, a young African American missionary in Angola, returned to the United States and became a vital link between American students and Angolans. She enabled a number of networking opportunities with those imprisoned. My office arranged campus visitations across the country for her, and she helped the MSM launch a countrywide solidarity campaign for the liberation of the Portuguese colonies. When Fred Brancel was released from prison, he worked tirelessly with MSM leaders.

From Mozambique came Eduardo Mondlane, a leader of the liberation forces, who had a profound influence on American students. Eduardo was in the United States as a Methodist scholarship student. He was a great leader of his people, the son of a Mozambican chief, highly intelligent and articulate and deeply committed to the liberation of Mozambique. He was tall and charming, brilliant and eloquent. During the long period when he could not return to his own country, he taught anthropology at Syracuse University and worked on the staff of the United Nations.

Eduardo spoke on campuses and student Christian movement events across the country. He was a charismatic leader, but when he worked with the MSM student committee on the seminar, he worked side by side with them, relaxing over coffee, talking far into the night, explaining fine points of political or economic analysis, telling stories of his people, their suffering, their victories. When at last Eduardo Mondlane was able to return to Africa, it was at the invitation of Tanzania, where he directed the Mozambique Institute, a training center for FRELIMO, the Mozambican liberation movement. I visited the institute in Dar es Salaam after Eduardo became its director.

It was a terrible shock to me and to all who knew him when word of Eduardo's assassination reached us in February 1969. Eduardo had eagerly opened a package, thinking it contained a new book. It was a time bomb. Mozambique, Africa, and the world had lost a great and irreplaceable leader. And American students had lost a friend they greatly admired and respected who gave his life in the liberation of his people.

With the courageous witness of African leaders and the flow of first-hand information, MSM became caught up in the desperate situation of the people of Southern Africa. Students began to recognize important common themes in the U.S. civil rights struggle and the revolt against colonialism in Africa. They saw links in white racism, economic gain by the oppressors, and the arrogance of rulers confident that superior military or police force would eventually prevail. They witnessed the fact that neither Africans nor African Americans intended any longer to bear the yoke of suffering.

The change that took place in young people in the course of one week in the citizenship seminars was amazing. In New York, they mostly listened and learned—through lectures by Africans, briefings with UN staff, observing UN units in session, and visiting with various delegations related to Angola, Mozambique, Portugal, and the United States. Theological reflection and worship were integrated into the daily schedule of the seminar. The discussions grew heated as issues began to emerge. By the time they reached the capital, students were loaded with new insights and many disturbing questions. They met strategic congressmen on key committees related to Southern Africa, as well as State Department and Pentagon officials. They explored American connections to colonialism and sought ways of influencing and changing policy. After the seminar, the student campaign went into action. Some actions were national, but many were local campus initiatives: demonstrations, fund-raising for Angolan students who had escaped, telegrams of protest, a strong statement by the Board of Missions.

A significant change was taking place among U.S. Christian students. Their concerns were shifting from service to justice. In the 1950s, they had largely focused on service and building relationships through programs such as student exchanges, study abroad programs, and international work camps. Now, through their participation in the civil rights movement, they began to cross racial barriers and work in programs of literacy and voter registration. Through organizations such as Students for a Democratic Society (SDS), they began to organize urban poor people. The student Christian movements, including the MSM, also organized such programs. Internationally, they grew more and more concerned about the systemic causes of injustice.

As the students' analysis went deeper, their desire to know more and to see for themselves also deepened. They wanted to travel and to see conditions in Latin America firsthand. They wanted to understand the context for the revolutions breaking out all over. They wanted to understand the role of the United States. Therefore the 1963 seminar on Latin America was followed in 1964 by a Latin American Study/Travel Seminar. The Methodist Student Movement, in cooperation with the National Student Christian Federation (NSCF), sponsored the seminar in several Latin American countries, including Mexico, Guatemala, Peru, Chile, Argentina, and Brazil. Our group of U.S. students, campus ministers, and staff began with an excellent week of orientation in Mexico and then traveled south. In each country we visited, we met with a variety of persons to help answer our questions: What is happening in your country? What are the causes of injustice here? What is the role of the United States in your country? What is the role of U.S. churches?

Some of our most valuable contacts were members of the student Christian movements. We were excited to be in direct contact with them. Although these movements were small, most of them were vitally involved in social and political issues. Our conversations ran far into the night as we pursued our questions and they pressed us for explanation of U.S. policies and what we were doing about them. Sometimes the depth of their theological understanding amazed us, and their willingness to take risks on behalf of their people challenged us to look at our own commitments.

Lane McGaughy, MSM president, elmira Kendricks Nazombe, and I left the seminar after Guatemala. For three weeks we attended the General Assembly of the World Student Christian Federation. It had been scheduled for Brazil, but a coup d'état necessitated a last-minute shift of venue to Embalse Rio de Tercera in western Argentina. The WSCF brought together delegates from student Christian movements in more than eighty countries. It was difficult, as well as inspiring, to be among students of such diverse backgrounds and rapidly changing conditions. On everyone's mind was the coup in Brazil, symbolic of these times of upheaval everywhere.

The WSCF delegates strove to find a way to express their calling as Christian students and their desire to make their unity concrete. The French word *présence* captured their imagination. By the end of the meeting, their statement on "Christian Presence" had been signed by students from all eighty countries. The statement said, "We use the word 'presence' to describe a way of life. It does not mean that we are simply there; it tries to describe the adventure of being there in the name of Christ. When we say 'presence' we say that we have to get into the midst of things even when they frighten us. It means for us engagement, involvement in the concrete structures of our society. . . . For us presence spells death to the status quo both in society and in the Christian community; we will not tire of pleading and working for the restoration of normal humanity as we see it in Jesus."

The U.S. students and I were impressed by the total commitment and vital involvement in social and political issues, the serious theological probing, and the daily risks taken by the Brazilians, the Cubans, and other students. We felt a sharp judgment on our "easy Christianity," and these encounters added urgency to our lives back home.

Lane, elmira, and I rejoined the rest of the seminar in Brazil, the final country our group would visit. For me, the visit in Brazil was the most memorable of all. We were fortunate that the Brazilian student Christian movement planned and hosted our visit, putting us in touch with valuable contacts. We traveled to three major cities, São Paolo in the south, Rio de Janeiro on the central coast, and Recife in the far north. We were impressed by the vast area of Brazil, so much larger than the other countries visited, and our travel from one end of the country to the other gave us greater opportunity for exposure to the Brazilian situation. Everywhere we went we were confronted with destitute people, suffering because of poverty. Because the coup d'état had just occurred, it inevitably formed the backdrop for our visit and discussions. As we explored the role of the United States in Brazil, we learned information that was new and shocking to us. For instance, we were told that our country had assisted those who carried out the coup by taking aerial photographs of every square mile of Brazil, with the proviso that the United States would keep its own copy of the photographs.

Margaret Rigg, an artist and the art editor of *motive* magazine, made a unique and valuable contribution to the seminar. In each country, she arranged for our group to meet outstanding local artists, see their work, and talk with them. Our visit with an artist in Rio stands out for me. As we met in his studio, the agony of the Brazilian poor surrounded us, pounded in on our sensibilities from every painting on the walls. We spent hours with him, and I came home with some of his art pieces as lifetime reminders of the poor people in Brazil.

Another unforgettable encounter was in Recife, where many of Brazil's poorest lived. Recife was the home of Dom Helder Camara, noted Roman Catholic bishop of Northeast Brazil. We went to his "palace" for our appointment and waited in the large audience room with its elevated "throne." I was reflecting on church hierarchy when he came into the room. His entrance is etched in my memory. I didn't realize at first that he was the bishop. He was very small of stature and humble in appearance, dressed in a simple, unadorned cotton cassock. He came into the room before we were even aware that he was there. Dom Helder, as he was fondly called, quietly suggested

that we move our chairs in a circle, and then he joined the circle. With ap-
pealing intimacy, he had us make the circle as small as possible so that he
"could hear." He began by asking each one of us to introduce ourselves. He
asked us questions about ourselves, the purpose of our seminar, what we had
seen and learned. Then he began to talk about his flock in Recife.

He was so gentle, so strong, so beguiling, so committed to justice for
the poor of the earth. He spent a long time with us, telling us about conditions in Recife and what he and others were trying to do. He discussed the
issues and questions we raised. Sitting beside him, I was deeply moved by
this quietly impassioned champion of justice. The visit with Dom Helder was
an unexpected blessing of great worth. His words filled us with encouragement. He welcomed us as allies in the work for justice for the world's poor.
As we walked through the streets of Recife among the "wretched of the earth,"
we saw them now through Dom Helder's eyes.

Back in the United States, we seminar participants reflected on our
learnings. We had heard bitterness toward the United States expressed again
and again in many Latin American countries, by students, artists, clergy, journalists, and theologians. We were often shocked by the intensity of their hostility. We had experienced powerful feelings of national pride among the Latin
American people. We had seen devastating and pervasive conditions of poverty and oppression, conditions that demanded change and would lead to revolution. In each country, we had met Christians who were compelled by their
faith to take great risks to work to alleviate the suffering of their people. We
had deepened our understanding of the meaning of solidarity. It seemed clear
that U.S. students must more carefully examine their assumptions about
United States military, financial, and cultural involvements, including the
church's involvements. To dig more deeply into the causes of injustice in Latin
America, they decided that the next year's UN/Washington seminar would
again focus on Latin America.

As students' desire for direct contact and involvement across national
boundaries increased, some of us were working on a plan to provide deeper
and more extensive opportunities through the Frontier Internship in Mission
program. Margaret Flory, Student World Relations staff of the United Presbyterian Ecumenical Commission, envisioned the Frontier Intern program and
was its first director. The idea grew out of the 1959 Athens conference, with
its emphasis on frontiers. Interns would serve for two years on one of the
strategic frontiers, such as sites of racial tensions, new nationalisms, uprooted
people, and university/world. Each intern engaged in study and service on
subsistence support. From its conception, the program was ecumenical. It be-

gan in 1960 as a pilot project of the Presbyterian Ecumenical Commission, with the Methodist Church and United Church of Christ soon joining in as active co-sponsors. I worked closely with the program for a number of years.

Here was the opportunity young people were seeking to cross international boundaries and join others already at work on mission frontiers. The carefully selected assignments were opportunities for young adults to explore and experiment with new possibilities of service. The program's distinctive features—flexibility, economic discipline, and freedom—attracted outstanding candidates. As a member of the team responsible for intern selection, orientation, and assignment to projects, I was deeply impressed by the candidates' excellence. It was thrilling to participate in interviews with these young people and anticipate their development and future contribution. Even more impressive was their continuing commitment when they returned to the United States. They made linkages across boundaries and eventually built strong networks with students and others dedicated to justice around the world. Among those who worked as Frontier Interns were Tami Hultman in South Africa (see chapter 7), and elmira Kendricks Nazombe in Kenya (see chapter 4), and Alice Hageman in Paris at UNESCO headquarters and at the international headquarters of the World Student Christian Federation in Geneva (see chapter 9).

Ruth?" It was my friend and colleague Peggy Billings on the phone. "What should we do about Dr. King's call to come to Selma?" There really was no question. We had to be there. That week in early March 1965, the movement had attempted to march north from Selma to the capitol in Montgomery to demonstrate for the right of African Americans to vote. They were brutally stopped. Before many days they would make the attempt again. This was the time of preparation. In the next few minutes we made our plan. Peggy was calling from Florida, where she was on a field visit. I would fly from New York to Atlanta. We would meet at the airport, rent a car, and drive to Selma. First, Peggy would consult with Thelma Stevens, and I would consult with Ann Porter Brown, the new executive of the Board of Missions. They immediately gave their blessings. It seemed entirely appropriate to them that Peggy, the secretary for race relations, and I, secretary for student work, should represent the Woman's Division and the Board of Missions in Selma in response to the call. Peggy had grown up in Mississippi and had been a missionary social worker in Korea. Both experiences proved invaluable in the coming weeks.

As our rented car approached Selma, we were reminded that it was the county seat of Dallas County, one of nineteen Alabama counties described as the Black Belt because of their heavy African American population. A majority, 57 percent, of county residents were African Americans, but only 0.9 percent of those eligible were registered to vote. The Student Nonviolent Coordinating Committee (SNCC) had begun organizing in 1962 in Selma, the birthplace and stronghold of the White Citizens Council.

We crossed the Edmund Pettus Bridge, by now familiar to the whole world through gripping television coverage of the first attempted march from Selma to Montgomery. There the marchers had met the force of hundreds of baton-wielding Alabama state police, who unleashed dogs on the marchers. Many demonstrators were injured. The world watched in disbelief and dismay as fellow human beings were beaten while demonstrating for their rights as American citizens. The march had to be canceled, and it was then that Dr. King sent out the call for supporters to come and participate in the second attempt.

We drove to the Brown's Chapel area of Selma. It was hard to believe that this was my country. We saw massive barricades, a multitude of state troopers cordoning off the area and holding their weapons high. Everyone going in or out of the area had to pass through a police checkpoint. This was incomprehensible to me. How could I understand the fear and hostility this represented? The show of force made what was happening inside the barricades all the more dramatic.

The heart of all activity was Brown's Chapel, with subsidiary activities in other nearby churches. Peggy and I spent the next two weeks of our lives inside this surrounded African American neighborhood. Families opened their homes, welcoming us with beds and heartwarming hospitality. Brown's Chapel provided food for body and soul. The women of the neighborhood ran an amazing kitchen and served up a seemingly never-ending supply of the most delicious southern cooking. Inside Brown's Chapel was a nonstop combination of rally, prayer meeting, and old-fashioned hymn sing. We had inspired preaching, glorious singing, laughing and weeping, eating, and sometimes sleeping—and through it all, courage, deep joy, and the power of the Spirit. For the first time, the reality that I had experienced in China in the little church at McTyeire was apparent to me in my own country. I was part of the church ALIVE!

Tensions in the white community ran high. A couple of times we were asked to give a movement person a ride to Montgomery. Somehow we got through the checkpoint, picked up our passenger at an appointed spot, and started our trip. Sometimes our passenger hid on the floor in the back seat. I didn't know just how high tensions were until I heard later about the murder of Viola Liuzzo, who was shot as she chauffered African Americans on that same road the day after the march.

Before long we began to hear that the second attempt to march to Montgomery would be starting. Then we heard that the march was peaking too soon and that preparations in Montgomery were not completed. Some Southern Christian Leadership Conference (SCLC) organizers approached Peggy and me and others in Selma and asked us to contact networks of people who would recruit volunteers to come to Montgomery and help prepare for the arrival of the marchers and the thousands of supporters expected there on the day the march arrived. Peggy and I found phones to contact our networks. Peggy contacted Methodist women, and I, the Methodist Student Movement. On March 15 I reached Bill Corzine, staff advisor to the National Council of the MSM. The recent decisions and actions of NCMSM, as well as two major conferences, the NSCF Athens conference in 1963 and the MSM national conference in 1964, had focused on the critical importance of the civil rights movement in our history. Bill called MSM president Charles Rinker and the chairperson of the Civil Rights Committee, Jill Hultin. The four of us devoted ourselves to an emerging strategy for Methodist student participation in this decisive phase of the civil rights struggle.

The day the march began, Sunday, March 21, all of us in the Brown's Chapel community made our way early in the morning to the Edmund Pettus Bridge with considerable trepidation and determination, trying to be ready for whatever might come. But this time, national and world attention was focused on the march. This time there was protection for the marchers. This day the march began without a hitch. Leading the march was Dr. King, linking arms with Rabbi Abraham Heschel, the great Jewish human rights advocate, and Eugene Carson Blake, president of the National Council of Churches. They were followed by the entire Brown's Chapel community. Some of the MSM leaders were there: elmira Kendricks Nazombe, Jill Hultin, Charlotte Bunch, Charles Rinker, Bill Corzine.

As we looked up, a great flock of huge birds seemed to be hovering over us—the sky was full of helicopters. At first I didn't know why they were there, and it was scary. They were television and military helicopters, a protection for the marchers, in fact, and they followed us for quite a distance. Peggy and I marched that first day from morning till evening. When we reached an encampment that had been set up to provide a place for marchers to sleep that first night, we caught a ride back to Selma, got our rented car, and drove to Montgomery. It was time to begin the work that the movement had assigned to us.

·

Our MSM strategy had begun to work. Bill Corzine and a few other leaders had come ahead to Selma to plan with SCLC leadership. In the next few days nearly one hundred Methodist students and campus ministers from all over the country arrived in Montgomery. MSM volunteers were directed by staff of the Montgomery Improvement Association, working with the MSM National Council. They were asked to help with housing, transportation, and community mobilization. At first the students were thinking about housing a hundred or so people coming from outside, but it soon became clear that they had assumed no such small responsibility. The marchers would arrive in Montgomery on Thursday. By Wednesday, the MSM still had to find housing in African American homes for several thousand people for the following night.

A number of the SCLC leaders were organizing evening rallies in black churches in Montgomery before the march arrived. One evening I attended a rally in a church packed with mostly young, black activists. Young people were hanging out the windows, standing on each other's shoulders. They were singing and dancing in the aisles. Andy Young was in charge of the evening. At one point he asked all of the older church members, many of them quite elderly, to stand up. "I want you to look at these people," he said to the gathered crowd. "These are the faithful members of this church. They're the ones who have been preparing for us all their lives. Because of their faithfulness for many years, we have this place ready for us to come together at this moment in history." I thought, Perhaps that's what I've been doing since I returned from China, where my life's real commitment to justice began. I've been working with students to prepare for a time such as this.

The next day, March 25, 1965, the marchers arrived. President Lyndon Johnson had federalized the National Guard and soon troops began to appear. Thousands of people arrived from every part of the country. It was a great ecumenical outpouring of Americans—Catholic nuns, Jewish rabbis, Protestant clergy, black and white, marching row after row, singing freedom songs. An estimated six thousand clergypersons came.

As the massive march made its way slowly up the great broad approach to the capitol building, I was fortunate to find a place to sit on the steps in front of Dr. King's church. Here is where the Montgomery bus boycott had begun in 1956 when Rosa Parks refused to move to the back of the bus because "it was a matter of dignity." In this city, forty-two thousand African Americans had refused to ride the buses, some of them walking as many as fourteen miles a day until change had come.

For me, the experience in Selma and Montgomery symbolized a kind of closure, a coming fully around. In a profound way this was in continuity with my time in China. During those weeks in Alabama, I personally experienced, for the first time in my own land, a situation of intense fear and oppression. Out of this experience and the leadership of Dr. King and other African Americans, I received some important and life-changing lessons. Some of them reinforced what I had learned in the Chinese Revolution; others were completely new. In China I had come to know about the power of the Spirit that comes to people as they take up the struggle for their own liberation. In Selma, too, I saw the power of the Spirit. But in Selma we experienced power in a melding together of political action and religious faith and morality. This was Dr. King's way. He refused to let politics and religion be separated. For him, it was not *whether* they mix, but rather how to establish as great a degree of congruence as possible between the nature of the God we worship and the nature of the human action that we undertake in God's name.

Sitting there on the steps of Dr. King's church and seeing the marchers approach the nearby Alabama capitol building, I could begin to realize some of what might lie ahead. This victory over Governor Wallace and Sheriff Clark and the forces they represented had unmasked even deeper layers of white fear and violence. At the same time, SNCC and SCLC were growing apart, as SNCC became disillusioned with a nonviolent approach. The U.S. involvement in the Vietnam War was on the increase. But by late spring Congress passed the Voting Rights Act, which would become the law of the land.

Within the student Christian movement, MSM was phasing out of existence in order to become part of the ecumenical University Christian Movement. Beyond that, before the decade ended, in the midst of assassinations and social turmoil, the U.S. student movement as we had known it would change greatly with the dissolution of UCM. Meanwhile the Woman's Division, as part of a merger of much of its mission work with the World Division of the Methodist Board of Missions, was deciding to eliminate its "lines of work" with children, youth, and students. I was moving to a position with the World Division to organize a new office of University World, focusing on students and faculty overseas. In the future I would work closely with denominational and ecumenical youth networks and the World Student Christian Federation. I would travel widely to be present with and support students who were organizing, studying, and struggling in Africa, Asia, the Middle East, Latin America, the Caribbean, and the Pacific.

Especially important to me in the years ahead would be work with the WSCF Women's Commission, for which I was the first advisor. For years I had worked with wonderfully able young women and excellent older female colleagues. But with WSCF women and urban and rural poor women I began to analyze sexism in a serious way and to see the profound structural implications of the exclusion and oppression of women in the United States and globally.

The Selma to Montgomery March in the spring of 1965 was a critical historical event. For me personally, Selma was a watershed. It brought me into full re-membering, a coming together of my experiences in China and the United States. It was in China that I had first seen the absolute necessity of radical social change. I had seen the depth of suffering caused by injustice that gives rise to revolution. I had come to know that people working together can change history. I had for the first time experienced the Living Church. In Selma it was all there again, here in my own country. It came together for me in Selma—full circle.

CHAPTER 2

Jeanne Audrey Powers

~~~~~~◠

*The Church is the only institution I
know that pays its employees to subvert it!"* This statement, by a conscientious objector seeking alternative service through the US–2 Program of the Board of Missions of the United Methodist Church, has haunted me, motivated me, and sustained me ever since I heard him say it in 1970. Now, as I write this, when my disappointment with the United Methodist Church has become excruciatingly difficult to bear, his statement reminds me that "committed subversion" is, in fact, an invitation the Church continues to offer. When the Body of Christ refuses to be part of the continuing incarnation of Christ in the world, this statement is a powerful witness to the vision that this young man had caught from the Church. As I reflect on my own experiences of Christian nurture and development, my calling to ordained ministry, my service as a campus minister and as a national staff person in missionary personnel and ecumenical offices for the denomination, I see that subversion is an identifying characteristic of my own life and ministry.

When I began my ministry in the fall of 1959, I had never had a woman seminary professor, had never read a book written by a feminist theologian, had no women models for ordained ministry, looked to ordained men exclusively for professional company, had almost no experience related to segregation or the "black experience," had no friends or colleagues of another race, and knew no one, other than myself, who was gay or lesbian. This description says far less about me as a white, upper midwestern, mainline Protestant "girl minister" (as a Minneapolis newspaper photo caption identified me) than it does about the culture of the time. I was alone, charting new territory at every point in my life. What was it that shaped me, that pushed me forward, that planted the seeds of whom I would become and what my ministry would look like? What enabled me ultimately to claim "subversion" as a primary form of ministry?

Y̆ou can be anything you want to be. You can do anything you want to do."
These were the messages I heard in my home, and they served me well as a
child and youth in a lower-middle-income family in Mankato, Minnesota, in
the 1940s. Only after I began my campus ministry did I realize that this
Horatio Alger outlook didn't work for most people. An only child, I grew up
in a family that was clearly matriarchal. My widowed grandmother and my
mother had been teachers; my two aunts never married, lived at home, and
held responsible jobs, one as a court clerk for a judge and the other as an
administrative assistant to a county agent. My aunts' friends—single women
who were teachers, secretaries, or clerks—became part of our family life, were
often in our home for meals, and went with us on outings. My aunts were
among the first to learn to drive and to purchase a Ford car, which they drove
on long trips to canoe and take photographs. Although I was unaware of it at
the time, all these women served as role models for me.

My mother married in 1927 at the age of thirty-two and gave birth to
me five years later, at thirty-seven, a very late age to start a family in the
heart of the Depression. What a glorious twelve years she had before her marriage! An elementary teacher through and through, she saw that profession
as one that would open the world for her—and it did. Following two years of
teacher training at Mankato State Teachers College, where I, too, was graduated forty years later, she taught in several different places. The children of
Eastern European immigrants on the Iron Range of northern Minnesota were
among her favorite students. But it was a two-year assignment in Panama
that became a primary influence on the rest of her life. She answered a newspaper advertisement for teachers for the children of workers building the
Panama Canal. World War I was raging, and there were threats of German
submarines all along the coast. Many southern Minnesota newspapers reported
on her adventure. "I swam in the Atlantic and Pacific oceans on the same
day," she used to boast. It was her way of saying that the teaching profession
offered unique opportunities for a young single woman. "The sky's the limit
of what you can do," she told me. I believed her.

I was never "programmed" for boyfriends and marriage, never told not
to excel or compete with boys. I was never prohibited from playing boys'
games—I beat them at ping-pong—and was never reminded to "act like a
lady." At seven, I was given the choice of a magazine subscription. I chose
Boy's Life, and I loved it.

My father worked for an electrical construction company headquartered
in St. Paul. He was often assigned as superintendent on rural electrification
projects around the country. My mother and I frequently joined him and lived

temporarily—from three weeks to a year—in seven states from Wyoming to New Hampshire. Everywhere we lived, my mother and I went to the Methodist church, just as her family always did. My father was raised an Irish Catholic loyalist and a pro-union Democrat, but he was not a practicing Catholic, so he turned my religious development over to my mother's family, which was Welsh, Republican, and definitely not pro-labor. Methodist Sunday school provided consistency in my life, no matter where we were. Thanks to my mother's teaching nature, we used every opportunity to learn about the areas where we lived.

You must find God's will for your life." This was the message I received from my Sunday school teachers, and, more important, from six years of weeklong summer church camps. It was the predominant theme of my life from ages fifteen to thirty. This did not mean that God would write in the sky what I was supposed to do. Rather, I was to make a spiritual journey with God as my companion through everything, and prayer would help me stay alert to the signs of God's will. No book has ever influenced my spiritual life more than Leslie Weatherhead's *The Will of God.* I believed that God had a special plan for me, and that it was my responsibility to find it. I prayed fervently that I would be open to receive God's word in every decision I made, from what college major to pursue, to my choice of a profession, to how to use my summer vacation. Each experience I had would reveal God's hand and word to me if I "let Him in." This was a time of deep piety for me, and while my theology has totally changed, I regret that my spirituality of that period has never been matched since.

I entered Mankato State Teachers College (now Minnesota State University) in 1950 and lived at home all four years. My father died during my freshman year, and my mother was now settled permanently in our family home. I had, however, intended to transfer to the University of Minnesota, as a social work major, until the unexpected happened: I was elected junior class president—the first woman to hold that position. I took this as a sign that God wanted me to remain at Mankato, where I became involved in the Methodist Wesley Foundation, believing that my public witness as a Christian was important.

If they give a free trip, then American Youth Hostels must have a program." My mother was encouraging me to answer a notice she had seen and apply to the American Youth Hostels (AYH) for a free trip. All I had to do was write on the topic "Why I'd like to go to Europe on a bicycle." I resisted her urging for a year, but finally my mother's memory of her Panama trip and her teacher's eye for learning experiences prevailed. Without question, the AYH trip was the primary foundational experience of my life.

Eight years after World War II, Europe was still in a state of chaos: destroyed buildings, displaced persons, scarcity of food. Memories of the war and the Holocaust were fresh in the minds of people who had lost family members, homes, and their sense of well-being. Apart from American servicemen, government employees, and the wealthy, few Americans traveled to Europe. There was no tourist industry. Who would want to go there under such conditions? But the youth hostels were open, and students were traveling.

Of the offerings available through AYH, I chose France, Belgium, Holland, and England. The program put ten students together with one leader and refused to accept more than two people who already knew each other. This was a key factor in my willingness to apply, because, as a small-town Minnesota student, I could look forward to joining others who would also be "alone" on this new venture. We bicycled 1,400 miles in eight weeks, and I got to know students from Stanford University, Ohio State, Harvard, and other schools. One of our group was the first Jewish person I had ever met. She and her family had been on the last boat out of Hamburg the day after Kristallnacht. Of course, we met many people along the way who had actually lived through the war's devastation and not simply read about it.

This trip showed me how inadequate my college education had been, and it led me to claim the world as my community. Despite my good grades in college, I felt like a dunce in this group. My Speech and English major had trained me to coach debate, declamation, and drama, but I was woefully lacking in a good liberal arts education. The others knew European history, the reigns of English kings, the political background of both world wars, the maestros of music, and the geniuses of painting. They were well prepared for all the castles, cathedrals, museums, and theaters we visited. I was angry that my guidance counselors had not encouraged me to apply for scholarships to elite eastern women's colleges. My family assumed I would work my way through college, which I did, but what was my education worth?

After the trip, I turned to self-discipline and the Wesley Foundation to supplement my education. The magazine *motive* challenged me beyond my natural ability, and the YWCA's *Intercollegian* put me in touch with social justice issues. I was determined to spend one hour a day in the library reading things outside my major, even on subjects I was not initially interested in. I began reading *Christian Science Monitor* cover to cover and paying attention to footnotes and bibliographies in scholarly books. I stuck to this discipline because I wanted more out of my senior year than good grades. As I was to learn later, anger is a wonderful motivator.

Becoming aware of the world, past and present, was a gift of the hosteling trip. Because few civilians had been to Europe (and certainly not on a bicycle) or spoken to a person from another country, the Mankato paper published stories on my trip. I became every organization's program of the month and gave about seventy presentations over the next year, showing slides of people we had met, of bomb damage, and of European life. Every picture provided a story of people whom I wanted the audience to see as neighbors. Because the Europeans we met on the trip were amazed that "rich" Americans would travel on bicycles, stay in hostels, and eat bread and cheese in a meadow for lunch, we were invited into personal conversations that still elude most tourists. We learned what a bad image Americans had in their minds, and we worked hard to distance ourselves from that "ugly American." The primary goal of my presentations on my return was to show the audience how we were regarded and to awaken them to the need for a new understanding of world community.

*B*ut Mr. Danforth, we already have a woman from Minnesota in the program, and you remember your rules: we will never have more than one person from a state."

"I don't care. I want that girl."

I was about to graduate from college with no idea what I wanted to do with my life when I heard about the Danforth Foundation. William H. Danforth, founder of Ralston-Purina Foods, believed that there was a place for serious Christian scholars in higher education, and numerous programs for graduate students and faculty had been developed. The program that captured my attention was the Danforth Graduate Program. Approximately twenty "Danny Grad" women were chosen each year, all of whom had splendid college grades, proven leadership, and expectations of becoming successful in their chosen fields. In addition to those qualifications, they had also realized in their senior year that the student Christian movement had become more important to them than their original plans. Having achieved what they prepared to do, they no longer wanted to do it.

Through a peculiar and wondrous set of circumstances—"God's will" again—I became a Danny Grad, joining with twenty-two other women, mostly from liberal arts colleges, for a monthlong training period at Camp Miniwanca in Michigan and then assignment to a college campus that had to be at least a thousand miles from home. Although I was initially devastated to be assigned to Towson State Teachers College in Baltimore instead of a big-name university, I realized later that the assignment, which was the result of careful observation and evaluation of my needs and hopes, was a wise choice for me.

Besides being required to meet with the whole group twice a year and to write monthly letters for a community packet, our assignments featured some unusual elements. We were to develop a disciplined prayer life. We were to spend two hours each day reading books or other material in fields that we had not read previously. We were to visit colleges and universities within a two-hundred-mile radius for their Religious Emphasis Weeks. In addition to room and board and an adequate stipend, we were each given $25 a month as a "happiness fund," to be spent however we chose, though we had to give an account of it. One month I took a blind student to her first symphony, and during exam time I brought donuts and cocoa to a college dormitory. Having this extra give-away money was marvelous for one who had always scrimped and saved.

That year, as I attended Middle Atlantic student conferences and observed campus ministry units in the colleges and universities I visited, I experienced the nationwide student Christian movement for the first time. Many of the friendships I made with other Danny Grads have lasted more than forty years, and because of the Danny Grad year, nearly all of us entered professions totally different from the ones for which we had prepared.

*D*o not be anxious about tomorrow; tomorrow will look after itself." The Danny Grad year, 1954–55, gave me the time I needed to stall, sort out my priorities, and decide what would come next. If I didn't want to teach, what *did* I want to do? I was sure that God was using that year to reveal His (*sic*) will for me, and I felt I was making crucial decisions that would set "the plan" for the rest of my life. The Towson-Baltimore experience had been the most urban and eclectic of any of the Danny Grad assignments. My campus visits ranged from an all-black college in Virginia to Yale University in Connecticut. Holidays with students from Maine to Virginia exposed me to the intensity of East Coast life, and I knew I wanted to remain there. My reading time during that year was almost entirely in theology, and I began to feel called to go to seminary for one year. Women were not ordained in the Methodist Church at that time, and I had no idea what seminary was all about. I only knew that I wanted to study full time for one whole year reading theology and hearing lectures about the Christian faith. I longed to deepen my faith, and seminary seemed to be the way to do it.

Having decided that Princeton Theological Seminary would offer the best climate for spiritual growth and rigorous theological study, I set out for Princeton in the fall of 1955 with seventy dollars and a one-way bus ticket. It was the first time I had taken seriously the promise that if "our Heavenly Father" looks after the birds of the air and the lilies of the field, then I had nothing to fear about managing a year, convinced it was God's plan for me.

I stood in a long line to register on the first day. At the desk, the line separated in two directions, and I was asked if I was in the Master of Religious Education or the Divinity program. I had no idea. I only knew that I wanted to take the most challenging courses Princeton offered. I was told that the Bachelor of Divinity (now called Master of Divinity) program would probably be the one to pursue, and so I asked which program took the least time. Each was a three-year program. Had it not been for that, I probably would have avoided the Bachelor of Divinity and completed the usual religious education program expected of women students. You can see why I believed so strongly that God was guiding each step of my life.

I finished the paper at three a.m. and it wasn't even due the next day." The Princeton year was the finest period of academic study I have ever experienced. Knowing little about biblical history, struggling with the required Greek, reading philosophy, and exegeting the English Bible, I finally learned what makes for a real education. Neoorthodoxy was the primary theological school of thought there, and visiting lecturers included all the big names of that time, such as Reinhold and H. Richard Niebuhr, Emil Brunner, and Paul Tillich. President John A. Mackay, a colleague of John R. Mott, founder of the World Student Christian Federation in 1895, was my professor of ecumenics, a required course for all first-year students. Chapel services exposed me to national and international leadership in the Presbyterian Church and the Reformed tradition. The written and preached Word became important to me as never before. Public prayer began each class and every meal. The dining hall mixed the students at round tables of eight, where stories of faith journeys were shared and strong arguments about theology or recent lectures kept us engaged. The Interseminary Movement exposed me to students at other East Coast seminaries. It was during that year—1956—that the Methodist Church voted to admit women into the itinerant ordained ministry. Now there was an actual vocational calling to realize.

During that year in seminary, I began to see myself in preparation for the campus ministry. Because I did not believe Greek and Hebrew, which Princeton required, to be crucial for such a ministry, and because I longed to meet Methodist counterparts to the national Presbyterian leadership I was coming to know, I contended with God over my desire to remain in Princeton's extraordinarily stimulating environment versus my need to prepare more specifically for the Methodist campus ministry. I didn't want to leave Princeton, but I felt God's active leading to do so.

The summer before, I had participated in an American Friends Service Committee work camp in Mexico. I was assigned to a site where conscientious objectors were usually assigned. Some were idealists or humanists, some were motivated by Christian or political convictions, and some were rigid pacifists or escapists from American life. All, as you might imagine, were individualists. It was a difficult assignment, living in a primitive mountain Indian community during the week, sleeping in our clothes and not washing for five days, and trekking a dangerous and mountainous eight miles back and forth to our camp on weekends. I became an ideological pacifist, even though the practical relationships in this heterogeneous "team" never seemed to benefit from such theoretical convictions.

This was my only point of contention with Princeton. The "just war" theory was taken for granted in this heavily neo-orthodox climate, and a pacifist point of view was not even given consideration. After visiting two Methodist seminaries, at Drew and Boston Universities, I reluctantly transferred to Boston University School of Theology (BUSTH) because of its Methodist roots, its strong pacifist perspectives (Martin Luther King, Jr., had finished there the year before I came), and its very specialized program in campus ministry. It was a painful decision. My experience, however, led me to hear a new call to parish ministry.

Only in retrospect have I realized that the feminist movement was taking shape in me as I worked on my bachelor's degree in sacred theology, which I received in 1958. Women seemed to be appendages to the seminary. My criticisms of its ethos were dismissed. When denominational appointments were being discussed and district superintendents were conducting interviews, women tended to be excluded. Minnesota Methodist offices had never shown a bit of interest in me. I was angry at God for pushing me to leave Princeton and angry at BUSTH for its group-process teaching style, its philosophical rather than biblical theology, and its refusal to give a hearing to neo-orthodox perspectives. Vehement arguments with my teachers forced me into a far more conservative theological position than the one I held when I entered. One faculty member told me, "I've heard about you and I don't want you in my class."

Yet when fellowships were given for additional graduate study, and there was a debate among the faculty about whether I was a good representative of the seminary, the primary spokesman for Boston's personalism school of thought said, "When BUSTH claims to be a liberal seminary, it means that we recognize a variety of theological perspectives, not a fixed position." Because I was one of the few who had taken courses in Greek, I qualified for the Lucinda Bidwell Beebe Fellowship and chose to take a year of noncredit study at St. Andrews University in Scotland. This enabled me to reflect on what I had learned, or not learned, in both seminaries and to begin bringing together the disparate theological streams with which I would enter the ordained ministry.

I 'm sorry I can't make it then. I already have plans for the summer." Just before I left for Scotland, I was ordained as a Methodist deacon (the first step in the ordination process), although the Twin Cities newspapers labeled me "one of the first Methodist deaconesses" (a title belonging to a distinct group of laywomen). Appearing before the Minnesota Methodist ordination committee was not as grueling as it is now, and most of the members focused on their memories of my often inappropriate behavior at junior and senior high church camps. They were proud to be ordaining a woman, and were less concerned with testing my abilities than with displaying their smugness at being open to implementing the controversial Methodist General Conference action of just two years before—the decision to ordain women.

A rare Methodist in Church of Scotland territory, I participated in a small University Methodist Society and was introduced to the Student Christian Movement of Great Britain. It was a very creative time in Britain, with new understandings of mission and liturgy. Shortly before the end of the term, I was asked by the Minnesota Cabinet, the appointment-making body, if I would accept an appointment in June as the half-time associate director of the Wesley Foundation at the University of Minnesota's St. Paul campus. With the other half of my time, I would be the first state director of the Minnesota Methodist Student Movement. Although I said yes, I also simply announced that I planned to travel through Europe and wouldn't be home until mid-September. And so I arrived in Minnesota the day before classes began. Ah, the naïveté of the young!

John Wesley said, "The world is my parish," and so was mine to be. In the 1950s, Wesley Foundations were usually staffed by the pastor of a congregation, who served as the director, and an associate director. The pastor-director preached sermons stimulating to college students, worked with the board of trustees, oversaw Foundation property (if it had any), advocated for funds from the Annual Conference, interpreted students' needs to the Church, and did pastoral counseling with students. The associate director, almost always a woman from the local community, had few functions and no specialized training. Her chief responsibility was to work on programming (usually a Sunday evening meeting) and be a mothering presence to students having difficulty adjusting to college life. Because the Minnesota Methodist Conference had never appointed anyone to a full-time campus ministry apart from a local church, and because my two half-time jobs made me a full-time employee, I was to be the associate minister, in name only, at the nearby local congregation. I participated in each service, preached occasionally, and taught adult classes. The Wesley Foundation board chair later had to explain to the church members that I was not supposed to be a full-time pastor to them, and they were not providing any of my salary. As a clergywoman, I seemed not to fit anywhere.

Minnesota, at that time, had three state university campuses and five state colleges, each with a Wesley Foundation. Only the Minneapolis and St. Paul campuses of the University of Minnesota had Wesley Foundation buildings. The rest met in local churches. Wesley House on the St. Paul campus, which served students in agriculture, forestry, home economics, and veterinary medicine, consisted of a lounge, two small rooms—one used as a chapel, the other as an office—a two-room apartment for a caretaking couple, and six rooms on the second floor that housed twelve women students. In the basement, there were two workrooms, a full kitchen, and a large room that served as an eating co-op for about forty students. The women's housing and the co-op made this building unique. It was exceptionally well planned for significant ministry and for income to support the Foundation's work. It was in this building that I had my office and worked in my two half-time appointments. I did my own secretarial work.

The Woman's Society of Christian Service in each local church named a secretary of student work. This local church officer communicated the names of college-bound students to the pastor/directors of the Wesley Foundations at their new schools. Included in this letter was an invitation to an orientation day to find out more about the religious groups on campus. My first responsibility, my first day on the job, was to meet the Methodist students who had come for this orientation. Although the St. Paul campus was nicknamed the farm campus or the "cow college," I was unprepared for the predominant number of students from farm families who showed up, looking as if they'd just come from the fields. One young man named Bill, with tight dirty jeans, perspiration odor emanating from his shirt, and a raucous laugh that barely disguised his discomfort, made more simple grammatical mistakes than I had ever heard in a university community. The word "hayseed" named it all for me, and having so recently come from a rich international experience, I wondered what kind of work I could do there. In retrospect, I wonder how, with that elitist attitude, I could have had any ministry there at all.

A tradition at St. Paul Wesley was a Chinese meal on the first Sunday of the fall term. Only chopsticks were available, and the seats were pillows on the floor. The meal was followed by a get-acquainted period, introduction of the leadership, the distribution of *motive* magazine's orientation issue, a carefully developed worship service, and a square dance. For almost all of the students, it was a night to remember: their first experience of ethnic food and dancing in the church, which would have shocked some of their home congregations. The evening provided an example of high-quality Christian community, models of student leadership, intellectual stimulation, and an opening to the world and a form of church life they had not known before. They recognized that the Wesley Foundation would provide certain challenges that they wouldn't encounter anywhere else on campus or at home.

At twenty-seven, I felt not much older than some of the students with whom I worked. It didn't take me long to realize how much I had to learn from these independent, responsible, honest, capable, self-initiating young people. Some of them had held their family farms together during high school while their parents were ill; nearly all of them were 4-H members who had raised their own animals and won ribbons for it; most of the men had been Future Farmers of America; and many of them—men and women—knew how to prepare food for large families and hired hands. All of them understood teamwork and mutual accountability because they had had a part in running "little corporations." They brought these qualities to Wesley House and the Foundation program.

There are many stories I could tell. As I came to know Bill and slowly tried to help him with social graces, I learned that he had been turned out of his home after eighth grade and had worked for two years as a hired hand for a neighbor, in whose barn he lived, before he returned to high school. His teacher told him he should follow the industrial arts program because he wasn't "college material," but he chose the regular academic track and was now working his way through the university. It was Bill who discovered that *motive* magazine provided superb resources for the deputation teams we developed to share worship and programs with Methodists in small towns across the state. The Methodist Student Movement's magazine, *motive,* was the most influential religious magazine for college students of its time. Inspired by *motive,* Bill completed his Ph.D. and is now teaching at a land-grant university in the South. There is no question in my mind that the Wesley Foundation "saved" Bill's life.

Our eating co-op at Wesley House was unique in Minnesota. Each semester two people were elected manager and dietitian, to plan three meals a day and order food. In return, they received free board. Dinners were prepared by a team of four co-op members who rotated tasks. The meal was served in sit-down family style, beginning with grace, and including introduction of guests, announcements, and enthusiastic conversations. Foreign students also participated, and one Hindu graduate student, in particular, was incorporated into the leadership. Simply by engaging in the life of the program, he became a magnificent teacher for students who had never had a personal relationship with someone of another religion and had never had their faith tested by other points of view. The co-op was a critical factor in the success of the St. Paul Wesley Foundation.

It was easy to have study groups when this relatively small building was already bustling with students. *Your God Is Too Small* by J. B. Phillips gave students perspective on the biblical understandings they had brought with them to the university. For many, the classic *The Bible Speaks to You* by Robert McAfee Brown provided their first coherent understanding of Scripture and the nature of its authority. Bishop James K. Mathew's *To the End of the Earth* was their first step in studying the Scriptures, and *Honest to God* by Bishop John Robinson challenged their Sunday school theology. *The Death of God* by Thomas Altizer frightened some, and *The Sun and the Umbrella* by Nels Ferré gave them grounds for a beginning ecclesiology.

Mission was a major theme of our study and action. The Methodist all-church study, *Our Mission Today* by Tracey K. Jones, helped them understand the Church as a corporate community and take responsibility themselves for its mission, in word and deed. Eugene Stockwell's *Claimed by God for Mission* and *The Congregation Seeks New Forms* and George Webber's *The Congregation in Mission* gave new meanings to the terms "missionary" and "local congregation." The students discovered that there was excitement in "being" the Church. Harvey Cox's *The Secular City* opened up the world in which Christ goes before us and meets us there.

There are many theaters in the Twin Cities, and students studied the scripts together before seeing plays. *J.B.,* based on the book of Job, dealt with the problem of evil, and *Death of a Salesman* offered a commentary on American society and a critique of capitalism. Films by directors such as Ingmar Bergman and Federico Fellini were enthusiastically discussed. Most of the students had never read these kinds of books and plays before, had never seen a film with subtitles, and had never imagined that some of these themes belonged in church. They were beginning to develop a critique of the Church, to ask questions about how it carried out its mission, and to make demands based on what the gospel required. The 1960s generation was being shaped.

As state director of the Methodist Student Movement, I was frequently asked to arrange for outside speakers at the eight Wesley Foundations. I always knew there would be a ready audience at Wesley House. After meeting visitors during dinner, the students would engage them in further conversation and frequently stayed longer than expected.

African independence movements were in the news, and attention was focused on atrocities committed by the Portuguese in Angola. Several Methodist missionaries there had been imprisoned and tortured, and students were mobilized to write letters on their behalf. After his release, the missionary Fred Brancel itinerated to many campuses. This exposure to the situation in Angola was unforgettable. Students discovered a part of the world they had hardly heard of before and were drawn into personal connections with it. They could identify with these modern missionaries, who were committed to freedom and human rights. "Salvation," they learned, had many meanings.

Sunday evening programs introduced students to contemporary issues: Can we have a Catholic president? Is Christian vocation broader than church-related work? What's ahead with DNA? What about "the pill"? Does Vatican II matter to Methodists? How much do we have to believe to be Christians? What does it mean to be a Christian in a Marxist society? We also examined divergent points of view, from the fundamentalist extremism of Billy James Hargis to Rudolf Bultmann's controversial "demythologizing." Hearing outstanding speakers of different colors or religions from themselves was a new experience for most students. Since these were not liberal arts students, the Sunday programs provided them with a broader education than they were getting in their courses during the week. The magazine *motive* forced everyone to stretch and triggered wonderful arguments at the dinner table. One student later said to me, "You helped our minds work in a better way than our studies did."

Cell groups, with disciplines for personal life and prayers in community, used Dietrich Bonhoeffer's *Life Together* as a crucial guide. Michel Quoist's *Prayers* and Malcolm Boyd's *Are You Running with Me, Jesus?* suggested new ways of praying in private and in public worship. John Baillie's *Diary of Private Prayer* gave students a more evocative and specific language of prayer than the "we just . . ." prayers they were accustomed to offering.

The World Student Christian Movement's *Student Prayerbook* was in frequent use, and *Cantate Domine*, published by the World Council of Churches, became part of our worship, linking us with students around the world. Donald Swann and Sydney Carter provided new kinds of music and text for our worship services. Carter's "Lord of the Dance," which I brought back with me from England, was an immediate hit. The students participated for the first time in Wesley's Order for Morning Prayer and his Covenant Service, but they also listened to Duke Ellington's jazz mass, featured Loyce Houlton's dance company in worship, and used nontraditional Christian art for reflection and meditation. Corporate worship became much more than devotional exercises. Geoffry Beaumont's "Twentieth Century Mass" was sung at major events, and they learned the Nicene Creed in the process. This matched the renewal of worship taking place in all denominations.

I saw myself as a coach, a caregiver, and a challenger. My style of enabling leadership among students was to facilitate their own confidence in what they were doing. This approach required me to spend a good bit of one-to-one time with each student who had a particular public responsibility, such as chairing a meeting, developing the worship, or introducing a speaker. Many of the students had lacked leadership opportunities in high school. They were the ones who had ridden a school bus from farms some distance away and couldn't stay at school to participate in extracurricular activities. We began by talking about how they saw their roles, and then discussed ways they could be fulfilled. I reacted honestly to their ideas, offered my suggestions, and encouraged them to think about other possibilities. The phrase "knowledge is power" was not yet in use, but I felt it important to share background information on controversial matters and the perspectives I brought to the issues. It's amazing how much authority student leaders had when they knew the campus minister would not take issue with them publicly. The time for sorting out differences is before the moment, and the time for criticism is afterward, in private. During their "solo performances," the students knew I believed in them.

Over the months and years, they also knew that I cared about them. Truth be told, I had no other life than campus ministry—and I loved every minute of it. Being single, I was often invited to eat in the student co-op or with the caretakers (former short-term missionaries in then Southern Rhodesia). After study and preparation at home in the mornings, my days at Wesley House went from 12 noon to 12 midnight, with counseling, correspondence, meetings, programs, and many conversations. My friends were the students. I shared my own experiences, expressed my own doubts and difficulties. I entered into their lives, their learning, and their losses. I always had time for anyone, even when I was under pressure, and they soon recognized that this was more than a job for me. It was my calling to their "congregation."

Incorporated in this style of work, of course, was challenge. One might say I was subverting their belief systems. I recognized that I intimidated some, and I worked hard to share my confidence in and caring for them. Calling students' unreflective convictions into question opened the door to acting on new ones. Some students, of course, did not want their worldviews, their Christian faith, their relationships, their studies, or their value systems challenged. Others, as they said, kept "coming back for more." Ultimately, what I was about was prodding them to grow beyond their expectations and to replace their conventional beliefs with transforming faith. And they did.

My other half-time position as state director of the Minnesota Methodist Student Movement expanded the circumference of my ministry and of my student friends throughout the state. In addition to the eight Wesley Foundations, there were Methodist groups at Hamline University (Minnesota's Methodist college), Macalester College in St. Paul, and at St. Olaf and Carleton colleges in Northfield. No one had held this exact position before, so I began with what there was—a president, a small state council, and a fall meeting—and operated in the same style as I did at the Wesley Foundation.

I had attended one National MSM conference in college, but had not realized how important these Christmas-week conferences would be for the students in Minnesota. Three months after beginning my ministry, I drove my VW bug, crowded with three students, to Athens, Ohio, for the 1959 Ecumenical Student Conference on Christian World Mission. After that, I organized buses, and we usually sent 150 students or more from Minnesota to these significant and exciting ecumenical conferences and to MSM and Student Volunteer Movement conferences. Athens, Urbana, Lawrence, Lincoln— the names of these cities carry memories of life-changing experiences for many. These five-day, intense national events with upward of five thousand students were among the things the Methodist Student Movement did best.

The MSM used the arts in profound ways. One quadrennial conference, with the theme "Covenant for a New Creation," featured subsections on painting and sculpture, drama, poetry, photography, and film. Erik Hawkins's internationally known dance troupe offered modern dance that was stunning and puzzling to many. "Endor" by playwright Howard Nemerov and an oratorio, "The Invisible Fire," by Cecil Effinger were commissioned works, with students playing leading roles. Ed Summerlin's jazz quartet, recorded at the conference, was heard in Wesley Foundations throughout the country while Sister Mary Corita Kent's lithographs and posters visually taught an activist, justice seeking theology.

National and state summer work camps offered students a practical experience of service and exposed them to needs they had not previously seen as personal. During inner-city weekends of cleaning, painting, and restoring dilapidated homes, engaging with families in poverty, and working on school playgrounds, we slept in sleeping bags on church floors. That is why I can now sleep anyplace and never need privacy. A week at Red Bird Mission in Kentucky gave two carloads of students a better understanding of Appalachian people, and a week each year at Rust College, a black Methodist college in Mississippi, served as a foundation for Minnesota students' participation in the growing civil rights movement.

One student from each state MSM attended the model United Nations under Ruth Harris's leadership and also the Christian Citizenship Seminar, which had a different theme each year. The seminar was usually a radicalizing experience, as the students received briefings at the Church Center for the United Nations in New York City and in Washington, D.C. Being confronted by political and economic issues in an international setting and by blunt critics of the United States during a time of cold war American patriotism could be shocking. Their worldviews would never be the same, and their support of the Church's role "for the life of the world" became indisputable. The Latin American Study/Travel Seminar was an outgrowth of the Christian Citizenship Seminar. Limited in number of participants, this seminar visited eight countries, and St. Paul Wesley was fortunate to have one of its students included. Mary Kraus, a "farm girl" and home economics major, became a short-term missionary in Brazil and later an ordained minister, pastor, and district superintendent. She is but one example of the many career and life changes that involvement in the MSM provoked.

I asked certain students whether they had ever considered going to one of these events. Often the idea had not crossed their minds, and being singled out by a campus minister and urged to think about it was the planting of a seed that brought splendid fruits. Usually the response was, "I can't afford it." Other campus ministers registered the same complaint: "Our students don't have the money to do these things. They have to work in the summer." Remembering the admonition I received from Princeton Seminary when I arrived there, poorly prepared and poorly financed, I repeated, "If you're willing to pay part of it, I'll do everything I can to make it possible." The student's willingness to pay something was critical, because I believed there had to be a sign of real commitment. I was not about to work on behalf of someone who expected a free ride.

Getting the funds took hard work on my part. The student and I discussed possible sources: parents, relatives, favorite school or Sunday school teachers, friends, community organizations, or the hometown congregation. I made most of the requests—on MSM letterhead. For example, I wrote to the student's pastor, with copies to appropriate people, indicating how proud the congregation could be of its student member. I explained the project in detail, and said that the student was not only willing to pay a portion of the expenses, but eager to share the experience with the congregation on their return. The Methodist Woman's Society of Christian Service in local churches frequently found students' support. Sometimes it meant shoveling snow or painting a barn, but I can't remember a single time when a student who genuinely wanted such an experience missed the opportunity because of lack of funds. Given the climate on college campuses through the 1960s, I wondered if the funds came through because hometown congregations were so grateful that their students hadn't "lost" their faith.

My parents are asking me, 'Where did you get all these ideas?' And I tell them that I learned it in church. You started me there. The only difference is that I'm acting on them now." I recruited students from throughout the Minnesota MSM to attend the major demonstrations in Selma, the 1963 March on Washington, Jesse Jackson's March on Poverty, and the 1968 Democratic Convention in Chicago. Each time students returned from such events and told of their experiences, the circle of awareness widened, and others became motivated to participate. The Minnesota MSM president, Beth Moore, who was also a St. Paul Wesley student, participated in the 1964 Freedom Summer voter registration drive in Mississippi spearheaded by the Student Nonviolent Coordinating Committee. She was being trained in nonviolent resistance when it was reported that three summer volunteers from the previous week, Andrew Goodman, James Cheney, and Michael Schwerner, were missing. As the students who were about to depart for Mississippi listened to reports of the search and prayed for the three men's well-being (they were, of course, later found murdered), all students were given an opportunity to return home if the danger was more than they or their families could bear. The climate of fear and sobering reflection brought frequent phone calls from worried parents.

Several months later, at our Minnesota MSM conference, the director of the Minneapolis Urban League spoke to us. His language was raw, his style abrasive, and his statements bold. His focus was the emerging concept of black power and self-determination, and he questioned the purpose of the well-meaning, idealistic students who had participated in the voter registration project. At one point, Beth, remembering the fear she had carried all summer, reacted to him out of her own experience in Mississippi. He responded in a rather verbally abusive way, and I immediately became defensive and protective of her. Somewhere in the shouting, Beth or I used the term "black problem." He nailed us: "Black problem? This is a *white* problem!" This was a major lesson for me. Looking back now, I'm sure we both wonder how we could have framed our response that way.

It was probably this experience that left the Minnesota MSM fearless enough to interrupt an event featuring three bishops as speakers. This was one of a series of large events held across the country to recruit for the ordained ministry. I was skeptical from the outset, believing that it is the experience of mission, not episcopal lectures, that creates an impetus for religious vocation. When the students heard which bishops the Council of Bishops had assigned to speak, they were appalled. One of them was an outspoken opponent of Martin Luther King, Jr., the Montgomery boycott, and the sit-in strategy. In fact, it was precisely to him and a few other church leaders that Dr. King wrote his famous "Letter from a Birmingham Jail." In addition, the team was to include Bishop James S. Thomas, the first black bishop elected after the Methodist church eliminated its all-black central jurisdiction, who had given a stirring speech on racism at one of the national MSM quadrennial conferences. This strange combination led us to plan a demonstration at the event.

As the bishop we objected to was being introduced, a large number of students in the balcony began singing "We Shall Overcome," while others came down the side aisles with posters and signs. We read a short statement expressing our conviction that recruitment for ministry was better served by what we were doing than by the scheduled presentations, especially the one by the bishop in question. I don't remember much about the consequences, except for the warm and grateful words that Bishop Thomas gave us, though he had to be careful in his display of appreciation. It was the first time the Minnesota Annual Conference had been interrupted by a demonstration, and it was a first for the students as well. There were many more to come.

As the 1960s and the Vietnam War continued, the antiwar movement claimed more and more attention. Every single young man, every male college student, had to wrestle with what to do about the draft. Much of campus ministers' time was now spent in draft counseling, helping men decide whether to apply for an exemption by registering as preministerial students, to seek conscientious objector status, to go to Canada, or to refuse induction and face the consequences. Campus pastors assisted in getting papers filed and securing recommendations, as well as in sharing strategies for meeting with draft boards and locating meaningful alternative service. Integrity was always an issue, but for most campus ministers, including myself, the goal was to find as many ways as possible to "escape the draft."

Parents were often a problem, and conversations with students' parents were part of our work. Parents needed understanding and pastoral support, especially if they opposed what their children were doing. Parents' Day helped initiate a pastoral connection. They came for the morning church service, which emphasized the relationship of the Church to the university and the mission of the Church in the world. Tours of St. Paul Wesley House were followed by a meal in the co-op and worship. We had an opportunity to explain the Foundation's programs, and parents met one another and got a better sense of what their children were being exposed to.

Resistance came at a number of points. The idea of spending hard-earned money to go to conferences was difficult fore many parents to comprehend. This was especially difficult when their children participated in actions that were controversial. Many local pastors were also resistant. Expecting that our role was to "keep the youngsters in church," they were distressed when their own long-haired students severely criticized the conservatism of the Church and made their dissatisfaction public. Campus ministers were often on the defensive, because we knew these same pastors would be making decisions about denominational funding of our campus ministries.

By the time I left this position, in 1969, after ten years, our annual state MSM conferences were attended by about 250 people and had a waiting list, because no retreat centers could handle a larger group. Nearly every Wesley Foundation now had property, and professional campus ministers had been recruited for most of the state colleges and university campuses in the Minnesota Conference of the United Methodist Church.

I still believe that even the Church can be reformed." Looking back on my work at the Wesley Foundation, I realized that the challenges its programs offered and the community of faith and action it fostered were of critical importance to the students. I, too, as a clergywoman, was being shaped by a ministry of subversion. When confrontation and challenge are necessary for transformation, then "the Protest-ant Principle" is at work. "Taking on the church so that it may correct itself implies using public opportunities and private strategies. I had been radicalized. In 1969, I left the campus for a national church agency, helping college students prepare for mission service.

The feminist movement in the church, in which I became an active role model, and the movement for full inclusion of gays and lesbians in the church both belong to my identity. Like the others, the ecumenical movement in which I served my remaining twenty-three years demanded faithful commitment, an illuminating vision, and a persistent critique of the church's willingness to accept the status quo.

And so I have chosen to swim against the stream in many areas of controversy, because I truly believe that the Church is the Body of Christ, called to share its message of healing, reconciliation, and salvation. Although I have been dismayed by the actions of the United Methodist General Conference on a variety of matters, my commitment to the life and mission of the Church has never wavered. I have continued in ministry not simply because I want to "belong," but because I believe in its transforming Spirit. I am confident that the Church is always renewing itself.

In 1976 I withdrew from an imminent episcopal election because I could not, as the first woman bishop, and for the sake of the Church, live my personal life under a magnifying glass. But from that moment on, I have tried to open doors and raise the glass ceiling for women of all colors, to work behind the scenes for the election of women to the episcopacy, and to be present to younger ordained women.

I have been a lesbian all my life. I've never known my identity otherwise. I knew that my partner would not be welcome in this church arena, and without her, I could not have had the kind of life I would need to sustain me through difficult times. I knew, though, that at some time during my active ministry, I wanted to come out as a lesbian. I wanted to send a message to the United Methodist Church that one who has responded to the call to ordained ministry for thirty-nine years, and offered many gifts to it, would have no place to make those contributions if the Church knew that I was a lesbian. I wanted my identity to be very public and to create "cognitive dissonance" in the many who, though valuing my ministry, did not yet accept that homosexuality is also a good gift of God.

The opportunity came just months before my retirement, after twenty-one years, from the New York City–based United Methodist Church's General Commission on Christian Unity and Interreligious Concerns. I was invited to give one of the four sermons at the biennial convocation of the Reconciling Congregations Program, which seeks full inclusion of all persons in the life of this denomination. I would be among friends, for the convocation would be in Minneapolis, which was still "home" and where I still had many friends from my campus ministry days. And so, on July 15, 1995, at Augsburg College, I became the most prominent woman in the United Methodist Church to come out as a lesbian. A journalist friend had advised me to write my own press release to tell my story the way I wanted it to be heard, because it was sure to make the news anyway, and it did—on television and in the national news. I saw my action as a political act, an act of resistance to false teachings that have contributed to heresy and homophobia within the Church. I stated that I would not withdraw from the ministry or surrender my ordination papers.

My coming out was not a statement of withdrawal or disillusionment, but rather an affirmation that the Church is also a gift of God. Believing that, I will never give up on it, even in its institutional form. If my "subversion" keeps the Church restless about its understanding of homosexuality and the Christian faith, then I will have continued my commitment to work for justice and to be a change agent in the Church and the world. Ultimately I believe this is an act of faith in the Christ whose redemption is ever new.

CHAPTER 3

Rebecca Owen

~~~~~~~~~~~~~~~~~~~

$\mathcal{D}$addy blamed the Methodist Church when I, a white child-woman, aged twenty, was arrested in Lynchburg, Virginia. He was correct, though I didn't know it at the time. Late in the afternoon of December 14, 1960, two African American and four white students entered Patterson Drug Store, sat at the lunch counter and ordered coffee. I was in this group that was quickly arrested for trespassing and locked up in the city jail. What had happened to Becky Owen, a scholarship student at Randolph Macon Woman's College, that she not only was involved in this act of civil disobedience, but had worked over the past few months to organize it? What might the Methodist Church have had to do with this unseemly behavior?

As a young child, I loved the story of Methodism's founder. John Wesley's heart was strangely *warmed* and he was called away from the affluence and formality of the Church of England to minister to the poor in the mines and factories of England and to the "Indians" in America, much like what they told me Jesus did. I have longed for such a conversion from my earliest memories. But the gospel was to first warm me, in an unwelcome way, one Friday afternoon in Saluda, in rural eastern Virginia, in the fall of 1952 when I was twelve. Along with two other seventh-grade girls in a Bible class, I sat in the study of a young, gay Baptist minister, who was soon to be fired and to move to New York. We had heard that the Ku Klux Klan had been marching in the adjacent county, and Reverend Hall asked us if we had any thoughts on the matter. I had many thoughts that I explained confidently. Of course integration was God's will, but it would be immoral to push it on the colored people before they were ready. They would only suffer and be humiliated in white schools, where white children would be so far ahead. Everything separate but equal was what they preferred, except for a few agitators, mostly northern. Furthermore, whites had to be very careful, for it was well known that if you gave them an inch they would take a mile and the next thing you knew one of them would be marrying your daughter. Naturally, no thoughtful Christian person would really support the Klan, but it might have a teaching, cautionary role if outside agitators were out and about. Furman Hall said quietly, "Becky, you seem to know a great deal about what Negroes want, but if integration is God's will, how do you know the timing of God's will?" Blood rose hot to my face and neck and I wanted to disappear. My Daddy was just about perfect, as far as I could tell, but at that moment his beliefs were in conflict with the gospel. I said not another word, but my shame lasted much of the fall. I remember waking up sometimes at night and recalling that moment and pulling the covers over my head. I may have been secretly happy when Furman Hall lost his job and went north. Although I liked him very much, whenever I saw him I wondered about the timing of God's will, and I felt frightened.

It was hard to set the matter of race aside, because Jesus was an important player in my prepubescent emotional volatility. After all, I planned to be a missionary to Africa and dedicate my life only to the highest and holiest calling. I longed for Jesus to call me unambiguously according to my terms. My mother Dixie said that I had always gone to extremes and sat on my high horse, and some truth lies in these labels. Nevertheless, on relations between the races, I understood that Jesus Christ and Furman Hall would be of one mind on the matter, and I had my first inkling that the gospel was revolutionary.

The daughter of Methodism, I grew into adolescence with my rural church, one of four on the preacher's circuit, serving as the center of my intellectual and social life. No child my age lived within walking distance. My family had no phone and no television until I went to college. Mama Dixie considered television uncouth, and Daddy had enough of the telephone at the bank where he worked and didn't want another damn one bothering him at home. My sister was pretty worthless as far as I was concerned. She was the beautiful petite blond, popular with boys, a cheerleader and homecoming queen. I was very tall and very skinny and brunette. I couldn't compete and convinced myself that such grapes were sour. I always studied hard, and the family saying was that my sister was smarter, but Becky studied harder. So as a teenager I turned more and more to the church, where I found acceptance. My home church's concerns centered around replacing the wood stoves with oil burners and whether to install a bathroom, which was deemed unnecessary because everybody lived nearby and in an emergency one could use the bathroom at the gas station.

When I was a child, the main pull of the church was those Bible stories. I loved the sound of Scriptures read aloud, and I was totally curious about the Bible characters and especially about Jesus. Sunday after Sunday, year after year, I tried to figure out who this man-God was and was continually surprised that my friends had so little interest in him. From my earliest memories I think I was waiting for him to call me. And the church also gave me pleasure. I loved *Together* magazine, which to the best of my memory must have embodied that sweet ignorance of the fifties. It served perhaps as my Brady Bunch, with its perfect families doing seasonal things with the blessings of God and country. And best of all was the sweetness of my own Centenary Methodist Church's annual Christmas pageant. Satin bathrobes, striped towels, scarves, and summer sandals turned acned farm boys into adoring magi and shepherds. Blue and white cheesecloth transformed a chosen blond girl into the virgin mother. Lesser beings were sheeted and crowned with Reynolds aluminum halos to make up the heavenly host. Dark-haired, skinny Becky Owen was always an angel, never the virgin mother, but that pageant remains more grand for me than any theater I have witnessed as an adult.

During adolescence, the larger world of the Methodist Youth Fellowship (MYF) opened for me. The Purdue National Conference in 1955 marked my leaving the state of Virginia for the first time. The conference was a little over my head theologically. I expected a great revival, with five thousand students dedicating their lives to Jesus. This did not happen, but all was not lost. I held hands for the first time with a boy from Oregon, and other events paled in comparison. Purdue also marked the first time I was part of an integrated gathering. African American and white students stayed in the same dorms, ate together, and attended events together, and African American speakers addressed us. Jim Crow was absent at Purdue; I was surprised at times that it seemed to be no big deal. I remembered Furman Hall's talk of the timing of God's will. The time had come for integration, at least at church conferences. I was not able to escape the feeling that there should be some relationship between what I heard in my larger church and the segregation I knew in my community. I returned home deeply puzzled and talked with my MYF leader and other persons whom I respected. I was rebuffed, but it was suggested that I might give some of my outgrown clothes to a colored family. For the first time I felt resentment toward my church, but I quickly became quiet.

The following summer, when I was sixteen, I attended the Southeastern Regional Missions Conference at Lake Junaluska, North Carolina. The events of this week further unsettled my white southern tribal values. I joined a boycott—a word unknown to me heretofore—of the Junaluska pool and entered discussions about the injustice of the conference's segregation and about larger injustices. For the first time I was among real live missionaries! Two memories stand out: both made me blush. News broke that the Russians and East Germans were building the Berlin Wall. The missionaries made so many references to this event that I asked what the wall had to do with Jesus Christ, implying that our thoughts should be with Jesus, not politics. A gentle response let me know I was out of step, but I wasn't sure why. A second question I still cringe to remember fifty years later was, "How exactly do you convert a heathen to Jesus Christ?" Another gentle response let me know I was not only out of step, but had fallen on my face. I was still hoping for a proper conversion myself, and thought the answer to my question might help. I had little idea at the time that my world was being turned upside down and that, indeed, amazing grace was rebirthing me and thrusting me repeatedly into the abundance and suffering of the larger creation that lay outside my tribal boundaries. And quite consistently blushing, not fervor and ecstasy, was to be my response to the Living Gospel.

At Junaluska I learned from John "Tex" Evans, the powerful yet gentle, cowboy-like mission director of Henderson Settlement in Kentucky, that students worked at the home mission each summer to help cover for vacationing staff. I wanted to sign up on the spot, but he told me to write him in the spring. I did, and the following June of 1957 I set out by Greyhound bus for Pineville, Kentucky. The mission lay in a hollow thirty-five miles distant and Tex told me to say goodbye to city life, which meant telephones, movies, and restaurants. A girls' and a boys' dormitory, a small frame Methodist church, a school, a small store and post office, a barn, a garden, a baseball diamond and a few staff houses, including the home of a resident deputy sheriff, constituted Frakes, Kentucky. Formerly the dorms housed children for whom school would have been otherwise inaccessible. Now about fifty children, most having been remanded to the mission by the court, lived in an orphanage-like setting.

Only in Soweto, South Africa, was I to see poverty that equaled that in the hollows that surrounded the mission. Children came into Frakes pulling red wagons to carry hundred-pound bags of sugar to bootlegging stills, their families' only means of support. They looked emaciated, and not infrequently there were mushroom-like growths from malnutrition on their knotty knees and elbows. I worked hard, stunned by the beauty of the mountains, shocked by this "other America," and nourished and encouraged by the staff. Tex's vespers, filled with Bible stories and often reaching an evangelical crescendo in the mountain dusk, seemed to me proper Christianity. The beloved hymns of my childhood also echoed in the hollow with beauty as they were sung by the mountain people in their extant English accents, a replication of their earlier incarnation among the factory workers in England led by John Wesley himself.

Days after I left Kentucky, I experienced culture shock as I began my freshman year at Randolph Macon Woman's College (RMWC) in Lynchburg, Virginia. Finding myself in the middle of sorority rush parties made me bitter, and I was disappointed and frustrated with what seemed to me to be an almost uniform superficiality and lack of sensitivity. My first months were difficult and my reactions extreme. Amazingly, the Methodist Student Movement and the larger student Christian movement soon welcomed me as no sorority could, and *motive* magazine engaged me as no class or professor did. *motive* gave me unsettling postwar contemporary art, which made visible what cannot be spoken; Dietrich Bonhoeffer, who was to transform my southern fundamentalism; and a social gospel addressing events in America and the world, honed by the evil of World War II.

In 1957 I attended my first national Woman's Society of Christian Service conference, where internationalism was palpable and exciting. My junior year of college, I served as Virginia State Methodist Student Movement president, and was elected in 1959 to the National Council. My senior year, I was president of the Virginia Student Ecumenical Movement and an MSM delegate to the National Student Christian Federation. I returned to Henderson Settlement the summers of 1958 and 1960, and in 1961 I went on an MSM work-camp trip to Europe and was in Strasbourg for part of the WSCF conference, returning to the United States to attend the WSCF conference in Denver. Although this reads like a resumé, each of these events invited me and wrenched me away from campus life at RMWC, which was still, in my view, very much a finishing school, albeit with a sound academic standing. Over time, the mores of my well-bred southern white tribe seemed not only unjust but archaic and absurd.

The WSCF conference in Strasbourg and the WSCF in general hold special places in my story. On my "all"-white campus—African Americans were there only to cook, garden, clean our rooms daily, do our laundry, and the like—and in strictly segregated Lynchburg, "race relations" could easily remain at the periphery of consciousness if you wanted. After all, never in my life had I heard a single colored person in Virginia speak ill of Jim Crow. Jim Crow's efficiency and the silence it engendered between blacks and whites still amazes me. Nonetheless, I thought that my thinking had changed. I saw that I "used to be" a prejudiced person, but no longer was. I had, in a very broad-minded way, I believed, been with African American students in a variety of national settings. I silently commended myself on my lack of bias or prejudice. I liked the black students I was with, as I had liked the colored people who had been an important part of my life from my earliest memories. But at Strasbourg, I was continually asked by delegates from Africa about the mores of my white southern tribe. They gently sought me out and were puzzled by the Christianity of my people. They knew colonialism well, but what was this segregation that thrived in a democracy and was sanctioned by the southern church? Having long dreamed of the African mission field, I had not expected Africans to ask *me* how *I* could be a Christian and do nothing about the injustices that were woven into every moment of my life in the South. My conversion was arising from Africa, and I had so longed that it would be the other way around.

At the Denver conference, matters worsened. For the first time, I heard African American students, speaking with southern accents born of English and East African languages, describe what, indeed, it was like to grow up with Jim Crow. The silence ended definitively and concretely for me in Denver. I had read and heard of such things, but now they were spoken to me directly. The imperative of the Denver conference was unambiguous: if you, Becky Owen, are serious about Christianity and injustice, get the hell back to Lynchburg and do something. The action required seemed marvelously clear. Black students told their stories of lunch counter sit-ins, jail, and community organization. The U.S. student Christian movement had birthed a student nonviolent civil rights movement at its Athens, Ohio, conference in late December 1959. The Christian imperative, the timing, and the course of action were clear. Was I to be a part of the living Good News?

$\mathcal{R}$eturning to Randolph Macon Woman's College from the Denver meeting was far less confusing than arriving three years earlier to face sorority rush week and initiations into the cult of young southern womanhood. Once again on my high horse, according to Mama Dixie, I had a clear task: to initiate nonviolent direct action to challenge segregation. Yet without three women upon whose shoulders I stood—my grandmother, Ruth Harris, and Mildred Hudgins—I would have done nothing. Becky Owen would have remained frightened, ashamed, and lonely. Only embraced by the presence of these women, in whose persons Spirit was visible, could I act up.

Even when I was a child the shadow of another consciousness hovered within my own family. My maternal grandmother, born Catherine Sheppard in 1877, ranted and raved and was thought a man-hater and crazy. She also spoke of the Lord's will with certainty and intimacy. In the 1940s, she worked her "Nagasaki strawberry patch" with a hoe and picked the berries in the hot Virginia sun, one hand on her back, the other moving leaves quickly, gathering the berries. She called the work her penance for her nation's war crimes. The money from the berries went to a girls' school in Japan. She wanted women to lead the world. In that berry patch, she explained to me that mothers could no longer send their sons to war. One of her sons had been killed at Normandy, the other wounded. She thought women might find a better way.

She was critical of the church as well. She found her own church, Oakwood Methodist, more interested in a Sunday school room than God's world. She was very interested in the world, though she never left the state of Virginia. She read the *Christian Science Monitor* and pored over the heavy volumes of the *Interpreter's Bible*. The Richmond papers, she declared, had no reliable news. The Woman's Society of Christian Service, called the Missionary Society when I was growing up, was imperfect, but the best the church offered. *Together* magazine, she said, might as well be filled with recipes and how to fix cars, but *World Outlook*, the Woman's Society magazine, had more of a vision.

Miss Kate, as she was called, had a special love of China. To date, I have a few poppies I watch over very carefully that Grandma grew near the turn of the twentieth century from seed given her by a missionary to China. As a child I once asked her why she talked so much about China. Her definitive reply was that only the ignorant have no interest in China. The Chiang Kai-sheks were Christian criminals—the worst kind, to her way of thinking. At an Easter dinner, with fifteen or so gathered family members, Miss Kate proclaimed that no difference existed between the Kremlin and the Pentagon; both were under the dominion of the devil. The following silence was so deep and long that I thought for years the Kremlin and Pentagon must have to do with sex. She also said the colored people were sending the white race straight to hell, and whites didn't even know it.

Miss Kate's husband died of typhoid fever, when three of their seven children were still at home. Mama Dixie dropped out of college and taught high school Latin to help out. Grandma sold eggs, butter, milk, and frying-sized chickens to make ends meet. Her large, gracious house, named Liberty Hall, had no indoor plumbing until the late 1940s. To date I have not seen the bounty or goodness of her Sunday noon meals equaled. In the early 1970s, Grandma took my daughter on her lap and told her she was glad I was working in inner-city day care in New York. This work completed a circle, she said, because after the war, by which she meant the Civil War, Quaker women came from New York to Virginia and taught poor children. Most important, these Quaker women thought girls as well as boys must learn, and be taught the same things. This woman, soon to be a hundred, also told my puzzled but fascinated four-year-old that men might control the world, but they could not control her mind. Kate cherished education to the end of her more than century-long life.

I too believed for too long that Miss Kate was crazy. As a child I viewed her with considerable curiosity and am told I followed her everywhere. Eventually came respect, and finally great admiration. By 1960 Grandma was my spiritual and intellectual mother, though I might not have known it at the time. And in that year, serendipitously, she was joined by Ruth Harris and Mildred Hudgins.

Grandma's beloved Missionary Society gave Ruth Harris to the Methodist and ecumenical student movement. To me, Ruth Harris was utterly astonishing. Heretofore, what men were doing in the church and the world had been much more interesting to me than women's doings. My impressions of Ruth's life, especially its glamour, are different, I am sure, from her own thoughts of herself, but they reflect my wonder at meeting a *woman* whose life I could wish to emulate. In Ruth I saw a tall, intelligent woman, also beautiful, with huge brown eyes and an exquisite, expressive voice, honed by musical training. Her appearance struck me all the more because it had long been part of my consciousness that only unattractive women found a place in church work. I had learned further that women in full-time Christian work must give up everything interesting, sexy, exciting, and embrace a pale, emaciated (or obese), asexual, diminutive, constricted role. This image persisted for years in my unconscious, manifesting itself in my dreams. In my conscious life, Ruth definitively shattered it.

Ruth was also, in my eyes, a highly sophisticated New Yorker, a world traveler, an executive with an office overlooking the Hudson River. Later I was to find a letter I wrote Grandma Kate about eating Chinese food for the first time in New York, Thanksgiving 1960, with Ruth. Her eating with chopsticks and her savvy about the menu seemed more stunning to me at the time than her missionary work in China, but I wanted to tell Grandma I knew a Chinese missionary. Ruth's Christian faith was, in retrospect, more liberating for me than her person. For her, "acting up" for Christ and thereby being thrown into the world as a full human being was an integral part of faith. In the months following my meeting her, I was repeatedly trying to reach some understanding of social justice in the world, only to find Ruth already there offering support. And hers was a very special modesty that clouded the fact she had dropped the stones making the path I followed. She can only have been a wizard at diplomacy, as well, because, without fail, when funds were needed for some student project, Ruth found them somehow, somewhere.

Ruth Harris's work was formative in the student Christian movement's spearheading of the student civil rights movement. Her leadership and vision shaped the organization of the Athens Christmas conference in 1959, and without doubt she found a way to finance the new student population's presence. The conference brought together a substantial number of minority and international students, along with the white students usually in attendance. With the leadership and teaching of Martin Luther King, Jr., Jim Lawson, and others, students grasped the imperative to return to their communities and turn Jim Crow upside down. The presence of these same students at the NSCF meeting in Denver the next summer was the single most compelling impetus for my actions in Lynchburg.

Amazingly, a third woman appeared—this time an earthly guardian angel—in September 1960. The president of Randoph Macon Woman's College either erred seriously or acted covertly in bringing this 1927 alumna back as director of campus religious life. She clearly did not share his public views of what constituted a RMWC child-woman's graces. Mildred Hudgins didn't capture my imagination on sight as did Ruth Harris, but she was present on a daily basis, easing my conflicts, ameliorating my shame and fear, and, I think, loving me deeply. It was not so much that I stood on her shoulders as that she kept me upright with supporting arms. The magic of Miss Hudgins for me was that she was truly of my local white tribe, her family living a few miles from my Saluda home. She knew me as no one else did, for she had lived in her own way what I was living. Although we did not speak to her of our specific plans to sit in, not wanting to put her job in jeopardy, her presence was with us in all we did, and we spent, I am sure, hundreds of hours in her office. To the best of my knowledge she was the only white person in Lynchburg who, from the moment she heard of the sit-in, stood behind and affirmed our action. Most RMWC faculty and staff acknowledged respect for our courage, convictions, or whatever, but nevertheless thought our action foolish and detrimental to race relations. How we needed Mildred Hudgins's unambiguous support. Many times her presence reassured me I was not crazy.

Miss Hudgins, like Ruth Harris, attended her first interracial meeting while studying at Scarritt College. She was a missionary to Japan, and found her way into student work initially with the YWCA. Whatever the Y may have lacked with respect to theological erudition, it surely made up for in trans- formation of souls, broadening women's horizons through social service and more. How Mildred Hudgins loved the Y.

Mildred Hudgins's energy was indefatigable. Within a few weeks of as- suming her new position, she was fully a part of campus life. And she was very smart. Her goodwill toward RMWC and her faith in the college's po- tential made her an excellent diplomat both within the conflict-torn campus and to the outside world. Even Mama Dixie respected her enormously. But the details are not so strong in memory; what overshadows all else is the ha- ven her presence provided. And, oh, yes, she was very funny; with her we always laughed a lot. The importance of laughter is often overlooked in theo- logical discourse.

On December 14, 1960, with two days remaining before my twenty-first birthday, darkness raced in the cold gray afternoon, making its presence felt by three o'clock. We were six Virginian students, two African American and four white, from three colleges. Each of us had a different personal history and ancestral shadow; nevertheless, in that moment we could act together and would continue to be largely of one mind in the events to follow. Our com- monality was that each of us took the gospel very seriously and hated racial injustice. We made our way to downtown Lynchburg and entered Patterson's Drug Store as darkness fell. We sat together and looked expectantly at the serving staff. No one served us. Mr. Patterson, the manager, who had already refused to meet with us to discuss anything under any circumstances, appeared after some minutes.

Forty years later, as I reach toward that moment, silence screams. What- ever sounds people make in a drugstore in a southern town shortly before closing time stopped. Customers, black and white, seemed to slow their move- ments. Those in the store appear in memory like two-dimensional paper dolls seemingly drawn to the doors by fear, but also in fascination toward us and the imminent action. The spectacle of two Negro students sitting with four whites in Patterson's was unprecedented. Snapshots of faces also appear. White faces foreshadowed what was to come. I saw mirrored in white faces something obscene and horrifying—we were that to them. Rage, indignation, and self-righteousness were interwoven with contempt for what they wit- nessed. Never had I been seen in such a way. I knew in those forty minutes that I sat without speaking at that counter in the neon-lit darkness of Advent that I had stepped out of all that had heretofore defined me. To my people, whom I have come to call my white tribe, I had been a privileged daughter going to one of the finest schools in the South, where I was schooled not only in liberal arts but in the charm, gentility, and manners of white Southern womanhood. Now I felt, above all, I was utterly other—outside.

Mr. Patterson told us to leave the store because we were trespassing on private property—a puzzling concept since the store was open to the public. We did not leave. He told us again, and again we stayed put. The police were called and they advised us we were breaking the law and would be arrested if we did not leave. We remained seated and the police arrested us. Kenneth Green, an African American Korean War veteran, told me later that at the moment of arrest all he could think about was wishing he had been killed in combat and spared this reality of America in his face. We were herded through the bystanders and into the waiting police wagon. Here Lynchburg's sexual decorum conflicted with its segregationist values. First we were ordered to sit males to one side, females on the other. We complied. Someone from the crowd called out, "They're sitting with the niggers." Indeed, Lynchburg's paddy wagon was integrated, with white and African American women sitting side by side on one bench, and white and African American men on the other. Segregation outweighed sexual decorum and we were reshuffled, now with the men and women together, but the races separate.

We were taken to the city lock-up, booked on charges of criminal trespass, and allowed to make a phone call, just like on TV. I had Ruth Harris's New York number, having been assured of bail by the Methodist Student Movement, but a long-distance phone call was not permitted, nor was I permitted to call collect. Nevertheless, bail was quickly arranged through negotiations at Randoph Macon and elsewhere locally, and we were released about ten o'clock that evening. Again we were quickly segregated and hustled back to our respective colleges with no chance to debrief among ourselves. The corridors at Randolph Macon were dimly lit, its being later than our 10:30 curfew. I was glad, for I dreaded being seen by my own tribe as those faces in the drugstore lingered in my consciousness.

The narrative account of our arrest and related events is a matter of public record, insofar as they received much attention, both locally and nationally, especially in the *Washington Post*. Locally, there was almost daily coverage, often front page. Our arrest, our trial, our appeal hearing, and our incarceration most of February after we chose "jail, not bail" were all reported. The press covered subsequent sit-ins, our joining a case challenging the constitutionality of the recently beefed-up trespass law, our colleges' disciplinary actions, the forcible removal of a white Episcopal clergyman from the segregated court room by uniformed officers, and more. Editorial followed editorial in both local dailies. When news events were scarce, letters to the editor kept the story going.

Coverage by the *Washington Post* stood in sharp contrast to the local reports. Elsie Carper, a remarkable reporter, made Lynchburg her home for extended periods of time, and to my mind got the story right. Front-page *Post* headlines announced, "Assault on Lynchburg, 6 Students vs. Town Aligned in Sit-in Battle" and "Desegregation Attempt Pits Six Students Against Lynchburg." Carper's voice, more than any other, presented the events in Lynchburg in a larger perspective by implicitly leading the readers to see that this was not so much about six students versus a southern town but the manifestation of a wounded nation. Others would soon join the front lines, with the first "freedom ride" taking place the month after we were released from jail. Carper's coverage, I believe, also made Lynchburg a safer place for us. Lynchburg's cherished view of itself as moderate, law-abiding, and refined had been challenged, and overt racial violence, were it to come to the attention of the national press, would have further damaged the town's self-image.

Like my Daddy, Elsie Carper blamed the Methodist Church for our action:

> The students have strong ethical and religious beliefs. Many have taken part in the various campus organizations that are affiliated with the National Student Christian Federation.
>
> Inspiration has been drawn from *motive*, the publication of the Methodist Church for college students. The November issue of the magazine contains an article endorsing the "sit-in" movement and tracing peaceful civil disobedience in this nation.

In contrast, an editorial entitled "Respect for the Law" in the *Lynchburg News*, February 10, 1961, asserts that the students "threaten respect for the church." The favored hypothesis in the local dailies was that the sit-ins were communist-inspired, with letter after letter to the editors speaking of the role of the Communist Party in racial mixing and agitation. Our own statement, which spoke of the Christian imperative of brotherhood (sisterhood was not yet known to us) and social justice and outlined the tradition of civil disobedience in America—breaking a law and willingly accepting the consequences—was ignored or ridiculed.

Time in jail was easier for my fellow RMWC student Mary Edith Bentley and me than for others in our group, and far easier for our group than for those arrested later in Lynchburg and elsewhere. Perhaps Lynchburg believed our behavior to be an aberration, that we could not have been serious.

Before and shortly after we were imprisoned, the head of the bar association offered us the option of a suspended sentence if we would apologize or perhaps repent. Lynchburg did not want us in jail, I think primarily because of the national press, the concurrent strengthening of resolve in the black community, and the support that was arising from whites—including clergy, members of the academic communities, and the larger Church.

The letters I wrote my parents and my college roommate offer glimpses of concrete details of daily life in jail. They are, nevertheless, somewhat misleading in that I urgently wanted my family's approval and therefore spoke only of the support we were getting at a time when I felt banished and humiliated by my own tribe. I also felt guilty because my father was not well, and I did not want my parents to worry about my physical well-being. And of course Sergeant Watts, the jailer, read what we wrote. All this being the case, I highlighted the amenities of the city lock-up and downplayed its shortcomings as a winter spa, including one shower a week, no exercise, confinement to a small cell except for two weekly visiting hours, no privacy, and no access to news. We were allowed only two books and a Bible each, so it was difficult to keep up with our studies, and we could write one letter each on Mondays and Wednesdays. I did like the very southern food, and the time was indeed a respite and opportunity for reflection amid the larger turmoil. As I wrote my parents:

> Reading nothing but the Bible and Bonhoeffer, I'm getting pretty steeped in [Christian] thought. I'll have to be careful to do nothing radical when I get out. I think the Bible is probably the most revolutionary book I've read. I need this reading very much for comprehensives. Also many things take on new perspectives here especially Paul's thoughts. The same thought exactly came to me of our greater freedom and, indeed, I feel freer than I have ever felt. I really feel I am no longer bound by what people will think and that I have acted as I had to act if I were to be myself.

And later:

> From a selfish standpoint not considering the difficulties I have caused others I have found my time here probably the most fruitful 20 days that I have had so far as my personal thinking, studying & development. One thing that has struck me is what a privileged person I am from the fact of my birth and environment. This position is something we cannot escape and perhaps it is the greatest stum-

bling-block in our way to understanding Christianity. Jesus certainly did not come to the privileged of his day primarily, and those of position were least able to hear him. This is a burden we must bear and it is amazing to me that I had been so oblivious to it before.

I indeed presented myself as so well cared for those three weeks in the squat, yellow-brick jail that my mother, with her excellent southern breeding, wrote Sergeant Watts a thank-you note for his kindness to me.

Omitted from my letters were the meetings that evoked the most terror of the entire series of events. On three occasions, two middle-aged white men, well dressed in suits, vests, and ties, questioned me in jail. These men—so like my father, my uncles, members of my church—I would heretofore have seen only as benign and would have expected their approval, but they had come to interrogate me on behalf of a state judiciary committee that investigated communist practices. Though hardly Klan members or rednecks, their power over me seemed complete. And I was all alone; there was no lawyer (I was refused access to one), no *Washington Post* reporter, no fellow students, no Mildred Hudgins, no witness. They kept wanting to get to the "bottom of things" in the questioning, which seemed interminable, especially since I had no watch and no idea how much time was elapsing. They claimed to have proof of my communist connections, but wanted to hear my side of things. From their ample leather briefcases, they would take out their evidence at intervals and confront me with it. The first was a book sent to me in jail by Carl Braden, the husband of an RM alumna, on his struggle for civil rights in Kentucky. I had never heard of him, but was told he was a well-known communist agitator. Next, they confronted me with several issues of *motive* magazine that were addressed to me and could only have come from my college dorm room. My roommate later told me a woman she did not know came to the room to get things she said I requested and went carefully through my papers and belongings. They questioned me at length about *motive,* having underlined passages they thought particularly damning. A copy of a New School for Social Research course bulletin, the New School having been founded by European scholars exiled from the Nazis, was further proof of my un-American proclivities. And finally, their most conclusive proof was materials written in Russian with notes in the margins in my handwriting. I had a double major in Russian studies and religion and was the teaching assistant in the Russian department. The men purported to have my interest at heart. I was young, I was of a well-known Southern family, I was born and raised in Virginia. But I had been seriously misled. They would hate to see me serve years in jail for my youthful follies. Finally, they benignly agreed between themselves that if I promised to leave the state of Virginia after graduation, they would not initiate a trial against me for sedition. When I got back to my dorm room, one of the first things I did was look up "sedition" in the dictionary. I did leave Virginia and, curiously, I spoke of these men to no one for many years. The humiliation was perhaps that their power seemed absolute under the circumstances and that I was to flee to the sanctuary of the North as had so many African Americans before me.

I was not a happy camper much of my time at RMWC, but I was, nevertheless, surprised by the school's official response. Mary Edith Bentley and I were tried by the college judiciary committee the evening following our arrest. I was required to step down as the senior judiciary representative. The committee's mandate had heretofore been to handle questions of honor—that is, cheating, stealing, and the like. No question of our honor was raised, and perhaps the closest we came to a college infraction was a guideline in the handbook that no student was to behave in a way that would bring criticism to herself or her college. In my memory, we were convicted of conduct unbefitting a lady, but I can find no evidence this was the charge. Perhaps over time my memory reworked the facts and distilled the essence of my transgression—yes, transgression against segregated Lynchburg, but more against the white patriarchy that defined my status and behavior as a young woman.

The most stunning and humiliating event, however, was that, contrary to the committee's tradition of absolute confidentiality, the student chair of the committee, the president of the college, and the president of the student body soundly reprimanded us in an assembly that required the presence of the full student body and, I believe, the faculty. That event and the interrogation in jail remain the most utterly shaming, frightening, and disenchanting events of the time for me. Even as I write this I feel my hand wanting to move up to hide my face as I remember.

Disappointment with the church was another consequence. At Christmas communion service at my home church, almost no one spoke to me, the anger of the community was so great. The District Conference of Methodist Ministers in Lynchburg refused to pass a statement that simply supported our convictions while not necessarily approving our actions.

The vehemence of white racial hatred that lay largely unarticulated when the colored people stayed in their God-given place, a favorite idea of southerners, was to surprise me many times during my remaining months in Virginia. At a Christmas party in Saluda, the host, a highly decorated military officer, called me into his study. He told me he had fought the niggers in Haiti, the Pacific, and Korea. He explained further that the ones he would most like to fight were those right here in Middlesex County. He also conveyed to me that I was a disgrace to my family and my home town and inferred that I must have been driven by some perverse sexual desire for the African American male. The general's lecture was to push me to a broader, more political perspective, and I was to think of it many times the following year when I chaired the Methodist Student Movement's citizenship seminar on "A Conservative Nation in a Revolutionary World."

My family's response was varied. My maternal grandmother wrote me immediately upon hearing of my actions:

Columbia, Va.

Dear Becky,
Congratulations. Find God and tell the sick world also church.
Love,
Grandma

This simple, strong affirmation, albeit from a woman considered crazy, felt sacred to me. Over Christmas vacation my mother wailed repeatedly, "How could you do this to me?" However, although she had never visited me in jail, she did come to the trial and the rally that followed and was genuinely moved. She wrote Grandma Kate that she had "experienced a kind of conversion at the trial which I did not even know I needed." Still, Mama Dixie's struggle with decorum and refinement versus ethics is palpable as she writes of her worry that my actions might disturb my sister's upcoming wedding. In a letter I found years later, my sister and brother-in-law told my mother that I was acting like I thought I was Eleanor Roosevelt, a huge compliment I did not imagine at the time, and that my mother's coddling me and visiting me in jail would only encourage this behavior. The following summer, with my mother's full knowledge, my sister burned hundreds of letters I had received in jail as well as other highly valued materials, including telegrams from Martin Luther King and Robert Kennedy, that were stored in my closet in Saluda.

One favorite cousin, a law student at the University of Virginia, came to Lynchburg to visit and offered to help with legal research. The rest of the larger family were silent to the best of my memory. The sit-in has not been spoken of to this day. More southern decorum.

*A*fter graduation, with an A average and an honors paper on Dietrich Bonhoeffer, I fled Lynchburg and Virginia, as the men from the legislative committee had agreed I should. Perhaps I would have left anyway. I received a master's degree from Union Theological Seminary in New York, with my work in the MSM and NSCF counting as my fieldwork. I worked out of Ruth Harris's office organizing seminars in Atlanta that permitted black and white students to meet together. After finishing up at Union, I worked in Ruth's office with African students from Angola and Mozambique, and her vision continued to stretch and shape me.

Almost a decade of work with children followed. A brief failed marriage devastated me and led me into psychotherapy. In 1966, I married Anton van Dalen, and our daughter and son were born in 1968 and 1970. I was nurtured and belatedly awakened to many things in a woman's consciousness-raising group that began in 1971. My work with children was informed and shaped by women's issues.

Largely because of my own therapy, I was led to earn a Ph.D. in clinical psychology at the New School for Social Research, and I have worked as a psychotherapist for twenty years. Sometimes I still cannot believe that this work is so totally engaging and interesting to me. The AIDS epidemic brought an unexpected and tragic dimension to it. In the New York AIDS mobilization and the service of people of goodwill, I felt Spirit moving as I had not experienced her since Lynchburg.

A month in South Africa preceding Nelson Mandela's election prepared the way for a month's work in rural Ghana. Christians were the only ones working in the countryside with people with AIDS. Airline tickets provided by the Sisters of Loretta for a fellow psychologist and me were "missionary" discount tickets. Thus I made the journey I had dreamed of since early childhood with just the right ticket. On the coast of Ghana, I walked through the underground dungeons that imprisoned Africans until slave ships arrived. Rather fine tombstones mark the graves of clergy whose task it was to baptize the infidels. How could this have been? That day, I knew what I had permitted only to hover on the periphery of consciousness, and it was unprecedented darkness. I was surprised how much of my tribe's denial had remained intact for me for more than fifty years.

The December 14, 1960, sit-in again made front-page headlines in Lynchburg on December 17, 1999. The *News and Advance* reported that of the "20 most significant Events of the 20th Century in Central Va.," the Patterson Drug Store sit-in has been deemed number seven.

When the barriers between blacks and white began to be breached during the 1960s, the simplest human acts often wound up as acts of defiance. Ordering food, using a restroom, even walking on a sidewalk could take on profound significance.

For segregation had to be all or nothing. The legal structure of the "separate-but-equal" South was like a house built of children's blocks—if any part of it was taken away, the whole tower could collapse.

William Patterson knew that when he stood behind the lunch counter of his drugstore on Lynchburg's Main Street on Dec. 14, 1960 and confronted six college students.

This time, in my opinion, local reporter Darrell Laurant got it right. No outside perspective was necessary. And her conclusion stunned me:

The six were finally released from jail a few days early on "good behavior." But the civil rights genie was out of the bottle in Lynchburg, never again to be contained.

What a gift to have been part of uncorking that bottle.

CHAPTER 4

elmira Kendricks Nazombe

$\sim$

$\mathcal{W}$e were on the playground of our elementary school, both probably eight years old. She was white, and she had been my friend for at least a couple of years. She had a black patent leather purse with a shoulder strap. We were talking about colors and she told me, not in malice but as a matter of fact, that her purse and my skin were the same color. I looked down at the brown skin of my hand and tried to absorb what she was saying. I wanted to argue with her because my hand and the purse did not look the same color to me, but somehow I knew that disputing her would not change her mind. It was the first time I realized that skin color had to do with something other than fact.

Growing up in Cincinnati, Ohio, in the 1940s was full of contradictory experiences. We lived in a low-moderate, mostly black neighborhood where few people owned their own homes. It never occurred to me to ask who the owners were. Our house was a large, three-story, red brick building on what might have been nearly a one-acre lot. I was told it had once been the home of a mayor of Cincinnati. The Federation of Colored Women's Clubs (a predecessor of the National Council of Negro Women) owned it, and my grandmother was the custodian. My parents and I and a series of boarders lived on the top floor. Our house was right across the street from Lane Seminary, where a minister called Lyman Beecher had been president during the pre–Civil War period. His daughter, Harriet Beecher Stowe of *Uncle Tom's Cabin* fame, had lived there, and neighborhood legend had it that some of the houses of the seminary had secret rooms that were a part of the Underground Railroad. By the 1940s, the seminary had been transformed into a series of apartment buildings. Ironically, only white families lived in those apartments. One of my best friends, Pat, lived there. My mother sent me to a nursery school on the opposite border of the seminary.

Having had the benefits of nursery school, I was ready to enter kindergarten at age four. There were two schools in our area. One was a block and a half from my house, directly opposite our church. It was an all-black school. The other was a twenty-minute walk away and it was an integrated school. My mother chose to walk with me to the integrated school. That twenty-minute walk took me from the almost all-black neighborhood where we lived through a somewhat mixed neighborhood and into a white working-class neighborhood. No one talked to me about why I was going to the integrated school, but somehow I knew that my mother, despite her admiration for the black teachers at the other school, thought that the integrated school was better, even though there were no black teachers there. It was the school that my mother herself had attended. The enrollment was perhaps an equal mix of black and white students. In later years, looking back, I felt that one decision made a great deal of difference in my life. It was the beginning of my separation from the people of my immediate neighborhood.

Sometime in the late 1940s, while I was still in elementary school, my mother decided to train to become a practical nurse. Up until that time she had been a full-time housewife and a leading light of the PTA. As she moved into her nursing career, our lives began to change. She seemed more independent, and she established close relationships with other women in the training program. Her work assignments were at night, and days went by when my parents hardly saw each other or spoke. By the time I was in the seventh grade, my mother felt she could not continue in the marriage. For the next several years, my mother supported us by herself, never letting me be fully aware of how close we were living to the economic edge. Her strength was so quiet that it was many years before I recognized what a powerful example she had set for me about coping in difficult times.

During those years in Cincinnati, a test was administered to every sixth-grade child in the city. Those who passed were sent to the city's only college-preparatory high school, Walnut Hills. My mother had gone there. Out of my elementary school, five students were eligible: four whites (including my friend Pat) and me. It was another step away from the neighborhood The school drew students from all over the city—rich neighborhoods as well as poor. Perhaps 20 percent of the students were black. It was my first real exposure to class differences. For the next six years I was referred to by many in the neighborhood as "the brain." It was not a friendly designation. I remember that it hurt. During these years, though, it was the community of our church, Brown Chapel AME, that nurtured me both spiritually and socially. The church was in the neighborhood but not only "of" the neighborhood. Others from my church also went to Walnut Hills, and so the stigma was less pronounced at church.

Some of my earliest memories involve my maternal grandmother. Her name was Bertha Mae. She was and continues to be the single most powerful influence in my life. She was born in 1895 and grew up in Atlanta, and she was very intelligent. She was a writer and a poet and seemed to be able to create anything she set her mind to, from a dress or a hat to a basket made out of Popsicle sticks. She was larger than life, not in a bombastic way but with quiet, sure power.

Because my mother worked in what was called a "war plant" during World War II, I spent much of my early life as my grandmother's shadow. I went wherever she went, which was mostly to church. At three, I was one of the youngest regulars at our Wednesday night prayer meetings. Eventually I not only followed her to those places but also did what she did there. It was her self-appointed task to educate the congregation of our church. She organized the women of her church club —called So-Re-Lit for Social, Religious, Literary—to perform pageants she had written of black women's history. It didn't occur to me until much later that she was giving us a history lesson about women like Sojourner Truth, Harriet Tubman, Mary McLeod Bethune, and Madame C. J. Walker that was unavailable in my schools.

My grandmother also went outside our community and brought information back to us. On Fridays she dressed up and went downtown to one of the white churches for United Church Women meetings. I don't think I understood how barrier-breaking that was then: a middle-aged black woman from the AME church joining as an equal in an organization of middle-class white women. My grandmother never went anywhere as an inferior. I never doubted that she was an equal of the women she met with, because I always felt the power of her intellect. She went seeking people who were thinking as broadly as she was, and I unconsciously used her light for my own path. I am sure that it was from her that I first heard the word "ecumenical," even though it was many years before I knew what it meant. All that she learned at those meetings about the worldwide mission of the church she brought back to our own church and shared in the many programs she wrote and produced.

It was from my grandmother that I learned about poetry. She taught me about Phillis Wheatley and introduced me to Paul Lawrence Dunbar's Angelina Johnson "swinging down the line." One of the earliest poems I remember was one she wrote for me because I loved sweet potato pie. It began, "When I was young, and about so high, I just could not get my fill of good old sweet potato pie." She wrote serious poems about faith and commitment but also wonderfully humorous ones spoofing members of our church or community. Many years later, when my mother died, it was my grandmother's poem that I asked to be read at the funeral.

For many years, my grandmother took me with her on Sunday afternoons when she read her poetry at church and community teas and other programs. By the time I was eleven or twelve, I found myself taking over some of her poetry reading assignments when she was double booked. In that period, oratorical contests were very popular in the black community. My training with my grandmother gave me an experience and comfort in public speaking that helped me then and continues to affect how I carry out my work. She seemed to be a leader wherever she went. When I was ten or so and had become active in a Girl Scout troop in another church, she and my mother decided that they should become Girl Scout leaders and start a troop of our own. And so they did. I'll never forget how surprised (and proud) I was when my grandmother became one of the most popular Girl Scout summer day camp counselors.

For my grandmother, the church was the central venue for the pursuit of intellectual life. One of the highlights of my summer each year was to go with my grandmother to the learning program that our denomination held at Wilberforce University. I know now that it was in the tradition of the Chautauqua learning institutes. We even had a Chautauqua clap that we did. The program was called Tawawa, and teachers and theologians taught classes on a range of topics for youth and adults. In addition to the thrill of living for a few days in a college dormitory, my first exposure to theology was at those summer institutes. We had a seminary at Wilberforce, and seminary professors or leading ministers from our denomination taught some of the courses. I remember strolling around the campus with my grandmother as she engaged in deep conversations with the teachers about theological points. And of course there was an oratorical contest. I was awed by young people who got up and spoke so convincingly about themselves and their faith.

When I was in high school, the Federation of Colored Women's Clubs decided that my grandmother was too old or just did not project the image they wanted for the caretaker of their building, so she was forced to move. Finding herself nearing sixty and with insufficient work history to collect Social Security, my grandmother found she had no choice but to seek work as a cleaning woman in the homes of rich white families. For the next several years she supported herself this way. She did it not with bitterness, but with the zest that she brought to everything, giving the families that she worked for the benefit of her talent and intellect and earning their respect.

Perhaps, given the times, the church was the only venue of expression available to my grandmother. It was a venue where her talents and imagination were able to blossom. That reality became her legacy to me as I moved beyond Cincinnati to worlds farther away than either of us could have imagined.

*D*uring my senior year of high school, like everyone else, I was exploring college options. Maybe because my mother had kept me insulated from our economic situation, my first thought was that I wanted to go away to school. Although the University of Cincinnati was a perfectly good school, I really wanted to establish my independence. The school guidance counselor sent us to a bank foundation officer, a white woman, who was to help us arrange for a loan. In the initial interview she seemed agreeable to my idea of going away. Later, however, she made it clear that since we did not have much money, I should give up the idea of going away to school and go to the University of Cincinnati instead. Hinting that my mother would be indulging me if I did otherwise, she said that assistance was available only if I went to UC. My mother was a very soft-spoken, quiet, introspective woman. Her response was wonderful. My mother told the loan officer that I wanted to go away to school and that she would make it possible and that we would not be in need of any assistance that she could give. I'm not sure what my mother thought of herself then, but I have always cherished this as one of her finest moments.

In September 1959 I arrived at Kent State University, 250 miles from Cincinnati, ready to pursue my dreams. Kent State in 1959 had probably two hundred black students out of a total enrollment of eight to ten thousand. There were few, if any, activities for them separately, and the black community was far away on the opposite side of town. Since I arrived there knowing no one, I headed toward an unknown that was somehow known: the church. I believed, though I had never really acknowledged this, that the church was a safe place. There were no meals served in the dormitories on Sunday nights, and the religious student centers offered low-cost meals and discussion. I found my way to the Wesley Foundation, the Methodist Student Center. I guess I must have thought "Methodist" also meant African Methodist.

One reason I kept going back to the Wesley Foundation was an extraordinary couple who were the campus ministry staff: Joe Brown Love and his wife Ruth "Lady" Love. They were white southerners, and she was an avant-garde religious dance and theater person—eccentric but charming. I don't think the issue of race was ever spoken of directly during that time. Joe Brown and Lady did not act as if there was anything unusual about my participation in Wesley Foundation activities. I felt as if they treated me the same as other students. For the most part, that response was echoed in the students I encountered there. Three other Wesley Foundation regulars and I formed a quartet—called the Wesleyaires, naturally. We performed all over campus. I joined the Methodist women's sorority. But the most important thing the Wesley Foundation did was introduce me to ideas beyond my imagination.

During that first semester at Kent, I learned about the Ecumenical Student Conference on Christian World Mission that was to take place in Athens, Ohio, at Christmas. I took a bus from Cincinnati, traveling into the hilly, coal-mining part of the state that I had never been to before. My roommates were young women from other parts of the country, one from Oregon. A subtheme of the conference was "Frontiers of Mission: Racism, New Nationalisms." It was my first exposure to the independence movements sweeping the third world. The conference discussions challenged us to be active on these frontiers. It was the beginning of a much broader view of the possibilities for my own life.

The next year I attended my first state Methodist Student Movement conference. The Ohio State MSM was another place where expansive ideas were commonplace. The Ohio MSM president was also the president of the student government at Ohio State University, and I began to see that there was a connection between the ideas we were discussing within the Wesley Foundation and life on campus in general. It was at that conference that I first met Jill Foreman, a student at Ohio University. Jill was active in the YWCA there and knew my friend from childhood, Pat, who was YWCA staff at OU.

The state MSM and later the ecumenical movement were leading me in new and wonderful directions, but my experiences at Kent were loosening my ties to the Wesley Foundation. In my junior year I volunteered to lead a study group on Dietrich Bonhoeffer's *The Cost of Discipleship*. One of the potential class members, a young man from Kent, confessed to me that he had a problem accepting a black woman as the leader of the group. The revelation surprised me, because I had never sensed any animosity from him. He later married one of the other women from the Wesleyaires and went on to become a minister. I participated in the group but took no leadership role.

In the spring of 1961, black students and their allies on campus began to organize to picket the local Woolworth's to protest their segregated policies in the South, and later the Administration Building, over issues of discrimination. I didn't have to think twice about joining these efforts. For one thing, the 1959 quadrennial had also included southern students who were planning sit-ins. There was plenty of discrimination to protest against at Kent. There was the "random" dormitory room assignments that always placed black students together. There was also the absence of black students from campuswide student leadership positions, and the fact that student racial population ratios were substantially different from the racial population ratios of graduating seniors from Ohio high schools. I remember walking up and down in front of that Woolworth's in downtown Kent—more a sympathy action than a response to direct discrimination. Most students walked by us rather puzzled about what we were doing. My friends from the Wesley Foundation were conspicuous by their absence. I don't know if they understood why I felt that I had to be on the picket line or involved in those meetings. I never spoke to any of them about it, but I carried their absence in my heart.

Around the same time, I joined Panel of Americans, a diverse group of students who went around doing panels on the impact of racial discrimination and prejudice on our lives. We gave a panel at the Wesley Foundation, and the pastor of the local Methodist church attended the presentation. During my years at Kent, I had joined the local Methodist church and even helped teach Sunday school there. The young woman director of Christian education was a close friend, and the pastor's six-year-old was a special favorite of mine. After my presentation, the pastor questioned me about my perceptions of discrimination. It was his view that my perceptions were more a function of my own sensitivity than of any actual prejudice I encountered.

Shortly after that, I began questioning others about how welcoming the Wesley Foundation was of blacks and other nonwhite students. No one seemed to understand what I was talking about. Choosing to become heavily involved with the Wesley meant I was not involved to the same extent with other black students on campus. My roommates, of course, were black. The social life of the black students, it seemed to me, revolved around playing cards in the student union basement. Because I was totally inept at cards and didn't like the feeling of segregation that the basement offered, I stayed away. So I felt happy about my Wesley Foundation–centered life, but also uneasy.

An encounter with Rev. James Lawson, who came to speak at Kent, was life-changing for me. Reverend Lawson was a young, black Methodist pastor who had strong ties to the pacifist movement (notably the Fellowship of Reconciliation, a historic pacifist organization) and had been a part of the groups at the Athens quadrennial who had planned the sit-ins. He agreed to have breakfast with the Breakfast Club, a group of us from the Wesley Foundation. Confused about the conflicting messages I was receiving from my Wesley Foundation friends, I was encouraged by his assertion that it was important to become agents of reconciliation. He said that it was important for some people to choose to build bridges between different groups of people rather than working only within their own group. His words became an important part of my self-identity in the months and years ahead and one of the few sources of validation I had from within the black community.

$\mathcal{T}$ here followed a series of very wonderful experiences that shaped and changed me. The National Methodist Student Movement sponsored a Christian Citizenship Seminar every year—a weeklong exposure to world issues that took a group of thirty students to both Washington, D.C., and New York. The year that I attended, the theme was African nationalism. The keynote speaker was Dr. Eduardo Mondlane, the founder of FRELIMO, the liberation movement of Mozambique. Present also were African students who were associated with other liberation movements. One of these students was Jose Chipenda from Angola, whose life, time and time again, intersected my own in the years ahead. It was my first independent experience outside Ohio and my first exposure to a critique of United States foreign policy. It was my first real encounter with Africa.

In June 1962 a Wesley Foundation friend and quartet member, Margie, and I traveled to Evansville, Indiana, for the annual meeting of the National Methodist Student Movement, where there were MSM student leaders from all over the country. I met southern white students for the first time. Rebecca Owen, Gayle Graham Yates, and Charles Rinker did not match any stereotypes I may have had. But there were some difficult encounters, too. The president of the Mississippi MSM was a student at Ole Miss, and it was clear that he was less than completely convinced that James Meredith's challenge of segregation there was right. Although I can't remember how it happened, at the end of the meeting I found myself elected to the National Council of the MSM. Elected along with me that year was Charles Rinker, who was from the Virginia MSM. Charles and his wife, Lora, were newly married and honeymooning at the MSM meeting. Our first act as the new MSM Council was to agree to participate in challenging the segregation at the Methodist campground at Junaluska, North Carolina.

That fall we went to our first MSM Council meeting in Nashville, Tennessee. Several of the eight members of the council were seminary students and the rest were still in college. I found myself dazzled by the intellectual power and scope of the discussions. I was struck by the way in which women students like Becky Owen and Gayle Graham Yates challenged and led right along with the men students on the council. Becky was a heroine because she had been arrested in a civil rights demonstration in Virginia. Ruth Harris, a staff member of the Board of Missions, and Margaret Rigg, art editor of *motive* magazine, were part of the team of staff advisors who met with the council. Ruth and Peg were clearly the equal of any of the male staff in the room. Whatever the real power relationships were, they were not apparent in our deliberations. All in all, I remember being both excited and awed, although half the time I felt I had no idea what was being discussed. I knew I wanted to be like these students.

Other than brief trips with my family, this meeting in Nashville was my first real exposure to the South. Our small interracial group had most of its meals at a small restaurant not far from the offices of the Board of Education of the Methodist Church and not far from the Vanderbilt University campus. I ate most of those meals with unspoken anxiety as my companion. The South was unknown to me, and I couldn't know for certain what the other patrons of the restaurant would think of us. I got a partial answer later. After a lot of hard work—we had a bad habit of meeting from 9:00 A.M. until late in the night—we decided to go to a movie. When we got to the movie theater, we discovered that it was segregated. We had two choices: we could all go in but I would have to sit in the balcony, or we could not go. All of us were stunned. I felt hurt and embarrassed that we were in this difficult situation because of me. The rest of the council, on the other hand, seemed to feel embarrassed and angry that I should be put in this situation. We didn't go to the movie that night. I don't think we even talked about it very much afterward. But in my mind, we were bound together in a powerful way by that experience. For reasons that I did not fully understand, the reaction of the MSM Council to racism was different from that of my Wesley Foundation friends at Kent State. It was the first time I felt there were whites who were prepared to stand up for me. What I sensed, as much as heard, from them was that it was not just my problem but our problem together. It would not be our only encounter with racism.

The MSM Council was to be the voice of Methodist students to the church as a whole, and by implication to the national and international events that were shaping our time. For example, we considered it our responsibility to tell the staff of the Methodist agency in charge of missions what they were doing wrong. We urged them to include more flexibility in the activities and work camps that they organized for students. We tried to convince them that they needed to move from social service to social change projects, that nurture needed to be revolutionary. The board was probably horrified at first, but it did listen and consider changes. Eventually the MSM Council decided to lead by example and organized and staffed the Morristown project, a community organizing project in a black neighborhood in New Jersey.

We also felt free to express our opinions about international events and to encourage broad dialogue within the MSM. At the time of the Cuban missile crisis, we wrote to other students about the unilateral and dangerous nature of the actions of the U.S. military. I don't know what the students on campus thought. One new MSM Council member repudiated his participation in the council because he thought our positions jeopardized his future career in the State Department.

I became the MSM representative on the Commission on World Mission (CWM), one of the constituent parts of the National Student Christian Federation, which was the U.S. manifestation of the international student Christian movement. In contrast to student Christian movements in other parts of the world, which were ecumenical organizations, the NSCF was made up of several denominational student movements and was supported financially by the educational and mission agencies that sponsored student work. The Methodist Student Movement was probably the best financed, and its student leaders had the most freedom of action. The staff leadership of CWM and NSCF was almost exclusively male. In the CWM meetings I met many young people who had already spent several years in the mission activities of the churches in Asia and Africa. Also present were students from student Christian movements in Africa and Asia—including those of Nigeria, Indonesia, and South Africa—who challenged U.S. students to get more involved in the changes sweeping the world. Commission members were conversant with political developments in many parts of the world and convinced that the churches must be present in revolutionary situations.

It was through CWM that I found myself, in 1963, as a student member of the planning committee for another quadrennial conference in Athens, Ohio. The theme of the conference was "For the Life of the World." Its theological grounding was in Orthodox theology and included a Eucharist liturgy from the third century. Three thousand students participated. It was a deeply moving experience, each person there a part of a global faith stretching not only around the world and across cultures, but backward in time two thousand years. Because someone more prestigious was unable to come, I was asked, surprisingly, to give a response to Vincent Harding's platform address. In fact, I was sandwiched in between Harding, a gentle and powerful

Mennonite, and Ken Carstens, a white South African exile who had been fear-
lessly active in the anti-apartheid movement. In hindsight, I wonder what audacious thought made me feel I had something to say. It was at that conference
that I first tried, partially under the influence of Malcolm X, to get people to
use only my first name and to spell it with a lowercase letter. I remember
how nervous it made many people and how much I enjoyed their discomfort.

In the fall of 1963, I enrolled at Drew Theological School in the Bachelor
of Divinity program. The example of the MSM Council leadership was just
too powerful to resist. If MSM Council members like Becky Owen and Wayne
Proudfoot and Lane McGaughey were in seminary already, and Charles
Rinker and Carl Evans were planning to go, then seminary was where I should
be. During all those conferences and meetings, we had the opportunity to
meet many wonderful people who had chosen the campus ministry for their
profession. I watched and was inspired by women campus ministers such as
Jeanne Audrey Powers. I knew that there was a place for women in campus
ministry and I thought I could have such a place.

Drew was everything I wanted: the most exciting intellectual conversation that I had ever been a part of. Some things I had never experienced as
powerfully before, such as the ugly face of patriarchy, though of course I didn't
know that word then. There were about fifteen or twenty women enrolled in
the theological school and about two hundred men. Most of the women had
been encouraged to enroll in the Master of Religious Education program.
There was only one woman on the faculty. Her name was Nelle Morton and
she taught religious education and was the advisor for all the women students. A southerner from the mountains of Tennessee, she had a quiet dignity that was the best example that we could have at the seminary. A serious
theologian, she was denied the respect due her from the men of the Drew
theological faculty, but she continued to explore new ground and share her
insights with students. She helped us think about the connections between
real life problems and the lofty theological concepts we were studying. In
1995 it was Nelle Morton who organized a gathering in her house so that
Charles Rinker and I could talk about our experiences in Selma and Montgomery. Her very presence helped us know we had made the right decision
in enrolling in seminary.

For me, nothing can match theology for intellectual excitement. But
the equality that existed in the MSM Council meant that I was in no way
prepared for a situation where I would be challenged every day to justify why

I dared to enter a "masculine" profession. Sometimes it was an outright verbal challenge, but more often it was unspoken. Every day it was there.

The summer of 1964 found me in Latin America, rather than in Mississippi where so many other MSM members were. The World Student Christian Federation was scheduled to have its General Assembly in Brazil, and I was one of the delegates from North America. The MSM decided to use the occasion to sponsor a six-week study tour of Latin America, and because I was already scheduled to go to Brazil (later shifted to Argentina because of a coup d'état in Brazil), I was included in the tour. The tour went to Mexico, Guatemala, Panama, Peru, Chile, Argentina, and Brazil. We were a multiracial group of students, including Jill Foreman, who by now was also a member of the MSM Council, and we traveled with three of the MSM advisors, Bill Corzine, Ruth Harris, and Margaret (Peg) Rigg. In each place we met with politicians, student leaders, and religious leaders. It was a time of great ferment in Latin America, just after a coup had toppled a promising leftist government in Brazil and before the socialist Allende regime came to power in Chile. There were so many lessons to learn in each country. Peg Rigg helped us see the connection between art and revolution by introducing us to artists throughout the region who were reflecting and amplifying the voices for change. Almost everyone we met was fiercely critical of the United States and its policies.

Brazil was an especially important stop on the trip for me. It was the only country where we saw black people in large numbers. I had felt a discomfort in the other places and had been the object of much staring. But in Brazil I was overjoyed to find that there were many people on the street who looked just like me. I was pleased to be approached by a black Brazilian and urged to move to Brazil where, she said, I could be with my people. I did notice, however, that black Brazilians were not among those we met from the student Christian movement. One of the members even suggested that I was fraudulently a leader of the movement. At the time I didn't have the self-confidence to dismiss the comment or recognize the racism that lay behind it.

In Recife, Brazil, we were able to have an audience with the bishop Dom Helder Camara. I will always remember a diminutive man in a simple black clerical robe who refused to sit on his dais, but instead came down and sat with us and told us about going down to the local prison to ask for the release of his Protestant pastors. We went to the prison ourselves afterward, but were refused permission to see the pastors, so we stood outside on the street and sang a hymn. I wrote a poem about the soft, warm nights in Recife where we could hear the tinkling glass lanterns on the bridges while home-less children slept underneath, the harshness of their lives masked in the ro-mantic darkness. Probably none of us has been the same since.

After the Latin America trip, I joined Bruce Douglas, the NSCF presi-dent, for fraternal visits to two Catholic student national conferences. Then we came back to the annual fall meetings of NSCF, where I was elected presi-dent in what seemed to me to be accidental circumstances. I was consequently rather embarrassed to talk about it with my family and appalled when my mother showed me a newspaper clipping about my election.

In my year as NSCF president, I learned a few things about myself and about the limitations of the ecumenical student movement. The spring of 1965 was, of course, the time of the Selma to Montgomery campaign. A few months before, the NSCF had established the idea of recruiting students from the ecu-menical movement to volunteer in situations of civil rights crisis. The money was there and the actual students were in the process of being recruited. Then Selma's Bloody Sunday happened: marchers were brutally beaten by sheriff's "deputies" as they attempted to begin marching to Montgomery. The move-ment was calling for people to come down for a second march across the bridge. I reached out first to the community that I knew best, the MSM. By that time, Charles Rinker was president, and since he was also at Drew we talked about how the student movement might respond. Charles and I, after consulting with MSM staff person Bill Corzine, decided to go to Selma for that second march, which took place on a Thursday. I remember being fright-ened as we started walking toward that bridge. Charles and I were walking together, and we tried to solicit the advice of Selma movement veterans on how to pick out the least dangerous rednecks to be beaten up by. Charles had on a clip-on tie and joked about it as his nonviolent tie that would come off easily if he was grabbed by one of the beefy-looking "deputies" that stood along the side of the march route. Mercifully for us, no incident occurred.

Later that week the movement asked for volunteers to help mobilize the Montgomery community while the Selma to Montgomery march was in progress. Ruth Harris and Peggy Billings, also Methodist mission board staff, volunteered the MSM Council for the task, and we went into action. As many of us as could went to Montgomery. Charlotte Bunch, a new member of the MSM Council, and Jill, Bill, Ruth, and Charles were all there. At first we stayed at the Holiday Inn, where local white bullies tried their best to intimi-date us. Later we moved into the homes of people in the community. Every day we were inspired by speeches by the likes of Andy Young and Jim Bevel, but also by the quiet courage of the people whose doors we knocked on to ask for support of the march. It's still hard to believe how easily they accepted us into their homes and their community.

In the meantime, I tried to see whether we could put the ecumenical teams into action. The leader of the Northern Student Movement, the northern equivalent to the Student Nonviolent Coordinating Committee, kept urging me to use the team resources to help in the current crisis. But the truth was that students had no control over ecumenical student movement resources. No matter how I thought the funds should be spent, I could sign no checks and the staff was in no way answerable to student leadership. The funds for the ecumenical teams represented specifically designated giving that could not be redirected to the present crisis. Eventually, however, a few NSCF student leaders and staff did participate in Selma to Montgomery March events, but on a much smaller scale than the MSM.

It was a wonderful time to be in the student Christian movement. So much was happening. There was so much energy. The Southern Africa committee was just getting started, raising awareness and pressuring the churches to withdraw any investments in South Africa. The North American Committee on Latin America (NACLA) was doing the same thing for Latin America. This work was shifting the focus of the student movement from denominational relationships to social action. Lacking a central leadership group like the MSM, I felt that NSCF's work with their geographic issue committees should help set a new direction. Women students were key players in these new efforts. Women's leadership was also strong in the denominational movements. Keen Stassen of the Baptist Student Movement was active in the Northern Student Movement and continued to challenge NSCF to get more involved in civil rights activities. Eileen Hanson, president of the Lutheran Student Movement, added her voice. At the staff level, Ruth Harris and Margaret Flory were powerful mission board allies who provided support for our efforts and were anxious to link us to student Christian movements in other parts of the world. During that year I tried to find a way to balance and harmonize all these voices with the traditional activities of NSCF, such as the work of its Commission on World Mission. The reality of the NSCF, however, was that it was a creature of the denominational mission agencies, and the tolerance level of those institutions for challenge from within was limited.

Near the end of my term of office, I was asked by the Fellowship of Reconciliation to join, as a representative of Christian students, a group of interfaith religious leaders who were making a trip to Vietnam. That year, 1965, the United States had begun to dramatically expand its role in the war and the self-immolations of Buddhist nuns and priests began. This trip was an extraordinary opportunity. We arrived at the Saigon airport and saw bullet holes in the walls that were evidence of a battle only a few days before. We began an uncomfortable sleep that first night to the sound of mortar fire, after being told that the Viet Cong were no farther away than the street. Our goal was to meet with religious and secular peace leaders and also U.S. and South Vietnamese government officials. Thich Nhat Hanh was one of the Buddhist leaders we spoke with. I was one of only two women in the group. The other was the late Elsie Schomer, the wife of Howard Schomer, a theologian from the University of Chicago, who was also on the trip.

Later, in Hong Kong, the group put together a statement that became a full-page ad in the *New York Times*, protesting the war and urging movement toward peace. As the youngest and only student member of the team, I argued with the long-time pacifist members of the group for more aggressive language and less optimism about the role of the United Nations. I had no chance of winning these arguments. In the months that followed, I was involved in the National Council of Churches' International Affairs Committee and its deliberations about what the churches should do about Vietnam. Former Cabinet member Arthur Fleming chaired the committee, and perennial presidential candidate Harold Stassen seemed to turn up often at the meetings. I don't know whether it was because I was young or black or a student or a combination of the three, but the only role they ever allowed me to play at those meetings was to say the prayer at the beginning. As usually the only student present, it was hard to be heard amid the voices of former Cabinet members and a presidential candidate. But more important, although it was a time when large-scale student activism was just beginning, the National Council of Churches preferred the posture of diplomacy.

In September of 1965 I ended my term as NSCF president and also left seminary. The times seemed too urgent for the luxury of studying theology. My formal association with the student Christian movement was over.

*F*our years later, I found myself married, about to be in possession of a master of urban planning degree, and finally able to search for my place on the "frontier." The political events of the preceding four years—the escalation of the Vietnam War, the assassinations of Martin Luther King and Bobby Kennedy, the chaotic events of the 1968 Democratic Party Convention in Chicago—had seriously shaken the optimism we felt earlier in the decade, when everything seemed possible and we were all so certain that the revolution was just around the corner. Like so many others, my husband and I felt a need to get away from the United States. We wanted to see how it looked from outside, to try and understand what people elsewhere thought of the United States, perhaps to get some distance on the anger and shame that we felt about the actions of our country in other parts of the world. The Frontier Internship in Mission (FIM) program seemed a perfect vehicle for gaining that perspective. It would give us an overseas experience without the stigma we felt would be attached to being associated with the U.S. government if we chose the Peace Corps. I knew about the FIM program both from the 1959 quadrennial and from my years in the ecumenical student movement. Ruth Harris and Margaret Flory, the creators of the program, had been my mentors during those years, and some of my student movement icons had been Frontier Interns.

In those days, FIM was still based in the United States. Three denominations—the Methodists, the United Church of Christ, and the Presbyterians—jointly sponsored it. For us, that ecumenicity was a plus. Two things appealed to us about the program. First, because of its nontraditional approach to mission, we felt that we would be able to use our skills as urban planners. Second, the FIM program ethos stressed that each person, whether single or married, was to have a complete assignment. Wives were not just additional workers on assignments tailored to their husbands' skills. Although I am sure that I considered our marriage and our roles in a fairly traditional way at the time, the idea of having an independent assignment was important to me.

By the late summer of 1969 we had been accepted and were on our way, along with about twelve others, to orientation at Stony Point, the ecumenical retreat center just outside New York City. Two of the first people we met at orientation were Tami Hultman and Reed Kramer. Tami's connection to the University Christian Movement, Duke University, and Charlotte, as well as Reed's and my husband Jim's joint attraction to ping-pong, made us instant friends. The issue of male and female roles was not a topic of direct conversation during the orientation, but it was definitely a subtext. There were four couples in the intern group. Tami and Reed seemed to have the most highly developed sense of separate identity and equal partnership. During the course of the orientation, though, each couple had to rethink their understanding. We had an opportunity to meet former interns, and we saw firsthand the potential for gaps between the ideal of independence and the reality of one partner fully engaged and the other adrift—unfortunately, usually the woman.

An amusing incident brought home the difficulty of trying to establish independent identities. Near the end of the orientation, there was a luncheon for interns and representatives from the mission boards that were sending us.

Tami and Reed and Jim and I sat together. There were name cards in front of each place, and each of our cards was different. Mine had no last name, and the other three each had a different last name. The mission board executives were not entirely sure who was attached to whom or exactly how to deal with the four of us. Unable to resist the temptation, we were slow in helping them to sort out the relationships.

One other conversation at the orientation sticks in my mind because, as the only African American in the FIM class, it brought the issues of class and race home to me. One of the unofficial rules of the program was that interns did not have servants during their assignments. The origin of the rule was no doubt grounded in the desire of the program to avoid traditional missionary stereotypes. Of course, in practical terms, our subsistence salaries didn't make it possible for us to be too financially extravagant. The FIM orientation included, nevertheless, a discussion of the pros and cons of having servants. A central theme of the conversation seemed to be that having a servant implied that the servant was viewed as less than human. Phrases like "denying the humanity of the servant" seemed to come up often. It dawned on me that the conversation was entirely from the perspective of the "master" class. As the child of a mother and grandmother who had been workers in the homes of others, I knew without a doubt that they never felt a sense of inferiority just because they worked for someone else. It was inconceivable to me that anyone would think that they might feel less than human. The conversation gave me an inkling of how different my perspectives might be from those of other interns on the experiences that we were about to have. It gave me something to ponder in my own reactions.

Our placement was with the National Christian Council of Kenya (NCCK) in Nairobi. An added assignment was to work with my friend from my student movement days, Jose Chipenda, who had recently been appointed one of three co-secretaries of the newly opening World Student Christian Federation regional office. I guess because we were from the United States and because it was in the terms of our contract, the NCCK never questioned that both Jim and I would be fully participating in whatever work they found for us. They had a number of women in responsible positions, mostly on the social service side, and they didn't question that I would be a worker in my own right.

Our first work with the NCCK involved squatter settlements. At the instigation of a young U.S. woman volunteer, the NCCK had created a community development project in the large, sprawling squatter settlement known as Mathare Valley. Our task was to talk with community leaders of the settlements to work out acceptable plans for improvements and to figure out how the squatter would be able to pay for them. We learned a great deal about community economics, thanks to the patience of the community leaders. Although the head of the Town Planning Department, a career British civil servant, was skeptical of me—black, North American, and female—he tolerated me because I was an additional free worker, and because Joan Richards, a white American already working there, insisted on my working with her. Jim began with squatter work but eventually spent more time in the office, involved with a large long-range planning project that was under way.

The NCCK, in an effort to place its staff among the communities it sought to serve, had built staff housing in a neighborhood called Eastlands, on the African side of town. They gave us one of these houses to live in. Our house was next to a local market that had been a famous rendezvous point during the Mau Mau resistance period of the 1950s. It was called Uhuru (Freedom) Market. All of this helped us in our effort to shed some of our U.S. identity and learn more about Kenya. I am not sure what led to the decision to place us in Eastlands, but it was very important to me. In addition to the market, our house was surrounded by public housing projects, some of them among the oldest in Nairobi—one- and two-room units with communal water and toilet facilities. Only some of them had electricity. As new city planners, we couldn't have asked for a better vantage point for study.

Work with Jose and the World Student Christian Federation gave us an opportunity to share some of the analysis we were developing. Jose was working to create a student Christian movement in Kenya. Because of our past association, he looked to us for help. One of the first things we did was to prepare a slide and tape show on the housing realities of Nairobi to present at a student gathering. Later, in an echo of my MSM days, we helped organize and staff a kind of "revolutionary nurture" student work camp in a city in the Rift Valley, in which students were helping local NCCK staff to assess the need for a social service center. The students went to bus stops, markets, and other community gathering places to engage residents in conversation about their problems and needs. Jose also gave me the opportunity to work on the newly created WSCF magazine for the region, *Presence*.

The Frontier Internship gave me a place to test my skills. It gave me room to grow, with probably the fewest constraints ever in my life. I was a wife, but this did not limit the work that I could do. I was a woman, but I was working in a place where my gender was not an automatic cause to question my abilities. I was an African American, but because I was working in an African context, the color of my skin was not an automatic barrier. For once my color was a passport. I learned early that as long as I kept quiet and listened, I could be accepted in African-only conversations and thereby gain many rich experiences. Living in Kenya was a special time for me. It was such a relief not to have to think about race and racial issues all the time. To be able to live without the constant tension that living as a black person in the United States involves was important for my self-confidence. Being a North American could have been and sometimes was a roadblock, but not in the way I would have imagined. Those we met were much less critical of the United States than we were ourselves, and they saw more of their assumptions about U.S. behavior in us than we would have hoped. The FIM program allowed me to gain the "view from a distance" of the United States that I wanted and also a "view from a distance" of myself.

*I*t is hard to believe how many years have passed since those days as a Frontier Intern in Nairobi. Although I finished my internship and any direct connection with the student Christian movement in 1972, its influence on my life has been continual. I remained in Africa an additional two years and then returned again in the 1980s to live and work for another six years. In between, I had the good fortune to spend time as a staff writer with Africa News Service, that wonderful news source that was created by Tami Hultman, Reed Kramer, Bill Minter, and Ruth Brandon Minter—all former Frontier Interns— along with others. Africa News gave me a place to share my experience and concerns about Africa and to sharpen my skills as a writer. These experiences also helped make it possible for me to go on to work as a policy advocate, first in Washington, D.C., for ecumenical organizations, and later in New York for the National Council of Churches (NCCCUSA) and Church World Service. Each place I have moved, the battles have continued to be those we identified all those years ago in the student Christian movement: the struggle for economic and social justice in the United States and other parts of the world— in my case, particularly in Africa. The work for the NCCCUSA brought me back to the very places where I had sat as a student trying to convince what I viewed as an unnecessarily conservative church bureaucracy to take a more critical stance on U.S. policy on the war in Vietnam. I even found myself as the staff person for the successor to the international affairs commission that had so tried my patience.

In 1998 I left the NCCCUSA and moved to my present position. Again my past and my present and future seemed to be converging. I work now as the program director for leadership development and global education at the

Center for Women's Global Leadership at Rutgers University, a position that finally allows me to bring all of my history and skills to my work. It gives me a space to work with others to translate what I have learned into learning opportunities for others. The director of the center is Charlotte Bunch, another child of the student Christian movement and my friend for all these years. It truly feels like the past is the present and the future.

CHAPTER 5

Jill Foreman Hultin

$\mathcal{T}$o convey the depth and scope of the student Christian movement's influence on my life, it is necessary to begin with a snapshot of who I was in the fall of 1961, as I entered Ohio University in Athens, Ohio. I grew up in Quincy, a rural Ohio village of perhaps six hundred people. The hardscrabble town, which developed around the intersection of two railroad tracks, served the surrounding farm community with a grain elevator, a gas station, a hardware store, and my father's garage. There were no amenities or amusements beyond the small school playground and the local ballpark. The community was relatively homogeneous—poor, white, and conservative, with only a handful of people who had a college education.

For most families—certainly for mine—life was focused on hard work and the practical requirements of survival. My father was a mechanic who repaired cars, trucks, and farm machinery. Although we did not live on a farm, the pace and activity of our daily lives was still linked to the cycle of seasons. My parents worked long hours, and by the age of nine, I had a number of adult responsibilities.

The narrowness of that life was compensated by a rich legacy of interdependence and connectedness. My family, which included three younger sisters, was part of a large extended family of aunts, uncles, and cousins who all lived and worked no more than fifteen miles from one another. We spent most holidays engaged in large cooperative work projects—painting houses and barns or repairing roofs and fences. Those workdays were followed by potluck suppers, homemade ice cream, and hours of singing, led by my grandfather playing his fiddle and an aunt playing the piano.

The women in my family—my grandmother, mother, and aunts—were tireless workers who raised large families with few modern conveniences like prepared food or store-bought clothes. (We did not even have an indoor bathroom until I was nine.) They were proud of their self-sufficiency and frugality, and shared the gift of enjoying their work. It was not unusual to hear them singing in the garden or kitchen as they worked late into hot summer nights canning vegetables.

They also shared a deep faith, and formed the backbone of our small local Methodist church. They taught Sunday school and vacation Bible school, led the choir and the Woman's Society, and organized most of the special events. Whenever an individual or family in the community needed help, they organized both direct assistance and the church's "prayer chain," a telephone network that linked members of the community in spiritual intercession for the sick, dying, and grieving. Their lives were also governed by a strict moral code, which they taught us and expected us to carry forward.

While the church was always a fundamental part of my life, it was also a source of some tension. Even as a child, I recall distinguishing between church members and the "Church" as an institution. While my mother and aunts accepted much on faith, I was often critical and quick to judge ministers who did not explain their reasons or church members whose behavior I thought was hypocritical. I had a strong negative reaction to the emotionalism of the traveling evangelists who visited our church, sensing that they were more manipulative than genuine. One of my earliest responses to "bureaucrats" was indignation that Methodist district superintendents or bishops could make decisions for our little church without any need to listen, explain, or negotiate with our members. Despite these wayward feelings, I was not generally rebellious; in fact, I disliked conflict and worked hard to avoid it— even at the cost of some swallowed anger.

As the first person in my family to go to college, I do not recall actively yearning for separation or independence. I had won enough scholarships and saved enough money to ensure that my education did not cause any hardship. In many ways, I wanted to avoid any personal change that might distance me from my family. I had little experience beyond my community and was intellectually unsophisticated and apolitical. (In a high school mock election, I voted for Richard Nixon, but do not remember whether it was because John Kennedy was a Catholic or because he was a Democrat.) Temperamentally, I was intense, approaching life with an attitude that was almost entirely dualistic: good or bad, right or wrong, black or white, all or nothing. Ambiguity and irony did not yet register.

*M*y adjustment to life at Ohio University was not easy. I was shy, alienated from the social scene that largely revolved around drinking parties, and painfully aware that my educational preparation was distinctly inferior to that of my peers. Throughout my first year, I studied obsessively to overcome this gap and ensure that I could keep my scholarship. In the fall of my sophomore year, my well-ordered study routine was shattered by the Cuban missile crisis. As U.S. and Russian warships steamed toward a doomsday encounter, I was, for the first time in my life, utterly, existentially alone. It seemed that we were only days away from nuclear war, and I wanted desperately to go home. But ten-hour lines at every available pay phone made even phoning home impossible. Finally, misery drove me to the Wesley Foundation, the local Methodist campus ministry, where shared anxiety created a kind of intimacy among the students who gravitated there for comfort.

The campus minister, George Kennedy, led us through that traumatic week with a series of practical and eschatological "what ifs." If we were somehow spared from nuclear holocaust, he challenged us to consider the kind of witness the Church should be making to the world. What should we be thinking and doing about nuclear weapons, the practices of war and diplomacy, and the foreign policy of our country and its allies? These questions were beyond the boundaries of any individual or collective action I had ever contemplated. I had never thought about whether the Church had a responsibility for international affairs, and my inability to respond to these questions troubled me. When the crisis finally ended, I had little interest in returning to the isolation and single-mindedness of my earlier study routine. If the world was really so dangerously out of control, good grades no longer seemed like a priority. And if there were answers to the questions that had been raised that week, I needed to know them.

Throughout my remaining two and half years at Ohio University, George Kennedy was my teacher, mentor, and provocateur, challenging me to a more rigorous mix of faith and action. He argued that the Christian life had three primary requirements: a personal, spiritual relationship with God that changes our "way of being" in the world; relationships with others in which we model the same love and forgiveness that God has shown us; and a commitment to social justice—working to make life more humane and just for the poor and dispossessed. God's promises were to be fulfilled in the here and now, as well as in some time still to come, thus increasing the importance and urgency of our decisions and actions in the present moment. George used Scripture to make the case that Christians' commitment to social justice must be proactive, radical, and structural as well as responsive, individual, and personal. He stretched us through the reading of Buber, Bonhoeffer, Tillich, and Niebuhr, and took us to see plays by T. S. Eliot. And he reminded us constantly—with great passion—that sins of omission were as destructive as sins of commission. "Not to decide is to decide" was his mantra.

In the spring of my sophomore year, George pushed me to become an officer in the Ohio Methodist Student Movement, a responsibility that also led to my election to the National Council of the MSM and further involvement in the National Student Christian Federation and the World Student Christian Federation. The Methodist Church, as my sponsor, made enormous investments in my education and that of other members on the MSM National Council during the years I was actively involved. They sent us to New York and Washington for seminars describing the legacy of colonialism and the social and economic problems driving demands for radical change in Latin America and South Africa. We met with leaders of the United Nations, Congress, and the National Council of Churches to discuss U.S. foreign policy as it was affecting human rights and economic justice on other continents. On other occasions, I was sent to conferences and meetings in Latin America and Eastern Europe, where I was exposed to a broad international dialogue about the Church's responsibility to promote social and political justice on all continents. These experiences led me to feel I had a personal responsibility to influence the policies of both the Church and the U.S. government.

$\mathcal{D}$uring Christmas vacation of 1963, the National Student Christian Federation convened an international conference at Ohio University. President Kennedy had been assassinated one month earlier, and U.S. participants were still struggling with shock and grief . One goal of the conference was to build on Pope John XXIII's efforts to open the Church to greater ecumenism, by promoting a broader dialogue among Catholic, Protestant, and Orthodox students. The conference study book, *For the Life of the World,* had been written by a Greek Orthodox priest, Alexander Schmemann, who challenged Protestants' tendency to reject or withdraw from the "evil" of the world. Schmemann argued that human lives and historical events are the media through which God acts, and that the world is where we encounter the signs of that activity—in the form of truth, grace, and forgiveness. In contrast to the Puritan history of the United States, Schmemann argued that there is no schism between the sacred and the secular. Instead, our lives and our work may be simultaneously secular and sacred, depending on the attitude we bring to them. He believed passionately that the mission of the Church is to be engaged in the life of the world, learning (from all sources), struggling against evil (our own and that of others), working for social justice (on behalf of all human beings, regardless of race, religion, class, culture, or country), and doing all this from a sacramental perspective.

The conference had a number of speakers and many small group discussions about how to apply Schmemann's challenge to the events happening at that moment all around the world: the civil rights movement in the United States, the movements of national liberation in Latin America, Africa, and Asia; and the conflicting political and economic forces of capitalism and communism as they played out around the globe. In one of those groups, I began a dialogue with a man who had strong opinions about the extent to which Christians and the Church should use secular political power to effect social change. He and I debated the possibility of knowing whether one's actions are aligned with God's purposes and priorities, and the moral risks of doing nothing, as compared with the risk of taking action that may or may not be right. Eighteen months later, I married that man, and the debates of that week have been repeated many times over the past forty years.

S ix months after the Athens conference, I traveled to a number of countries in Latin America as part of a national MSM study/travel seminar. Our group's purpose was to learn more about the social, economic, and political revolutions occurring on that continent, and to see how liberation theology, the Church, and student Christian movements throughout the countries were responding to and supporting those changes. The group was led by Bill Corzine, who worked for the Methodist Board of Education as the chief staff liaison to the MSM National Council. Bill was a humble, facilitative leader whose quiet strength, powerful intellect, and wry, self-deprecating humor created a safe space for me and others on the council to grow. Peg Rigg, the art editor of *motive* magazine, was also a member of the group, as was Ruth Harris, staff from the Methodist Board of Missions. Ruth was a visionary leader who had created many of the Christian Citizenship Seminar experiences that were so important in broadening my awareness of international issues. She was the first person I knew who truly lived and worked from a global perspective. Ruth and elmira Kendricks, a member of the MSM Council and a theological student at Drew University, were traveling with the group, although they had to detour for several weeks to attend a World Student Christian Federation meeting in Argentina. One of the great gifts of that trip was the chance to deepen my friendship with elmira. She was brilliant, but had not lost a childlike sense of wonder, and I was in awe of her intellectual and spiritual insight.

In each of the countries we visited, we met with a broad spectrum of leaders—including bishops, priests, politicians, students, peasants, writers, artists, government officials, and generals in military juntas. We listened to their various perspectives regarding how Latin Americans could manage the crises facing their countries, and heard them describe widely differing methods by which they felt those challenges could best be addressed. Some of the people we talked with felt there was no realistic hope for social justice until the repressive regimes controlling their countries had been defeated in elections—or overturned by revolutions.

The Latin Americans were intensely interested in U.S. politics, and fascinated by the fact that we were an interracial group. They peppered us with questions about our personal involvement in the civil rights movement, the Church's position on civil rights, and who we thought *really* killed President Kennedy. In many Latin American countries, political conspiracies and political repression were the norm. As a result, they tended to view North Americans as politically naive, a judgment we strengthened by asserting that we did not think there had been a massive conspiracy behind the president's assassination. The Latin Americans were also deeply impressed by our political freedom and right to vote, and they urged us not to take that right for granted. As we traveled from country to country, we were told repeatedly that the foreign policy of the United States had a more direct impact on Latin Americans' lives than their own leaders and the economic and political policies of their own governments did.

Peg Rigg had arranged for our group to meet with artists and writers in each country we visited. She had a gift for getting them to talk about the sensibilities that informed their work, and helped us decode the symbols they used to represent their experience. As an English major, I was familiar with literary images, but discussing art was strange new territory. I was particularly fascinated by several artists who talked about "knowing" what was happening in their country—before they could describe it in words and before they knew what they thought and felt about it. One of our most memorable conversations was with Jorge Luis Borges, who though already blind, was continuing to write novels and poetry in the style we now call "magical realism."

We arrived in Brazil several months after a successful coup by a military junta. The country's colonial history, commodity-based economy, grinding poverty, and rapidly inflating currency all pointed to extreme instability. The Brazilian student Christian movement believed economic change was a prerequisite to social justice, and its members were involved in ongoing dialogue with economists, engineers, and architects about how Brazil's economy and infrastructure could be modernized. They had forged alliances with secular political movements advocating social change, and seemed to accept the inevitability of a political revolution.

In Brazil, as in most other Latin American countries, it was common to experience generalized anti-American attitudes, although, as individuals, we were usually treated with great warmth and hospitality. The Brazilians were especially open and generous in spending time with us. I recall a conversation with one of the leaders of the Brazilian student Christian movement, in which I asked whether his willingness to talk with North Americans caused others in his group to question whether they could trust him. He smiled, and answered, "If I only did what they like me to do, how could I be their leader?"

That summer's learning process was heightened by the fact that I had to listen so intently to understand what was being said in Spanish, Portuguese, or a translator's English. I was often awake nights replaying conversations—trying to be sure I'd understood what had been said and considering what I thought about it. I was overwhelmed by how many different interpretations could be made about the same facts or events, depending on one's interests and degree of self-awareness. Land ownership, wealth, and cultural history clearly shaped individuals' views regarding social justice and the appropriate speed of change. I could see how people without any stake in the present social order might feel few qualms about the destruction and death that might accompany a revolution. And the responsibility of leaders seemed to be an issue everywhere.

Our group returned to the United States in late August, just as the 1964 presidential election was hitting its peak. The Gulf of Tonkin incident had occurred only a few weeks earlier, and U.S. citizens were rapidly learning about the extent of America's military involvement in Vietnam. The prospect of an expanding war had personal implications for me, as my fiancé had just begun serving his commission as a naval officer on one of the ships involved in the second Gulf of Tonkin incident.

At the fall meeting of the MSM Council, we debated the "responsibility" question at some length and finally decided to send a special mailing to Methodist student groups around the country, expressing our concerns about some of Barry Goldwater's positions and urging support for Lyndon Johnson. We anticipated (accurately) that for a church organization to advocate a political position would be controversial to many of our members. And we were not particularly enthusiastic about Johnson. But our discussions with the Latin American student Christian movement were still fresh, and we felt we should act—despite the ambiguity of the situation. Not to decide was to decide.

Although my religious and political perspectives had been evolving rapidly, I cannot recall the extent to which I had discussed those changes with my family. But during that fall of 1964, I learned that the letters I had sent home from Latin America and the controversy surrounding the MSM's special mailing on the election were unsettling to my family. One of my aunts thought I must have been influenced by communists. My parents were troubled by both the political content and the intensity of my views, and I was deeply disappointed by their reactions. We seemed unable to discuss these issues in a way that did not exacerbate our mutual sense of loss. My precollege clarity about the need to remain unchanged was not working out as I had hoped.

In December 1964, Martin Luther King, Jr., was the keynote speaker at the MSM's Quadrennial Student Conference in Lincoln, Nebraska. As the chair of the MSM's civil rights committee, I introduced Dr. King to the assembly of thousands of students, and he delivered a powerful sermon on the civil rights movement as an instrument of social justice and an opportunity for the church to lead in purging the evil of racism. I sat behind him on the podium that night deeply grieved and ashamed as his message recalled an incident I'd been involved in during the week of the August 1963 March on Washington.

I had worked that summer as the night desk clerk of a small hotel in Ohio, and one evening a black family had come in to request a room. I was registering them when the hotel owner intervened, taking the paperwork from my hands and announcing that the hotel was full. It was an obvious, humiliating lie, but the family left without protest. The owner then turned on me, screaming that I would be fired if I ever let another Negro into her hotel. I was shocked and upset, and when I got home after midnight, I wakened my parents with the announcement that I could not continue to work for a racist establishment. My parents were troubled by my outburst. They believed I had a responsibility to finish the job I had accepted, and that it was the owner's prerogative to make the rules. I felt their view was a weak rationalization, and argued that although they had raised me to be a Christian, they were now directing me to be a hypocrite. As I became increasingly overwrought, they became more firmly entrenched. Finally, despite my conviction that returning to the job was morally wrong, I did not have the courage to defy my parents.

Following Dr. King's speech in Lincoln, the winter months were dominated by television and newspaper stories of escalating violence against black citizens and civil rights workers demonstrating for the right to vote and for an end to segregated facilities. By early March, the MSM Council talked by telephone about whether we should respond to the events occurring in Alabama, which now included daily marches in Montgomery and a planned long march from Selma to Montgomery. Finally we decided that a small group of MSM Council and staff members should go to Montgomery to assess the situation. I saw this as an opportunity to make amends for my previous failure, and I called my family to inform them that I intended to go to Montgomery. They were adamant that I should not go, but this time I was clear.

In preparing for the trip, we got very specific advice from civil rights workers in Montgomery: Do not come unless you have your own bail money. Do not come unless you have been trained in nonviolent resistance. Do not come unless you are prepared to face violence. If you decide to come, dress and act like clean-cut, middle-class college students. People may not mind watching black folks attacked by horses and dogs and billy clubs, but they won't like watching it happen to their own children.

My fiancé, supportive as always, wired bail money. When I arrived in Montgomery, I joined other members of the MSM Council and staff, including Bill Corzine, elmira Kendricks, Charlotte Bunch, and Charles Rinker. Charles, the president of the National MSM at that time, was a clear thinker who radiated intelligence and strength of character. Charlotte was smart, strategic, and quick to assess alternatives and make decisions. She was a natural "take charge" leader who could also work in a team and bring out the best in others. Over the years we worked together, Charlotte became my alter ego, the person with whom I did my best thinking.

We conferred with officials of both the Southern Christian Leadership Conference and the Student Nonviolent Coordinating Committee. The Montgomery branch of SCLC needed additional help. They wanted the MSM to help mobilize the black community to participate in the last leg of the march from the outskirts of Montgomery to the State House downtown, and locate people willing to provide shelter to march participants when they reached the city. SCLC anticipated that anyone without housing would be a target for violence. So our volunteers were divided into teams with local youths and sent door to door through the black community to sign up people willing to march and people who would open their homes to us.

For the first few days, our group stayed in a downtown motel, as we needed multiple phone lines to call campus ministers and student leaders around the country asking them to come to Montgomery. (Nearly a hundred people agreed to come.) We were a biracial group, and as a result we experienced a lot of petty harassment. When we were not using the phones for outbound calls, they rang incessantly with obscene callers and "breathers." Anonymous hands pounded on our door at all hours. When we tried to eat in the coffee shop, we were surrounded by sheriff's deputies and bystanders who shouted insults and threatened us. Several times during those days, we observed the deputies talking with men who appeared to be federal agents. Although we could not know the reasons for these conversations, they increased our sense of unease and paranoia. We had all participated in interracial projects in our home states, but none of us had experienced an environment as menacing as Montgomery.

When our calls were finally completed, the SCLC staff found homes for us to stay in the black community, where we would be safer. The way black families in Montgomery extended themselves to total strangers was amazing. They welcomed us as family, supplying us with shelter, food, and transportation—even though this action substantially increased the likelihood that they would be targets of future violence. It seemed ironic that we should feel so at home there, almost as if we had reached the eye of a storm.

In the evenings of the week and a half we spent preparing for the marchers, Andrew Young, Hosea Williams, Jesse Jackson, and others on the SCLC staff spoke in the black churches in the community. Like Dr. King, they were powerful preachers, propelled and sustained by the Old Testament's stories of God's promises to his people—and the New Testament's vision of how those promises would be fulfilled. Each night, the churches were packed with community members, civil rights workers, and volunteers. One night we arrived at the service too late to get inside. The building was already surrounded by a crowd, and there were some people standing on the shoulders of others, listening at the windows to hear and glimpse the speakers. I remember experiencing a flash of recognition that this must have been what the early Church was like, when Peter or Paul came to preach to first-century communities actively thirsting for the Word.

Days later when the marchers from Selma reached Montgomery, their ranks had swelled to ten thousand. Our volunteer teams worked through the outdoor rally and entertainment and through most of the night, registering marchers and making sure that each person had a map and a guide to the assigned home. The National Guard had been mobilized to "protect" marchers from acts of violence, but it was difficult to take much comfort from the protection of troops with fixed bayonets, live ammunition, and Confederate flags on their uniforms.

On the morning of March 25, we were finally free to join the rest of the marchers. I had been alert and anxious since arriving in Montgomery ten days earlier, but during the hour and a half that the march was assembling, I was overwhelmed by fear. I could imagine the National Guard troops stationed on rooftops and in helicopters opening fire and mowing us down. I chose a place somewhere in the middle of the march and the middle of a row, reasoning that the first and last marchers, as well as the ends of rows, would be most vulnerable. I could not comprehend how foot soldiers through centuries of war have lined up to march into battles they had so little likelihood of surviving.

Eventually the lines began to move, and there were waves of marchers ahead of me and behind me as far as I could see. Within a few minutes, people began to sing. And somewhere along the way that morning, my fear was replaced by the extraordinary awareness of being a bit player in an unfolding moment of history, a witness to the transcendent grace of "one Body, filled with the Spirit." Like the Israelites fleeing Pharaoh's soldiers, we were protected. No sharpshooters, horses, dogs, or police clubs were turned against us that day.

After the march, while a friend and I were working our way through the crowd to the train station, an angry white man shoved me into a doorway and punched me several times. With adrenaline pumping, I was unable to feel the love and compassion Dr. King urged us to show our enemies, but I was able to comply with the instructions on passive resistance. Late that night, when our train pulled into Memphis, newspaper headlines announced that Viola Liuzzo, a white civil rights worker, had been killed by snipers as she drove away from the march.

*I*n June 1965, two and a half months after the Selma to Montgomery March, I left the university with my undergraduate degree. My family had welcomed me back from Montgomery with relief, but political tension had reached even my sheltered hometown. Word of my involvement had led to death threats for my family, and my father had gotten into a fist fight with a man who charged into his garage to challenge him for having a "nigger-loving" daughter. In the years I had been away at school, the country's mood had shifted to an anxious awareness of the fragility of life, peace, and social order. It was no longer unthinkable that families or communities could be divided by political differences.

The week following my graduation, the MSM held its national conference at the Ecumenical Institute (EI) in the heart of Chicago's inner-city ghetto. The institute was a striking model of the Church at work in the world. Its members, most of whom were ordained ministers and their families, were living in a campus-style community as an urban religious order. This group had rejected the spiritual indifference that characterized much of suburban life and the life of many local Protestant congregations. Some of its members were leading community organizing and job creation activities in the neighborhood surrounding the institute, using tactics developed by Saul Alinsky and the Woodlawn Organization. Others were leading groups like ours through a dramatic training program they had created to challenge the worldview and theological assumptions of participants. Some were working at outside jobs to support the work of all those engaged in the EI ministry. Every family—and there were many with young children—participated in a discipline of morning and evening worship, and each also took vows of poverty and sharing of resources.

The institute challenged us to get clear about how we were going to live out our religious beliefs. Were we prepared to give up our middle-class advantages to live side by side with the poor? Would we use our income to support more people than just our own family members? Did we believe that inner-city schools were worth saving—and would we enroll our children there? Were we prepared to use our intelligence, networks, and resources to create jobs where there were now only burned-out buildings? Would we go back to Sunday-only churches—or would we join them in action? We were deeply impressed by the work of the institute, and within the following year, several members of the MSM Council joined new EI communities forming in Los Angeles, Minneapolis, and Washington, D.C.

During that week in Chicago, I got a telegram from my fiancé saying, "Wedding off. Will call on Thursday." Several days later his ship docked, and he called to say that he had just received orders to return to Vietnam immediately. This meant it would be impossible to marry in July as we had planned. After several frantic phone calls discussing options that were all bad, we finally decided to get married in Ohio the following weekend. Eight days later, he caught a plane to Hawaii to catch up with his ship, while I sat at the airport, studying a map to figure out how to drive through the massive urban sprawl of Los Angeles to the apartment that would be my new home. The deep roots and close connections of my past seemed like a surreal dream in contrast to this new life alone in a city of millions. It took some getting used to.

Change was the operative reality on many different fronts that summer. The war in Vietnam no longer seemed like an abstraction halfway around the world. Draft notices were increasing sharply, and antiwar protests and Vietnam teach-ins were being organized on campuses. In West Coast harbors, ships were being loaded with weapons, troops, and body bags. In August, riots broke out in Watts, spreading quickly to other urban ghettos, first in Southern California and then to other cities around the country. The rage expressed in those riots seemed to overwhelm the patience, nonviolence, and willingness to suffer that had characterized the southern civil rights movement, with its religious and spiritual roots. In a short period of time, the movement's leadership shifted to younger, angrier men committed to "black power" and willing to consider the legitimacy of violence.

*T*hree months after my arrival in Los Angeles, I was accepted into the Coro Fellows Program, a postgraduate internship in public affairs—a program designed to give a dozen new graduates with leadership potential an in-depth immersion in how our system of government really works. The objective of the program was to strengthen individuals' capacity to influence the system, regardless of whether they held positions of power. My assignments included projects with a labor union, a business, a city manager's office, and a political campaign. As a result of the summer riots, many different organizations—both public and private—were struggling to rethink what they were doing and how they needed to change. The internship provided me with a crash course in California's geography, economy, politics, and culture, as well as a lot of basic information about how governments and other organizations function. I left the program impressed by the extent to which solutions to serious, real-world problems were made possible—or impossible—by the assumptions, rather than by the skills or expertise, that stakeholders bring to the negotiating and decision-making process. I also glimpsed the role that strategy and money play in shaping the issues that get addressed and the questions that get asked.

At the NSCF's fall meeting, in Chicago, many of us felt that the country's social and political environment was changing rapidly, and we were looking for a way to play a more direct role in that change. For those of us who had experienced the "organic" power of the civil rights movement and the liberation movements abroad, the federation's structure was an anomaly. Although the federation had sponsored many of the powerful experiences that had nurtured our growth, in other ways those events seemed to have happened in spite of the way we were organized, which was more like a legislative body. Some of us felt we needed a more flexible structure, less driven from the top by the decision making of multiple denominational church hierarchies and more directly responsive to and supportive of the needs of local campuses and communities.

Not unlike the Reformation debates about Church polity, we were struggling not only with problems of our organizational structure but also with issues of governance and the role of leaders. The "Congregationalist" approach we were considering meant that at both the local and the national level, individual "members" would determine the movement's priorities and approach, with less direction by professional staff employed by the various denominations. After several more meetings during that academic year, in June 1966 the NSCF voted to create the University Christian Movement (UCM). Charlotte Bunch, from the MSM Council, became the first UCM president, and I became one of five regional vice presidents of the UCM, as well as the national president of the Methodist Student Movement.

During the following year, my life involved a great deal of travel from campus to campus around the country, meeting with MSM groups and campus ministers as well as with secular organizations that were increasingly becoming "the movement." If the NSCF was having difficulty with issues of structure and decision making, the movement was having them to the tenth power. A great deal of meeting time was spent in doctrinal disputes regarding assumptions and analysis as well as strategy. I was often frustrated by these debates, in part because the range for "right thinking" seemed rather narrow and in part because they frequently marginalized me. Several people I had worked with in the South would not even talk with me when they later learned I was married to a naval officer.

I could empathize with the anger that was now fueling the black power movement, but was not clear how that rage could be transformed into energy for community building. I was grateful that demonstrations and community organizing were beginning to shift public opinion on the war, but was not convinced that they generated much insight into sustaining peace. What I thought we needed was a concrete vision of a desired future, and a set of strategies and compatriots who could make that future real. The brightest spots I experienced in that year of travel and meetings were the small, informal clusters of women who were beginning to meet on university campuses to discuss their own experiences and concerns.

When I was not traveling, I was living in an experimental community in Los Angeles modeled after the Ecumenical Institute in Chicago. My husband was stationed on an island off the coast of California that year, which allowed him to fly home most weekends. We were both attracted to this community's goal: empowering neighborhood residents to take responsibility for their own lives and futures. The group's members had made a conscious decision to give up middle-class comforts to live with people who were without privilege or power. Members also committed to being strategic, intentional, accountable, and disciplined. The discipline included participating in regular group worship, meetings, some communal meals, and other celebrations. To minimize personal differences and maximize productive problem solving, group members agreed to discuss problems or concerns with the whole group in regular meetings—avoiding any divisive "side talk" or complaining. Although I had a vague twinge of unease about the group's leader, an articulate, visionary minister who worked as a consultant to a number of churches, my most significant concern about this new venture was the potential loss of independence and emotional space for an uncertain group process.

Twelve of us moved into a set of concrete block apartments on Century Boulevard in south central Los Angeles. Our first project was a rent strike in the apartment complex, which was in terrible repair, with several courtyards having open sewage and rats. After several months of working together and with the neighborhood, the "shadow side" of our leader began to emerge. Although he was adept at a range of roles—visionary, mentor, theologian, and priest—he had a strong belief in his own authority and an even stronger need to be in control. He was a master of psychological games and used them to the detriment of anyone who disagreed with him. Even minor disagreements could be quickly elevated to a level of such intense psychological battering that reasonable people simply dropped out and let him have his own way. He kept us off balance by lifting some members up while triangulating and humiliating others. The discipline we had accepted created a perfect "catch-22": to raise a serious concern with the whole group required preparation for full-scale psychological battle, yet to plan a group approach to problem solving was a violation of the code.

Although the rent strike succeeded, our internal life continued to deteriorate. The discipline, as enforced by the leader, essentially required us to disconnect our intellects from our emotions. Negative feelings were judged to be "neurotic" and evidence of the "failure to give up middle-class values." Criticism of any aspect of community life was seen as a projection of an individual's inability to commit. My gut rejected these judgments, but I lacked the intellectual and psychological experience to successfully defend myself. I was particularly crippled by the internal split between my intellect and emotions. I saw great value in the way EI taught theology and in the strength of the community model, so it was hard to admit I couldn't live with it. I had not experienced such an intense internal dichotomy since that August day in

1963 when I went back to work at the hotel, knowing it was wrong. Although I continued to battle the leader, I also internalized his accusations and doubted myself. My husband, Jerry, was gone for much of this period, so he only heard about the conflict from me, although he could see I was suffering and that the group was in trouble. I needed to talk through my feelings, but everyone in the group was avoiding one another—lest each be accused of "side talk" and "plotting."

It should have been clear that I did not have to choose between my head and my feelings—or between self-interest and the interests of the group. Both should have been possible. But struggling to understand what was happening and why, in the midst of the conflict, without the benefit of others' wisdom, contributed to significant confusion and exhaustion. After several months of bad dreams, I woke up one night with the sudden clarity that I was in some kind of psychological or spiritual death march—from which I needed to save myself. A few weeks later, the movie *Dr. Zhivago* precipitated a denouement. I experienced the portrayal of Zhivago, the individual able to see the benefits of the revolution but unable to support its brutal excesses, as unbearably close. I did not want to be like Zhivago—I had spent the last four years believing that "not to decide was to decide." I did not want to be a person who abandoned commitments—but I also knew that I could not remain in the community.

When my husband and I went to tell the members of the group that we were leaving, we found that most had come to the same decision. In fact, most were already packed. So our experiment ended ingloriously, with little accomplished beyond a successful rent strike. Although I was only twenty-four—fifteen months older than when I entered the community—I had changed. My belief system and my experience were at odds, and I didn't know how to get them aligned. I felt that I had personally failed, but didn't know what I could have done differently.

In June 1967, the National Methodist Student Movement voted to phase out its national denominational hierarchy over a two-year transition period, while continuing the effort to bring local and state student organizations into the UCM. The vote did not answer worrisome questions about how the transition would be accomplished, but my term on the MSM and UCM was over, and I was relieved. Someone else would have to carry that process forward. Most of the people I had grown up with in the movement had moved on, and I felt ready to move on myself. I recall Ruth Harris's concern that we needed to stay in relationship with the Church if we hoped to have some influence on it. But at that point, I had no idea how to think about—let alone take responsibility for—the future of the Church. I was not sure I could trust my own judgment.

The summer of 1967, I attended my first national feminist conference in Chicago. The unhappy experience in the Los Angeles community had raised my consciousness about the damage caused by paternalism and leadership centered on assumptions of male authority. It felt good to be in a meeting with women talking about how to change our own lives and attitudes—as well as trying to change others' attitudes toward us. A number of the participants seemed clear that our heads, hearts, and way of living and working needed to be aligned if we were ever to be whole, healthy, and truly free.

Although I still did not know what I wanted to be when I grew up, Marshall McLuhan seemed to be on to something in his books on media and globalization: I needed a better tool kit. Media seemed to be having an extraordinary impact in shaping individuals' expectations, and I thought this was an arena that needed a change agent. So I went back to graduate school to learn television and film production, and spent the next three years writing, directing, and producing videos and films. For my MFA production at UCLA, I borrowed $10,000—a fortune in those days—and made a theatrical film about women's issues called *Sisters*. It was a grueling but exhilarating process. Although I never fully recouped my investment, the film won several awards and I experienced a way of working that drew on all of me—even more than I knew was there.

During my last year of graduate school, I heard that the UCM had closed its doors, fracturing along the fault lines of race, class, and gender that were tearing apart many organizations—and the movement.

*I*t was easy to get hooked on the drama of the 1960s. Those days remain a point of comparison: the time I was where I needed to be, doing what I needed to do. My life since the movement has been blessed with a happy marriage, wonderful children, and good friends. Yet I've always had a lingering sense of alienation, of working in the system without accepting it or giving myself to it. This is different from the experience of most of my colleagues.

The student movement helped me understand that my mission was in the world, and I've worked in a variety of ways—as a university professor, a film and television producer, a government strategic planner, and for the last dozen years as an organizational consultant. In each of those jobs, I've tried to function as a change agent, challenging assumptions, helping people see alternatives, and helping them take the action needed to make those alternatives real. Throughout the last three decades, I've repeatedly observed that secular political action and programs without a spiritual dimension rarely lead to social justice or transformed lives.

Keeping the student movement's spiritual legacy alive in my life has been difficult. I have struggled to find a local church with strong theological leadership and a vital congregation. I've had to learn repeatedly that I am responsible for my own spiritual growth. My most frequent failure has been what my Shakespeare professor used to call being "ontologically impercep-tive," mistaking myself for God, placing my faith in strategy, intention, and effort, rather than in how I was *being* in the world. I embraced Paul's admo-nition to "run the race to win" because it appealed to my intensity, but I over-looked the balancing scripture that assures us we will not often succeed in this world. I wanted to win, often and splendidly.

Today I am clearer that being faithful is not the same as being suc-cessful. I am more patient and more grateful for progress a "chunk at a time." In recent years, I've reconnected with friends from the MSM Council and UCM, and have taken both strength and pleasure from seeing the ways that they have continued to run the race. In many ways, my life has come full circle in these thirty-five years—or perhaps "full spiral" is more accurate, because growth continues.

CHAPTER 6

Charlotte Bunch

~~~~~~~~~~~~~~~

$\mathcal{W}$hen I was in the sixth grade at Hermosa Elementary School in Artesia, New Mexico, in the 1950s, I earnestly bet my teacher, Mr. Damron, that when I grew up I would be a missionary in some faraway country. He was skeptical, but I was insistent. As a bright, adventurous girl growing up in a small rural town, I saw the missionaries who occasionally came to our local Methodist church to show slides and talk of their work in distant places as my role models—especially the women. They seemed to have exciting lives as women who traveled and yet also did good works. The next year someone gave me a book called *Girls' Stories of Great Women,* and I began to imagine that I might become a social worker, like Jane Addams, helping people in the United States. I was restless, searching for something that I did not know how to name. It was through the student Christian movement in the 1960s—the YWCA and the Methodist Student Movement in particular—that I was able to transform my vague ideals into a life as a political activist.

Now, in the early part of the twenty-first century, I direct the Center for Women's Global Leadership, which seeks to bring more women from all parts of the world into leadership in the global arena. I think a lot about what enables and encourages women to take action and leadership for justice and change in the world. Therefore I look back on my life and my generation of women activists in the 1960s and 1970s with a special interest in what propelled us forward and helped us to imagine that we could move into arenas where women were not expected to go and even change the world.

My childhood was full of mixed messages about what it meant to be female. The imperative that I should become a responsible, active citizen, however, was never in doubt. My parents were open-minded Methodists and middle-class professionals whose commitment to fairness and moderate politics often made them controversial in the conservative West Texas atmosphere of southeastern New Mexico, where we lived throughout my childhood. Artesia was a flat, undistinguished town of about nine thousand people with an economy that centered on its oil refinery and nearby ranches. There was empty space for miles in all directions. High school football was the town's primary passion, and its greatest source of fame was being featured in *Time* magazine in the late 1950s for having the country's first underground school that doubled as a bomb shelter.

My parents were pillars of the local church and active in civic affairs. They had planned to be missionaries to China, but were stopped by World War II. My father became a family doctor in needy rural areas of the United States instead, eventually landing in New Mexico because of his asthma. Our house was the local spot for visiting foreign students and people who passed through from around the world. One year, we were designated New Mexico's Methodist Family of the Year. My mother was a housewife who clearly enjoyed her civic activities more than housework, and she became the first woman elected president of the local school board. She had great integrity and was often the lone vote against proposals like spending money on the football team rather than on classroom equipment. My parents taught us to stand up for our principles, and that you can disagree with and be different from the people around you without being alienated from them. Although my parents were involved in local issues, traveled throughout the United States, and cared about the world, their political views were not sharply defined by ideology. Our home was busy and activist but somewhat apolitical.

I was the third and most adventurous of the four children. Our parents encouraged me, my two sisters, and my brother in many extracurricular activities. Growing up before we had television, I belonged to all kinds of clubs, and I accompanied my parents in some of their activities because I liked listening to grown-up talk. I was generally happy and outgoing but frequently bored and restless. I took every opportunity to go to camp (church, Girl Scout, or music camp—it did not matter) and to visit friends or relatives in nearby towns. I saw travel as an adventure and especially loved being put on a bus to go somewhere alone or with one of my girlfriends.

My curiosity and my desire to explore the world were encouraged, and I was rarely told that I should not do certain things because I was female. Yet something was missing. There was little discussion of what I wanted to be when I grew up, while there was much hand-wringing over my brother's future. I had a strong desire to do something meaningful and keenly felt the family imperative to be active, but no one seemed to think it important that I shape that into a career. There was pressure to perform well in school and to get a good education, but what I was supposed to do with that education remained fuzzy. This is the only clue I remember: when I chose to go east for college, unlike my brother and sisters who remained in the region, my father commented that men there might be more willing to accept such an independently minded woman. I did not realize how independent I was, and I assumed that I would someday marry, so his words made me uneasy although I didn't quite know why or what he really meant.

I arrived at the Women's College of Duke University in Durham, North Carolina, in the fall of 1962, eager but somewhat apprehensive about going to a big eastern school. Coming from the Southwest, I saw myself heading for the East Coast, with all the intellectual and political weight attached to that region. It took some time before I realized that others saw it as the South. I was not very confident socially and had inherited my mother's prejudices against sororities, so I did not join one. I did not know anyone at Duke, but my older sister Mildred had worked that summer at the Methodist Assembly grounds at Lake Junaluska, North Carolina, where she met Sara (Peachie) Evans, an entering freshman at Duke who was the daughter of the chaplain at Southern Methodist University in Dallas. I called Sara, and we gradually became close friends, growing into lives of political activism separately and together over the years. One of the first places we both found that met our needs for a concerned community was the Freshman YWCA.

The YWCA was strong at the Women's College, which was on a separate campus from the men's college, and it had a program of advisors for freshmen in every dorm. I joined the special Y program for freshmen and soon became part of its cabinet. We met weekly, and we read about and discussed issues facing us as women beginning college. It was a stimulating, women-only environment which encouraged our leadership and forged strong bonds of friendship. Some of us agreed to be advisors for freshmen in our dorms the next year, and one of our concerns was preparing for the racial integration of Duke's undergraduate colleges in 1963. The Y advisor, Bobbie Benedict, encouraged us to discuss racism and to think about how to support the seven African American students who were to arrive in the fall. Three of the seven were women and one was to be in my dorm. I felt both challenged and excited about the prospect of befriending her, realizing that I had grown up with no black friends in a town with almost no African American families.

Going to the Methodist Student Center when I arrived at Duke was a natural step for me, because I had been in Methodist activities all my life. I did not think of it as political at that time, but rather as a familiar place to find friends and community. The timing could not have been better. The Methodist Student Movement at Duke was a place of intellectual and political ferment, from the theological excitement generated by the Lay Scholars Program that Art Brandenburg had initiated to the social activism that was spawned by the black civil rights movement in North Carolina. At first I was intimidated by the discourse at the MSM, which included graduate students and faculty as well as undergraduates. But I kept going because they were welcoming and the atmosphere was exciting, with its ongoing discussion of events that were happening around us, from the Bay of Pigs to lunch counter sit-ins. We learned about civil rights demonstrations in the state, and a number of programs involved talking with students from nearby Negro colleges as well as with international graduate students and faculty from various parts of the world. Eventually, as part of this community, I got up the nerve to go to my first demonstration—an interracial pray-in outside one of the local segregated churches.

It happened gradually, but as I look back, I see that 1963 was the turning point in my life, moving me inexorably from timid moral opposition to the unfairness of segregation in the South to a wider political understanding of injustices in the world and a commitment to work against them. My participation in my first civil rights demonstration was sparked by a photo in the local paper of the police beating one of the black students from North Carolina Negro College whom I had met at the MSM. In the spring of that year, I participated in a Duke MSM study tour to New York City and met activists in Harlem and toured Greenwich Village. That summer I learned about poverty and racism in the North while working in an inner-city project for children sponsored by the Methodist Deaconess Home in Philadelphia. These opportunities helped me begin to understand race and class divisions throughout the country from north to south, east to west, including in my hometown, which was divided between Anglos and Mexicans. I read the recently published book *The Feminine Mystique* by Betty Friedan, which our YWCA director recommended for summer reading. This book confirmed my unarticulated suspicions about the prospects for educated women and helped clarify the fuzziness I had felt about having a career. Just before I returned for my sophomore year at Duke, which was now integrated, I watched Martin Luther King, Jr., deliver his "I Have a Dream" speech on television. I thought to myself that I should have been at the March on Washington, and that I had missed my chance to be part of that history. Later that year, activist students at Duke wept over the assassination of John F. Kennedy, fearing that it meant the end of our hopes for a new era.

The culmination of this life-altering year was my attendance at the quadrennial Ecumenical Student Conference in Athens, Ohio, during Christmas vacation. I had heard about the YM-YWCA Quadrennial Student Conference held over Christmas break the previous year and had wanted to go, but my father insisted that I come home to New Mexico for the entire break my freshman year. He had been the coordinator of one of the Student Volunteer Movement quadrennial conferences in the 1930s and assured me that there would be more such events that I could attend later. I was hungry for such experiences, and I held my father to his promise.

Through the Y and the MSM at Duke, I had begun to learn about political issues in the United States, but at Athens, I discovered the world. The theme of the conference was "For the Life of the World," and the world was very present in the program as well as among the participants, many of whom were international students. Speakers from South Africa challenged us about Christian responsibility to confront apartheid, a Czechoslovakian theologian talked about Christian-Marxist dialogue while the right wing was outside protesting the presence of a communist on the program, and Latin Americans spoke of the CIA and U.S. intervention in their region, which seemed on the verge of revolutionary change. Theologically the conference was also a mind-opener, with Catholic, Protestant, and Orthodox liturgies and inquiry interspersed throughout. The vision of a politically engaged, interracial, ecumenical Christian community electrified participants. There was a buzz everywhere.

After Athens I returned to Duke with a new sense of excitement about ecumenical endeavors that I took into the MSM, where I was now a regular participant. In the spring, at the statewide Methodist Student Movement annual conference, I was elected president of the state MSM, which meant that I went to the National Methodist Student Movement conference of state presidents that June in the Midwest. Here I was elected to the National Council of the MSM and met leaders of the council like Charles Rinker and elmira Kendricks from Drew University and Jill Foreman Hultin from Ohio, as well as the staff who worked with the council, Bill Corzine of the Methodist Board of Education and Ruth Harris from the Methodist Board of Missions Woman's Division of Christian Service.

The National MSM meeting was full of stimulating debate about the role of Christians in politics and the struggle for justice in the world. I will never forget the jolt I felt when a Chilean who spoke with great animation about the coming elections in his country added that as important as those elections were, voters in Chile knew that the presidential election in the United States would have more impact on their lives. This laid the groundwork for the MSM Council decision that summer to endorse a presidential candidate. We agonized over the dangers of a Barry Goldwater presidency and his threat to use nuclear weapons in Vietnam, while also seeing the limitations of Lyndon Johnson. We voted to endorse Johnson and to go "Part of the Way with LBJ." It was the first time the MSM Council had made an explicitly political endorsement, and our call to the churches to do likewise explained why we felt this was so urgent. Our move was met with considerable displeasure among many in the churches, and they let us know it.

There was great anticipation at the MSM conference about the Latin America study tour that elmira, Jill, Ruth, and others were going on that summer. I wished that I could be part of it. There was also discussion of the 1964 civil rights campaign called Mississippi Summer, and I agonized over my feelings that I should be going to Mississippi. But I was about to embark on a journey of my own to Japan. It was a trip I had been planning since my senior year in high school, when my family hosted an American Field Service student from Japan for the year. My family was going to Japan in the late summer of 1964 to visit him and meet his family. I had convinced my parents to let me go first for the whole summer and then meet them when they arrived.

I attended a YMCA work-study camp in Hokkaido on the theme "Our Responsibility in a Changing Asia." I was one of the few participating Westerners and one of only a handful of women. Half the participants were from Japan, and most of the others were from other parts of Asia. English was the common language, but the perspective was Asian. At first I was a bit confused. Gradually I learned the essential lesson that the world, its problems, and even how one discusses them can look quite different when viewed from another culture, country, or life circumstance. This dramatic paradigm shift, with the changes it brought in my perception of what gets called "reality," has undergirded my work ever since.

I returned from Japan with a greater interest in Asia, particularly in China, and with growing anxiety about U.S. involvement in Vietnam. I changed my major to history and began to shift my academic work more toward Asian studies. I wrote a paper for one class on the Chinese view of the Korean War that shocked many students, and I began to look for the few critical professors with an international perspective at Duke. In my last year, I pursued this interest further by working for two semesters on a senior history honors paper on the role of women in the Chinese Revolution. Although I did not really understand my topic as feminist, it foreshadowed where my life was moving.

Meanwhile, the MSM was becoming more involved in the issue of civil rights, which was now making the national news as violent backlash against the movement escalated. In December of 1964, Martin Luther King, Jr., was the keynote speaker at our MSM Quadrennial Student Conference. Fannie Lou Hamer from the Mississippi Freedom Democratic Party also spoke, and many sessions centered on how student Christians could be engaged in this struggle. When a national crisis arose a few months later in Selma, Alabama, over violence against demonstrators seeking the right of African Americans to vote, many of us were ready to respond. I also saw this as a chance to make up for not being at the 1963 March on Washington or in Mississippi for Freedom Summer.

When I got the phone call from someone else on the MSM National Council asking if I would come to Montgomery, I immediately said yes. I wanted to be there, but I knew that I had to convince my parents. Their initial reaction was negative. They were concerned for my safety; but finally my father broke down and said that although he did not want me to go, he knew that if he were a student, he would want to go. That was all I needed: to go with their understanding that I had to do this.

When I arrived in Montgomery to meet the other council members, we were to stay at the Holiday Inn. Some of the white members had been given rooms, but when the manager realized we were an interracial group, he balked. I will never forget how Peggy Billings, who was the secretary for race relations of the Woman's Division of the Methodist Church, picked up the phone and called the national headquarters of Holiday Inn. She told them that if they did not see to it that the Montgomery manager let us all stay there, she would make certain that nobody from Methodist Church headquarters ever stayed in a Holiday Inn again. I have no idea whether she could have carried out such a threat, but it was one of my most vivid lessons in using institutional power, and it worked. We were allowed to stay, although we were made so uncomfortable that it was a great relief to move into the welcoming homes of African American families a few days later.

Our task in Montgomery, to find housing for arriving marchers, was hard and occasionally frightening, and we were disappointed that we did not get to go to Selma or join the marchers on the road. Yet it was exhilarating to be part of that historic moment and to feel that we were playing a useful role. The sense of mission and interracial community we experienced in people's homes and at the church rallies, as well as in the march, fulfilled the vision of being together in the world that we had glimpsed at the Athens quadrennial in 1963. It could not last, but one can live for years doing this work on just a few moments like this.

Back at Duke, Sara Evans and I were in discussions with the campus YWCA over our decision that we would not compete against each other for the presidency of the Y the next year. We ran instead as a team to be co-presidents, which required only a yes or no vote. We won the vote, and our prefeminist assertion garnered us the "sisterhood of the year" award in the campus newspaper's sarcastic end-of-the-year review. Our position as co-presidents raised our profile as campus leaders at a time when we were both becoming increasingly alienated from mainstream Duke blazer life. One day, as we walked across the sedate and beautiful campus discussing whether to join the small picket line against the war in Vietnam at the Durham post office, one of the most conservative woman leaders crossed our path. We looked at each other and nodded, then took off on our bikes to the post office, where the more secular radical student group seemed surprised to see us.

Opposing the war in Vietnam was seen as a more radical move than supporting civil rights, especially in 1965, and whether to do so was very controversial within the civil rights movement. It involved making a political critique of foreign policy that was less idealistic and also engaged one directly in thorny debates over the left, communism, and cold war politics. I knew that my parents would not support me on this one. When some of us decided to go to Washington, D.C., in the spring of 1965 to participate in the first major national antiwar demonstration, I did *not* call home before I went. Later, when I told my parents I had gone, we had a difficult conversation that signaled my growing independence of them. Opposing the war seemed like the right thing to do as a Christian, but the march in D.C. was not the exhilarating community experience that the march from Selma to Montgomery had been.

The steps that were to determine the contours of my life in the student Christian movement in the next few years were taken in September of 1965 as the member groups of the National Student Christian Federation met to discuss how to create a new kind of organization in the United States. The World Student Christian Federation had long urged U.S. student groups to create a more ecumenical body. In most countries there was a student Christian movement that brought at least the Protestant groups together. Denominational student work, like that of the MSM, had a stronger tradition in the United States, and the NSCF only functioned as a confederation of such groups, with little latitude for direct action. In 1965 NSCF committed itself to a transformative process that was aimed at creating a truly ecumenical movement on campuses. David Robinson, a graduate student at Columbia University, was elected president of NSCF to guide this effort, and I was elected vice president. This increased my responsibilities at the national level, and I began traveling to New York almost once a month. I also had personal interests in spending time in New York as my future husband, Jim Weeks, had moved there from California to begin a year at Union Theological Seminary.

During my last year at Duke, I was already moving on into the world. I was serious about my academic work and managed to keep up good grades by working in the library over many holidays to make up for time lost going to meetings and marches. But when others started to apply for graduate school, I froze. The female professor I most respected, Anne Scott of the History Department, took me aside to warn me that my future career would be hampered unless I curtailed my political activities long enough to get my Ph.D. She assured me that there would be plenty of years ahead to be politically active. But it was 1966. I felt that history was being made now, and I was already too involved in the movement to step back. My experiences in the student Christian movement made me think that I could shape a life as a political activist. So I chose the movement as my career and never applied to graduate school.

The years I spent at Duke provided me enormous opportunities for growth and leadership development both on and off campus. As a woman, I had the best of both worlds. The women's college and the campus YWCA gave me a women-only space to learn about myself and develop leadership skills with other women, without the dominating presence of men who assumed that those roles were their prerogative. At the same time, I was also operating in a mixed-sex university setting. Most of my classes were co-ed, and the Methodist Student Center offered me a wider world in which to exercise my leadership. Although there was certainly plenty of sexism at Duke, and I felt it in some of my activities, I did not experience it in the MSM. Further, the unique moment at which I entered the MSM nationally was one when there were extraordinarily supportive adults present who encouraged our growth, including strong women like Ruth Harris and Peggy Billings, who clearly equaled the men as role models. Finally, I count myself fortunate that I had so many bright, strong women friends around like Sara, Jill, elmira, and my roommate Jan Poppendieck. Their presence enabled me to feel that as women, we could do whatever we thought it important to do with our lives.

I graduated from Duke on 6–6–66. One month later I was in Geneva at the World Council of Churches' World Conference on Church and Society, speaking on behalf of the youth delegates about the march we were going to lead

to UN headquarters to demonstrate our concern over the issues of war, racism, and poverty. The night before, the plenary session had voted down a proposal that the conference delegates hold such a public march. The student
delegates staying at the John Knox House sat up all night with a few radical
theologians like Harvey Cox, discussing what we could do. We then organized a march to be led by the students as a group of individuals attending
the conference, not on behalf of the conference, and invited all concerned
delegates to march with us. It was a moving moment as we took the power
we had to make our concerns heard and rallied considerable conference support to go out into the sedate streets of Geneva. I had been the NSCF student member of the organizing committee for the conference, so I knew who
our allies were there. But I had also noticed that, unlike the MSM, there were
few women speakers or delegates at this adult gathering. The photo I have of
the march shows only four or five women among the thirty-some pictured
demonstrators.

That summer I moved to Washington, D.C., to live in a communal house
with Jim Weeks, my fiancé whom I first met at the 1963 Athens conference;
Charles Rinker, who had finished his term as president of the MSM Council; Charles's wife, Lora; and the Wus, a couple they had known at Drew University. We wanted to create an intentional Christian community working in
the black ghetto and saw community organizing as a way to mobilize the poor
to take power over their lives and change society. Our fledgling project lasted
only a year, during which time we learned a lot, often painfully. Above all,
we came to understand that the role of whites was not to organize a black
community, especially at a time when black power was emerging around the
country, but rather to support their challenge to white power structures and
to educate our own community about racism.

In the spring of 1967 Jim and I got married in an alternative wedding
ceremony with vows that spoke not of obedience but of our decision to build
a life together around our commitment to social activism. Soon after, we left
for the Ecumenical Institute headquarters in Chicago for a summer training
program. Although we learned a lot about theology and strategic planning,
our tentative steps toward becoming part of their community ended as we
found their methodology rigid and too constraining. At the end of the summer, we moved into our own apartment in D.C., across the street from the
commune.

While I worked part of the time in the D.C. community project, my
primary commitment during 1966–67 was to build the University Christian
Movement (UCM), which had grown out of the ecumenical transformation

of the National Student Christian Federation and was founded at the NSCF conference in September 1966. I was elected its first president, Jill Hultin was one of several vice presidents, and Tami Hultman, another Duke student active in the YWCA, was elected secretary.

The birth of the UCM was a time of great hope. The UCM was our utopia. The vision behind it had been shaped by our experiences at events like the Athens quadrennial, as well as in secular settings like the Selma to Montgomery March. The Protestant student denominational groups who had worked to create it—the Methodist Student Movement was one of the most active—dreamed of a truly ecumenical Christian movement that would not only supersede our separate organizations, but also attract Catholic and Orthodox Christians, as well as be open to non-Christians who shared its mission. We called it the University, not the Student, Christian Movement because we believed that students, faculty, staff, and campus ministers could come together in a community of equals to address the issues facing universities. We imagined it as a movement, not an institution—a more flexible embodiment of the urgency of our times that could act more easily than its predecessor, the NSCF. We wanted to go beyond the previous history of churches sponsoring student work on campuses to an autonomous body that interacted in a creative and challenging way with the churches, yet was truly led by its members and not by church staff. We thought we could build this new vision out of the old student denominational structures, but the times we faced proved too challenging for such an ambitious dream.

In my year as president of the UCM, I traveled the country spreading the word of our vision to campus groups and to those in the church establishment. There was a sharp focus on ecumenism in the church world at that time, and we were generally received as pointing the way to the future. At some colleges, campus ministries had begun to work more closely together, even merging their staffs, creating what we hoped would be a local base for the UCM. What we did not yet realize was that some of this merging was also out of necessity, since church funds for student ministries were beginning to decline, especially as these ministries were identified with the rise in campus activism.

I also represented the UCM at many secular movement events, and this enabled me to get to know some of the leadership of organizations like Students for a Democratic Society as well as more mainstream adult groups like the Mobilization Committee to End the War in Vietnam. Because I was president of a national organization that often helped members of these other groups gain access to a constituency and/or support from the Protestant churches, I escaped much of the sexism in the left that other women experienced. Nevertheless, I sometimes felt patronized by leftist men. I was never quite sure if this was because I was a woman or a Christian. Overall, it was a busy and fulfilling year, during which I got drawn more and more into the secular new left, but I still felt safer entering there from the supportive space of the progressive Christian community.

In the summer of 1967 I passed the presidency of the UCM over to Steve Schomberg but continued to work as field staff for UCM on the national event we called "Process '67," which was to replace the old student volunteer quadrennial conferences held in Athens, Ohio. Process '67 was more than just a conference, as it centered around an experiment with Depth Education Groups, which were intended to bring together students, faculty, and others on campuses to engage in a dialogical style of education that would lead not only to understanding an issue better but also to more effective action for social change.

In the previous year the UCM had defined its "Organizing Principle" as "to work for social change through the reformulation of the university." Process '67 encouraged the formation of Depth Education Groups on campuses in the fall of 1967 and then brought thousands together over Christmas break for what was called "Cleveland Week." This quadrennial conference, moved symbolically out of the quieter college town of Athens to the urban hub of Cleveland, Ohio, centered on putting everyone, for at least two to three hours a day, in a Depth Education Group formed of diverse participants around a topic of common concern. Other aspects of Cleveland Week utilized television and other media forms, as well as featuring keynote speakers on social issues of the day. In short, it was a "happening" in late '60s style, but with an educational theory that the UCM hoped would also help build its constituency on campuses. The event was successful in many ways, but the more sensational media and hippie-style happening aspects of it overwhelmed the more serious effort at depth education.

For the 1967–68 academic year, I had arranged to do my work on Depth Education Groups in Washington, D.C., at the Institute for Policy Studies (IPS), a prestigious progressive think tank that the MSM had invited to help shape our annual conference in 1966. I held a student post under the tutelage of Arthur Waskow, one of the founders of IPS who was a leader in Jewish progressive thought, and Jim had a student position with another IPS fellow. I wrote an ambitious prospectus of vital questions about education and social change growing out of the Depth Education experiment that I wanted to explore. I did write a report for the UCM Annual Assembly in 1968, but my

other plans for studying this topic were cut short by my overwhelming discovery of sexism at IPS. My recognition of this sexism had, perhaps, as much
to do with my gradually evolving consciousness of myself as a woman in a
male-oriented adult world as it did with behavior unique to IPS. Nevertheless,
this was the place where I confronted sex discrimination in general and patron-
izing (and often worse) attitudes toward women within the left in particular.

At first, I thought that maybe I had gotten into an institution that was
too advanced for me, or that I simply did not know the language of the left
well enough. But gradually I realized that the men there simply did not listen to or take women very seriously—with the possible exception of Susan
Sontag and Hannah Arendt, who they often implied were the only women
on their level. All the classic things happened: I would be in a room with
mostly men and say something and nobody would respond, but then, some
time later, one of the guys would say virtually the same thing and they would
respond to him. I felt invisible. I did not have a lot of self-confidence in some
ways, but at the same time I was used to being taken seriously. After years
of being nurtured and supported in my leadership in the student Christian
movement and treated as a serious student at Duke, I was shocked and angry
at what I experienced. I probably became a feminist more quickly, precisely
because I was not used to such treatment. When Marilyn Salzman Webb, who
was associated with IPS primarily through her husband Lee Webb, suggested
that we form a women's group, I was ready.

We held our first D.C. radical women's meeting in January 1968, immediately after the Jeanette Rankin Women's Brigade for Peace, a national
antiwar march sponsored by Women's Strike for Peace, various church
women's groups, and others. I gave a speech on young women's views of imperialism at the rally, as a compromise speaker acceptable both to the church
women and to the more radical groups, who had argued over what youth
speaker to invite. The greatest stir there was caused by a New York group of
radical feminists who were not on the program but disrupted it with guer-
rilla theater, complete with coffins and talk about the connection between
maleness and warfare. Their actions upset some of the organizers but intrigued
me and many of the women there. Meanwhile, on the edges of the march,
women from the radical women's groups that had formed in New York and
Chicago a few months earlier were talking about what those groups meant
to them and the political discussions they were having. I knew about the Chicago group, because Sara Evans was part of it. These discussions at the Brigade encouraged us to go ahead with our group in D.C. and helped us see
ourselves as part of a national phenomenon.

FIGURE 1. elmira Kendricks Nazombe and other students at Methodist Student Movement Citizenship Seminar at the United Nations, New York, February 1962.

FIGURE 2. Methodist students participate in March on Washington for civil rights, August 1963.

FIGURE 3. Alice Hageman on assignment at UNESCO during her Frontier Internship, Paris, May 1964.

FIGURE 4. Jill Hultin introduces Martin Luther King, Jr., during the Methodist Student Movement National Conference in Lincoln, Nebraska, December 1964.

FIGURE 5. Ruth Harris among demonstrators at the Selma to Montgomery March, Montgomery, Alabama, March 1965.

FIGURE 6. Charlotte Bunch with youth delegation leading a demonstration at the World Council of Churches Conference on Church and Society, Geneva, Switzerland, summer 1966.

FIGURE 7. Tami Hultman, leading antiwar and pro-labor vigil at Duke University, Durham North Carolina, 1968.

FIGURE 8. YWCA students meet with Dorothy Height to promote the One Imperative–Elimination of Racism, USA, 1974.

FIGURE 9. Valerie Russell at the grave of Sojourner Truth in Battle Creek, Michigan, summer 1996.

After our first meeting, a group of about eight or ten women loosely connected with IPS specifically or the new left generally formed a radical women's group that met weekly. We spent months convincing ourselves that it was politically valid to meet separately and focus on women's issues. Ultimately the experience was so powerful that it justified itself. By summer, I had embraced the term "women's liberation" and began to change my political work in order to organize more women in what felt like a new direction for my life. When the UCM held its annual assembly in June of 1968, I delivered my report on the Depth Education Groups and helped create a women's caucus there, but my heart was beginning to move elsewhere.

Nevertheless, in many ways the student Christian movement was still my home base. In the summer of 1968, I attended the World Student Christian Federation General Assembly in Finland. This was a gathering held every four years of representatives of the student Christian movements (primarily Protestants) from around the world. I was active in the working group on student political action, which discussed the relationship between theological reflection and politics, the role of Christians in political life, and how to politicize nonactive Christian students. We also heard reports from WSCF study/action projects related to certain political issues, including a China study group that sought to bring the student Christian Movement into dialogue with the Chinese Revolution, a South African study group that was working for the divestment of church resources in South Africa, and a Middle East seminar that brought together Christian Arabs and Christians from North America and Europe to examine the role of university-based Christians in the region.

The work of the WSCF resonated with my political concerns and provided an opportunity to continue my internationalist interests. At the meeting in Finland, Richard Shaull, an ex-missionary from the United States who had been radicalized by his experiences in Brazil and who was also one of my political/theological mentors and allies, was elected to the presidency of the organization. I was elected to the Executive Committee as part of the more radical political faction at the assembly. Over the next four years, I attended annual Executive Committee meetings in Beirut, Geneva, Tokyo, and Addis Ababa. Each meeting included opportunities to learn about the region and to meet student Christian and other political leaders while there. It was an extraordinary international education. At the same time, the Executive Committee grew increasingly polarized between what was seen as the revolutionary political group, led by Richard Shaull, and the more conservative group focused on evangelism and maintenance of the organization, led by the WSCF general secretary from Finland, Risto Lehtonen.

After my return from Finland in the summer of 1968, I became immersed in the rapidly growing women's liberation movement and helped start more consciousness-raising groups in D.C. I went to Atlantic City for the first protest against the Miss America beauty pageant, where the myth of "bra burners" emerged from our throwing all that we found oppressive—including bras and many other things—into a "Freedom Trash Can." Out of the basement at IPS, several of us organized the first national women's liberation movement conference, held over a snowy Thanksgiving at a YMCA camp outside Chicago.

In the fall of 1969, I moved to Cleveland, Ohio, in order for my husband to go to graduate school and found myself for the first time being identified in terms of him, being called Mrs. James Weeks. When a party I had helped plan for the Movement for a Democratic Society was announced as being at the home of Jim Weeks, I became angry and began to hyphenate my name as Bunch-Weeks. While in Cleveland, I worked part-time at the Case Western Reserve campus ministry, having convinced them that they needed a woman on the staff for outreach to female students. I worked with Carol McEldowney and others to organize Cleveland Women's Liberation and began to write feminist articles to reach more women. Faced with considerable hostility toward feminism from the left in Cleveland, we began to reach out to women who had not previously been political and to develop a more autonomous feminist politics. While I found my time in Cleveland politically stimulating, I missed Washington and was happy to return in the summer of 1969 when IPS offered me a position as one of their first women "fellows."

Still connected to the student Christian community, I worked with the staff of *motive* magazine, a liberal student publication of the Methodist Church known for its avant-garde work, on a special issue devoted to the "woman question." At my urging, their lone woman editor, Joanne Cooke, had come to the national women's liberation conference in the fall of 1968. She then collaborated with me in making the issue one about the women's liberation movement itself. That edition of *motive*, published in March 1969, was one of the first women's liberation anthologies. All sixty thousand copies sold out in a few months. It created more controversy than any issue of *motive* in thirty years and contributed to the process of making the magazine independent of the church. It also furthered linkages between some women connected to the church and the women's movement. As Alice Austin, who had worked in the UCM office, wrote to me from Geneva:

Life has not been the same here since the women's liberation issue of *motive* finally reached me in June. I casually handed it to my roommate with the comment, "You might be interested in reading this," and she was instantly turned on. Sonja Hedlund arrived about that time for a visit and we three together have initiated the Women's Liberation Movement of Geneva. My roommate launched her first campaign when two Gentlemen friends passing through Geneva stayed at our apartment. They were reminded that they ought to help with the dishes after a WL discussion; towel and dishrag were placed in their reluctant hands.

In March of 1969, the UCM General Committee decided to disband the national structure of the UCM at a meeting held in Washington, D.C. It is still painful for me to talk about or even to fully remember what happened there, even though I was at the meeting and acquiesced in the decision. Since the annual assembly the previous June, I had stopped working as field staff for the UCM and was less directly involved in its daily operations. I was, however, still part of its life and an active member of the UCM Task Force on Ideology. The immediate catalyst for the break-up, best as I can recall, was a challenge from the black caucus that they should make up 50 percent of the governing body and/or control 50 percent of the resources of the UCM. The discussion that followed and the difficulty the group had in responding revealed the underlying tensions, ambiguities, and guilt that ran deep in the organization and went beyond the issue at hand.

In the midst of the debate, someone suggested that the organization should disband. I remember standing in the back of the room watching this unfold with a sinking feeling in my stomach that somebody needed to do something. I cannot remember if I spoke or even if I later voted, but I do remember thinking that I could not save this organization. I felt keenly that the old leadership had to let the new leaders lead, and the new president, Nell Sale, seemed relieved by this proposal. Further, I knew that my life was moving on somewhere else and that I could not lead the UCM now even if some people thought I should. I watched with sadness as our dream collapsed, and I carried a vague sense of guilt about this for years.

Today as I read the Working Paper on UCM Ideology that we had submitted in February of 1969, not long before the breakup, I see many clues to the deeper causes of the demise, as well as a reminder of the intensity and divisiveness of the late '60s era. We understood ourselves to be in a revolutionary moment, faced, as the paper states starkly, with an essential choice: "whether to commit ourselves to a reformist posture in relation to our society or whether because of our analysis to assume a revolutionary stance." The paper goes on to lay out a societal analysis of the power realities and oppressions of the time, including an analysis of the role of the university "within consumptive society." It ends with a vision of the new society and a call for UCM to alter its structures and priorities in order to be part of the revolutionary movement. It is the serious thinking of serious people. But I wonder now if we knew what it would actually mean to do this. Further, it is the kind of debate that was paralyzing, dividing, and/or destroying many organizations at the time.

The UCM earnestly wanted to be a Christian community that responded to the challenges of the secular world in a difficult time. But it simply did not have the time or the capacity to deal with all these secular conflicts, to overcome its own roots in a divided denominational history and develop a genuine local ecumenical base, and still survive, given its economic dependence on dwindling church support. Further, there were more divergent and urgent expectations placed on UCM than this rather small structure could possibly fulfill. Much more could and perhaps needs to be said about what happened to the UCM. But in a moment when there seemed to be no right way to move, it seemed better to let go than to go on pretending that it was what it could not be.

Political tensions similar to those that doomed the UCM also plagued the WSCF Executive Committee throughout my tenure on it. Considerable activity was, however, going forward on a regional basis, since we had decided that regions should set their own priorities. There was only one other woman on the Executive Committee, but as I became more involved with the feminist movement, I began to raise these issues and proposed the creation of a WSCF Women's Project. The idea was initially rejected and then approved, but only as a project of the North American region. In 1971 the WSCF hired Jan Griesinger to staff the project, and she tells her story in this book. I was happy to see another feminist carry on working within this structure as I was moving out of it.

In the early years of the 1970s, I was completely consumed by my involvement with feminism. During this time, I began to explore my sexuality and came out as a lesbian in early 1971. As a previous member of the editorial board of *motive*, I was involved in producing the final two issues of the magazine, on the lesbian and gay movement. As we wrote in the editorial to the lesbian issue: "In the aftermath of the controversy over the women's issue, the church began to reduce its support of *motive* and *motive* decided it could no longer function under the church. *motive* could not survive without church money so the staff and editorial board decided to close up shop, using the remaining resources of the magazine to put out one final gay issue." The gay issue was split into two parts: a gay male issue edited by a previous *motive* editor who had come out and a lesbian issue, which I helped edit with The Furies, a lesbian collective of which I was part in 1971–72.

It was fitting that the final products of *motive* were focused on gay and lesbian issues, both because *motive* had a tradition of being avant garde and because a number of previous staff members have come out over the years since it ended. It was also fitting for me that this was the end of my institutional relationship with the Methodist Church, because it was coming out as a lesbian that finally sent me out of the church. As a part of the new left and as a feminist, I had become increasingly secular in my orientation, but it was still possible to feel part of the wider Christian community and, indeed, to engage with it on political issues. The more feminist I became, however, the more impatient I was with the phallocentricity of Christianity and with the slowness of the institution to see how it oppressed women. When I came out as a lesbian in the context of the feminist movement, I was simply not willing to be affiliated with an institution that labeled me a sinner or denied me the right to enter its highest callings.

The church and especially the student Christian movement played an important role in training me to lead, giving me a global perspective, and teaching me how to live with values and purpose in the world. But as I took that mission seriously and found my calling, as well as my sexual identity, outside its prescribed boundaries, it no longer supported me or provided a context for my life. Yet I feel that my work today on feminism and human rights is still part of the struggle I began in the '60s to find a values-based politics that can give hope and vision for a better life for all—in community and with respect for our incredible human diversity.

CHAPTER 7

Tamela Hultman

Six months after the United States Supreme Court ruled against school segregation in *Brown v. Board of Education,* my father got a chance to say what was on his mind. At the age of twenty-nine, in the pulpit of the Seagrove Christian Church where my mother grew up, he took a radical step that altered the trajectory of our family's life. Seagrove is dead center in the state of North Carolina, a small town settled in the mid-eighteenth century by English potters attracted by its malleable clay soil and fertile farmland.

On that November morning in 1954, Robert Hultman, a sawmill worker, short-order cook, restaurateur, and Sunday school superintendent filling in for an absent pastor, preached a sermon about race and Christian values. Among the things he said was this: I don't mind what color man my daughter marries. If she comes to me and says she wants to marry a Negro, my question to her will be, "Tami, is he a good Christian?" Seven years old, sitting in the pew beside my mother and trying as usual not to fidget, I had no idea that we, along with the nation, had entered an era that would change us all. And I surely had no sense of the personal cost to my mother of the impending rupture of community ties.

It would be some time before we entered the familiar sanctuary for worship again. But my mother's calm, matter-of-factness as we left the church must have masked for me the drama of the moment, because what I recall is a pleasant feeling of shyness at being singled out in the sermon.

It didn't occur to me until recently, when an interviewer asked whether my father's first sermon had been prompted by the *Brown* decision, to wonder if it had been. Yes, he said as I then questioned him, it was. A few days later he produced a fragile, yellowed piece of paper. A handwritten note, signed by five deacons, demanded his resignation as Sunday school superintendent. The names are ones I recognized from later years of church homecomings and dinners on the church grounds—because we all go back for visits when we can—as kindly "uncles," free with hugs and well-wishes. On his deathbed, one of them told my father that the vote to dismiss him was the worst thing he himself had ever done. The wife of another told my mother that the action was the worst in the church's long history.

So I was lucky. At a formative age, I experienced the church as a source of possibility as well as pain, of reconciliation as well as rejection. And I was lucky in my extended family as in my nuclear one. My grandparent and aunts and uncles never wavered in their love and support. My mother tells me that shortly afterward, my grandfather came to her in excitement after poring through the Bible and its commentaries and finding scriptural endorsement for my father's views. It seems that Moses took a black wife, he told her. God was clearly on the side of interracial marriage!

Perhaps I have only conjured up the apt memory that the recessional hymn on the day of my father's race sermon was one of my favorites, a rollicking gospel song about reaping what one sows—in the sense opposite to the common use of that phrase.

Sowing in the morning,
Sowing seeds of kindness,
Sowing in the noontide and the dewy eve.
Waiting for the harvest and the time of reaping.
We shall come rejoicing,
Bringing in the sheaves.

Almost exactly twenty-seven years later, at the anniversary of an inner-city Philadelphia church he had earlier pastored for seventeen years while it made the transition from majority white to majority black and became a force for renewal in the community, my father paid tribute to my mother's courage. "Nobody," he said, in a voice hoarse with tears, "has sacrificed more for this ministry than Jean Hultman."

In a packed sanctuary, with a grandson looking on, my father ended his sermon with the kind of call to action we've all come to expect from him. Quoting Air Force sergeant and Vietnam veteran Leonard Matlovich—"They gave me a medal for killing two men, and a discharge for loving one"—he said it was time for the churches to catch up with the times and accept gay Christians as full members of the fellowship of faith. He also cautioned, an hour before we learned that the U.S. bombing campaign in Afghanistan had begun, that war is an evil the Church must resist.

"I was warned," said the minister presiding over the anniversary, "that you are a man who always says what you believe!" But his invitation to my father to come preach again, and the outpouring of congregational love, was new evidence of an oft-learned lesson. Faithful, careful work that honors the good in all people, that encourages them to believe in their own possibilities, that inspires them to dream of a world made new—and challenges them to create it—is the most potent change-agent we possess.

The power to imagine a new thing, supplemented by the songs and examples that show the way forward, was an instrument I would see used again and again. It was a tool that was equally empowering in the patient work of neighborhood organizing in North Carolina, in the antiwar demonstrations on U.S. university campuses, in the civil rights sit-ins and marches, in the cultivated resistance of South African townships, and in the contagion of West African democracy movements. The stories that women tell each other have been an integral part of those struggles. The worldwide church as both foundation and impetus for those struggles is a story that is only beginning to be told.

*M*y parent's search for a new church home was an adventure to me, an introduction to differing denominations and worship styles. More than one Sunday school teacher in the small town of Asheboro—a metropolis compared to rural Seagrove—must have been bemused when I explained that we were changing churches because my father had said I could marry a Negro. When we settled in the Congregational Christian Church, which, like the Seagrove church, would become part of the United Church of Christ, the range of activities was invigorating: participating in live Nativity scenes on the lawn, watching my father act in religious dramas (particularly memorable was the shepherd he played in his blue chenille bathrobe), and going bowling with the youth group—an activity my parents liked to chaperone because of the memories it kindled.

My father wasn't always a pacifist. When he met my mother in the Asheboro bowling alley, he was a dashing, eighteen-year-old paratrooper, a product of Swedish and Dutch immigrants to western Pennsylvania, and my mother was a fetching fifteen-year-old southern girl, there with her older sister. Before the evening ended, my father told her he intended to marry her and she promised to wait. Two years and a Purple Heart later, they fulfilled their pledge. It was a couple of decades before I knew about the Purple Heart, when I found it in a dresser drawer and probed for the story of my father's jumps into Germany behind enemy lines. By then he was a longtime peace campaigner, one of the first voices I heard raised against the war in Vietnam.

The source of my family's instincts remains a mystery. My father had few encounters with people of other races, growing up in a town where ethnic prejudice meant epithets about dirty Italians or dumb Swedes. My mother can't explain why her storekeeper parents never appeared to treat black or white customers differently. She doesn't know why she experienced such visceral anger, as a small child, when she heard a bus driver crudely order black riders to the back, but she remembers glaring with all her might when the driver tried to help her and her mother disembark. "He must have wondered for a long time," she laughs, "why a little girl would be so hostile to him." Whatever its origin, the familial tendency to tolerance was both a great gift and a powerful example.

Similarly exemplary was the presence of strong women on both sides of the family. My maternal grandfather owned two stores, but lost both because he was too soft-hearted to demand payment from hard-up customers. So my grandmother, Nettie Bean Lucas, became the entrepreneur, opening and selling a grocery store and a furniture store before acquiring the feed, food, and drygoods store, on Seagrove's two-block main street, where I spent many hours as a child and young adult. There my gentle grandfather worked for her, when he wasn't helping take care of six children, keeping the fires going in the woodstoves, or, later, trundling his giggling granddaughter, perched on a feedsack, up and down the aisles on a trolley. In impoverished Randolph County, they were better off than many, but they never owned much besides the store, which required constant labor, and the house they built, with two tiny bedrooms for eight people. And though they valued learning, only one child, a son, made it to college and became a teacher.

My paternal grandmother raised eight children alone after her husband died when my father was twelve. There wasn't much work for anyone in an Allegheny town where the coal had never been worth much, the major jobs were in the broom-handle and wooden toy factories, and the Depression hit hard, especially if you lived on the immigrant's side of the river. Eva Beesucker Hultman was a small woman, but she did large work, supporting the family by cleaning houses, taking in washing, and growing or picking what food she and the children could manage, gaining spiritual sustenance each week at the Episcopal church. When I was grown, she still worked as a maid at the local motel. My father's older siblings were able to get jobs through various New Deal schemes, and my grandmother believed fervently that Franklin Delano Roosevelt had saved her family as well as the world. She never let a remark against the Democratic Party go unchallenged.

My father was the only one of his siblings to attend college, a feat made possible by the GI bill, a motivating call to the ministry, and a willingness to work the night shift at Burlington textile mills while taking a full course load and pastoring three rural churches on weekends. My mother, an avid reader, supplemented the meager income by cataloguing books at the Elon College library during my school hours. She thought it her duty and her calling to take care of me, but she also told me constantly that I could do and be anything I wanted.

I took her seriously, imagining myself in faraway places, saving the world. While my father earned two degrees and moved to full-time ministry, I plotted how to skip a year of school and get on with the business of finding my place in the world. I had a strong urge to explore far-off places. Three things nourished that ambition: the books I read about fictional and real-life heroines, the missionaries who regularly visited our churches, telling stories about their work, and the visits to my Pennsylvania family. In those years, my Episcopal and Catholic cousins, with their incense and their rosaries and their catechisms, seemed as exotic as any foreigners, and their accents and manners were sources of endless wonder to a small-town southern girl and nurtured an enduring curiosity about other peoples and places.

The year after my father graduated from Duke Divinity School, I entered the university as a freshman, on a scholarship that included a component tied to a church vocation after graduation. For the first time ever, I was outside the close-knit circle of family, and I was ready for new things.

*W*hen I arrived in Durham in the fall of 1964, there were already groups of church-based students debating issues of race, class, and gender in the context of their beliefs, although they were dispersed in denominational outposts. At the United Campus Christian Fellowship (UCCF), the student organization affiliated with the United Church of Christ, John Kernodle, son of a prominent North Carolina physician who headed the American Medical Association, pushed us to think systemically and internationally, analyzing the power structures that perpetuated inequities. Spurring similar studies at the Methodist Student Movement were future feminist leader Charlotte Bunch, Jan Poppendieck, who married John Kernodle and went on to do groundbreaking research on hunger policies that became a nationally acclaimed book, and Dennis Campbell, who would become president of the National MSM and later still the dean of Duke's Divinity School. Presbyterians and Catholics and Jewish students had their own groups.

It was at the YM and YWCAs that we all came together. Every Duke student, religious or not, was involved with the Ys. Student activities fees funded them, and they ran first-year orientations on the then-separate men's and women's campuses. "Y Groups" of eight people gave Duke students their initial college identities and, in many cases, continued as cohesive units throughout the year. The upperclass advisors who led them served as role models and mentors for a generation of first-year students.

If we sought further involvement with social issues, we could interview for committees on the Freshman YWCA that planned programs and helped the "big" Y develop and staff community services. Interest was such that participation was competitive, and I didn't make the cut. Probably the interviewers deemed me insufficiently sophisticated, assuming as I did then that righting wrongs was a fairly straightforward matter of calling attention to them. Despite the assassinations the year before of the Mississippi civil rights organizer Medgar Evers and President John Kennedy, and the Birmingham church bombings that killed four young girls, the world still seemed a fundamentally good place where bad things sometimes happened.

If I was at least aware of racial discrimination, I was oblivious to gender issues and to the growing undercurrent of war in Southeast Asia. Somewhere Betty Friedan's book, *The Feminine Mystique,* and Gloria Steinem's exposé of life as a Playboy Bunny were being debated, and on other campuses the two-year-old Students for a Democratic Society was ramping up an antiwar campaign, but I was preoccupied by the social life at a university where men outnumbered women two to one.

Sophomore year changed all that. Noticing that Duke's handful of black students had been placed either together or in single rooms, I proposed to my dorm mate, Bertie Howard, that we room together. Attracted by her beauty and her lively personality, I wanted to get to know her better, but I had no idea how formative our relationship would be for me. The daughter of educators from Orangeburg, South Carolina, she made the passage from a segregated world to Duke with a rare grace. More than thirty years of friendship later, I realize, with a clarity that eluded me at the time, how extraordinarily privileged I was that she took the risk of rooming with me. She was a window on a world whose existence I only hazily comprehended, and she taught me depths of generosity and forgiveness that I didn't find again until I met South Africans like Steve Biko and Archbishop Desmond Tutu.

At the same time, Andy Moursund took me on as a project. The son of activists of the 1920s who had worked with the crusading independent journalist I. F. Stone, Andy both irritated and fascinated me, ridiculing my naive idealism, deploring my lack of feminist consciousness, and generally disparaging my view of America as a benign superpower, making the world safe for democracy. Meeting in a music course, we discovered something in common. My father had recently accepted a position in Cambridge, on Maryland's Eastern Shore, and Andy had spent time there with civil rights organizers and had many friends in the town. Though he found me impossibly uninformed, for some reason he believed I was redeemable, and after classes he introduced me to masterworks, while tutoring me in geopolitics. In the music listening room, to the backdrop of bombastic pieces like the "1812 Overture," he would read aloud articles from *Liberation* magazine, founded by the pacifist David Dellinger. He plied me with history and statistics, and I didn't know enough to argue with him, so I did my own research and gradually confronted the shallowness of my perceptions. On Sundays, he would take me with him to black churches, where everybody knew him and also welcomed me. I learned the hymns that were becoming anthems of the struggle. "Paul and Silas were bound in jail," we sang. "Keep your eyes on the prize, hold on!" "Ain't gonna let nobody turn me around." "Before I'll be a slave, I'll be buried in my grave, and go home to my Lord and be free."

My emerging awareness was bolstered by engagement with activities sponsored by the YWCA, headed that year by Sara "Peachie" Evans, whom I had met through Andy, and Charlotte Bunch. Sara and Charlotte had pioneered an unusual co-presidency, a model of work sharing that prefigured the attempts many women would make in the coming years to share jobs and thus slot them into busy lives. The group had a long history of social activism and racial justice advocacy, including participation in the first North Carolina meeting of the NAACP in 1934. Y women, in particular, had for decades worked with Durham's Edgemont Community Center as well as with a children's refuge. By the mid-1960s, the Ys were the epitome of thinking globally and acting locally: sponsoring major symposia on world issues, coordinating work with the Legal Aid Clinic at Duke Law School, and getting involved with a nascent effort at community organizing in low-income areas.

The culture of poverty that chained whole neighborhoods, black and white alike, was a reality I was slow to understand. I had lived with scarcity all my life, without ever feeling deprived, and I failed to recognize the economic and political systems that perpetuated privilege for some while leaving others trapped in a cycle of deprivation. I hadn't seen the link between low wages in the mills where my family worked and the lack of unions. I experienced no constraints on my aspirations, and so saw little virtue in the growing women's movement. And I believed that my friends and I were, as President Kennedy had said in a speech I revered, "a new generation of Americans," ready to bear any burden to spread peace and justice throughout the world.

Feminists have talked about revelatory moments, when something happens that clarifies power relationships and discriminatory policies, and they describe the instant of perception with the word, "Click!" I recall only one such moment, but it was powerful enough to come to seem like a "before and after"—a rounding of a corner from which there was no retreat. The incident was spawned by the Speaker Ban Law passed by the North Carolina legislature in the summer of 1963, limiting who could speak at state-supported institutions and intended primarily to exclude communists from campuses. In April 1966 Andy Moursund insisted that I go with him to Chapel Hill, where a First Amendment campaigner named Frank Wilkinson was about to creatively defy the law.

While several hundred students and onlookers gathered at the edge of the University of North Carolina campus on a glorious spring day, Wilkinson stood just beyond a low stone wall on the sidewalk of picturesque Franklin Street and quietly told his story. The son of devout Methodists, he had planned to become a minister until a visit to Bethlehem, where he saw a level of poverty he hadn't known existed, and he spent several months traveling in Europe and the Mideast, living among refugees and displaced people. Returning home to California, he worked with the Los Angeles archdiocese of the Catholic Church on poverty issues and became a public housing administrator. When he protested the housing authority's policy of racial segregation, he caught the attention of the FBI. When he refused summonses to testify about his political affiliations before both the California and the U.S. House Un-American Activities Committees (HUAC), he inadvertently became a poster child for anti-McCarthyism. He had belonged to no political organization, he said, but the Constitution was worthy of defense, and he found himself in a position to defend it. After his First Amendment test case lost by a vote of 5–4 in the U.S. Supreme Court in 1961, he served a year in prison. Now he had returned to the struggle, calling for the abolishment of HUAC. And he was filing a case against the Speaker Ban Law as a violation of free speech.

We couldn't know it then, but his suit would overturn the North Carolina law, HUAC would be abolished in 1975, and in 1987 the FBI would admit to withholding exculpatory evidence at his trial. The agency also released his 132,000-page FBI surveillance file, the largest on record. What I knew at the time was that this was a man whose life exemplified the spirit of Kennedy's inaugural address, a man who had borne a burden, paid a price, and opposed foes to ensure the survival and success of liberty. His was a life inspired by faith, informed by world affairs, and lived according to principle. It was the kind of life to which I aspired, and my state and my nation believed him their enemy.

Back at Duke, Andy and I encountered a friend of mine from the UCCF, a sweet young man, committed to social causes, who asked where we'd been. To hear Frank Wilkinson speak, I said. "Oh, that communist?" he asked, surprised. Suddenly, the injustice of that perception overwhelmed me and I burst into tears. Andy patted my back awkwardly as I cried bitterly on his shoulder, while my friend looked on in astonished dismay. "You're all right," Andy kept murmuring. "You're really all right now." And both he and I knew that he was speaking about more than that moment.

Through the National Student Christian Federation, which was affiliated with the Geneva-based World Student Christian Federation, Duke's campus denominational groups were involved in ecumenical programs at the national and international level. One of those programs was an annual study/travel seminar administered from the office of Margaret Flory, Student World Relations staff for the Presbyterian Church. Encouraged by John Kernodle, I applied for the summer 1966 seminar. The chance to travel abroad was what drew me; the study topic of Africa was incidental to my interest. Acceptance to the program provided my first experience with fund-raising—a skill that would prove crucial in the decades ahead. Without family resources, I had to write proposals and peddle them to various offices and agencies to cover the costs of the trip.

Designed to open the world to young Americans, the seminars were products of Margaret Flory's faith, born of her own experience as a church worker in Asia, that international experiences change lives. Thanks to her insistence that those experiences be as local and personal as possible, our group of a dozen people stayed in homes, college dorms, and community centers. Although we visited thirteen countries, that rootedness ensured an intensity of engagement that belied the trip's ambitious pace. Welcoming committees, usually led by Margaret's friends—who seemed to be everywhere—had prepared superbly organized programs. That our group was interracial, including a Georgia student whose mentor was that state's charismatic SNCC leader Charles Sherrod, and that we were led by a black university chaplain, Yale's Sam Slie, provided internal as well as external learning experiences.

There could have been no better time to gain an appreciation of the problems of development and of the global currents tugging Africa. Orientation stops in London and Amsterdam introduced us to international student Christian movement colleagues and to South African exiles who taught us freedom songs. Arriving in Ghana a few weeks after the overthrow of Kwame Nkrumah, we got a quick course in anti-imperialist movements and their limits. In Africa's most populous country, Nigeria, home to world-class universities and a sense of boundless energy, the first of a succession of military governments had been installed five months before our arrival. Weeks later, a second coup set the stage for the Biafran war that claimed a million civilian lives. In Congo, where General Joseph-Désiré Mobutu had seized power the previous November, fellow students introduced us to the risks of opposing a dictatorship backed by cold war "containment" strategies. The same month as Mobutu's military coup, Rhodesia's white regime, led by Ian Smith, had made its Unilateral Declaration of Independence from Britain and was busily consolidating power. In South Africa we were hosted by the Christian Institute, founded in 1962 by the breakaway Dutch Reformed Church pastor Beyers Naude, who quietly organized interracial meetings for us. Nelson Mandela had been on Robben Island for two years, and what was left of the African, Indian, and Coloured political movements was underground and on the run. Freedom hymns had become songs of the night.

Exhausted from the intensity, and needing a respite before facing the countries of East and North Africa, three of our group made a detour from Dar Es Salaam, Tanzania, to spend a day hiking. I still have a Brownie Instamatic photo of a small boy, about ten, encountered in a village on the lower slopes of Mount Kilimanjaro, who queried us incessantly about civilian casualties in the war in Vietnam, U.S. support for apartheid, and whether the CIA had been involved in the assassination of Kennedy and the overthrow of Nkrumah. It was the most striking example of a reality we first met among British and Dutch students and found over and over that summer—that people around the world did not see us Americans as we liked to see ourselves.

*I*nspired and energized, I returned from the seminar in time to attend the launch of the University Christian Movement in September 1966, which replaced the NSCF with a more inclusively ecumenical body and one more self-consciously committed to melding theological principles with political action. The conference was an exhilarating gathering, beginning what was for me a two-year process that I think of as becoming an active part of the historic class of 1968. Multiracial and international, the gathering was a rich mélange of cultures and religious practices. We learned songs in several languages. Catholic priests served communion to all who wished to partake. We debated and cried and laughed. We saw ourselves as breaking barriers, and we imagined that our collective strength could overcome any resistance.

To my surprise, I was recruited to be among the first group of officers, as UCM secretary. Margaret Flory delivered the message. "Oh, Margaret," I exclaimed, excited by the prospect. "I almost didn't come to the meeting. Isn't it strange that at the last moment I found a way to get here?" "Oh, no!" Margaret admonished, breaking into her infectious, trademark laugh. "Not strange at all. Not if you believe in divine providence!" Not being Presbyterian, I wasn't sure if I understood Providence in quite the way that Margaret did, but one thing I soon learned. Providence or not, the challenge was one to which I had difficulty rising. There were many impressive students, faculty, campus ministers, and church executives involved with the UCM, and our administrative sessions spawned serious discussions of a range of issues I was only beginning to grasp. I had always thought I had something to contribute to any group of which I was a part. Now, although I had a title connoting national leadership, I found I had little to say.

Among the many articulate people at executive meetings, the most formidable were Charlotte Bunch, UCM's president, and Jill Hultin, another MSM leader who was a UCM vice president. That two women could not only hold their own but could dominate a group that included many older, more experienced men was a revelation. The fact that it *was* a revelation prompted me to begin to rethink my assumptions about the lack of constraints on women's achievements. *The Feminine Mystique* hadn't addressed the realities of my working-class upbringing. These peers, who were as engaged as I wanted to be in the critical issues of our time, were more persuasive illustrations of the roles women should be playing. The fact that I experienced it as extraordinary revealed the flaws in my analysis. About feminism, and about everything else, I still had a lot to learn.

The Duke YWCA offered a way to continue reflection as well as action. A new Y advisor, Nancy Richardson, only a few years older than the students and a southern woman herself, offered the perfect foil for our quest for deeper understanding. She wore the mantle of administrative authority lightly—she was still searching for her own answers—and she supported our increasing militancy, even while she quietly worried about the consequences. As I became more involved, she encouraged me to take more responsibility, and I was eventually tapped to become the Y president for the following academic year.

The summer of 1967 proved to be another chance to acquire needed insights. Based at my parent's parsonage in Cambridge, I worked for the National Council of Churches' migrant ministry, visiting the camps of crop pickers on the Eastern Shore. My job was to assess needs for social services and assist families in obtaining them, but living conditions were so abominable that church agencies could offer only a palliative, and local government structures were unwilling to trespass on private property or to confront growers. Edward R. Murrow may have exposed the country's "Harvest of Shame" on television in 1960, but like most Americans, I had paid little attention. Suddenly the boycott of grapes picked by nonunion labor, launched by California farmworkers in 1965, made sense.

My co-worker on the project was a black minister, whose parishioners in nearby Easton fed me and comforted me and gave me courage during a tumultuous summer. The Eastern Shore, which one resident described as more like Mississippi than like the rest of Maryland, was tense with civil rights demonstrations led by Gloria Richardson, a SNCC worker from Cambridge. The town's main street, appropriately named Race Street, divided black neighborhoods from white ones more completely than anything I had seen, and relations across the line were hostile and growing worse. On July 24, SNCC leader H. Rap Brown came to town and made a speech that made headlines with its call to violent action. That night there was a shootout between demonstrators and police and much of the black section of town was destroyed by fire, eclipsing Gloria Richardson's years of organizing. For the rest of the summer National Guard troops occupied the town, and in the fall my father was once again fired for his views on race.

By that time I was back on campus, where teach-ins and symposia and antiwar demonstrations crowded out almost everything else. Sometime that year Nancy Richardson arranged a "meeting" between me and a YMCA leader who was my age but a class behind me. Only some while afterward did she confess she had been matchmaking. More than thirty years later it is obvious that her instincts were correct. Reed Kramer, from Tennessee, became a collaborator and a soul mate, and his support has never wavered. In the spring of 1968 he campaigned for and won the YMCA presidency, in a hotly contested campuswide vote, giving us our first experience at formally working together, which has endured for three decades.

On April 4, 1968, Martin Luther King, Jr., was assassinated. Through the long night that followed, as more than one hundred U.S. cities erupted, Y officers joined other students to develop a response. The result was a march to President Douglas Knight's house by nearly five hundred of us. Invited in, we stayed two days, then marched to seat ourselves on the main Duke quadrangle, in front of the imposing Gothic chapel, where the numbers swelled to two thousand, nearly half the undergraduate student body at the time. For two weeks we stayed on the quad day and night, visited by singers like Pete Seeger and Joan Baez, the draft resistance activist David Harris, and local black leaders. On Easter morning, the dean of the chapel, James McCleland, who had given me the last chunk of funding I'd needed to go to Africa, threw open the doors and served us communion where we sat. Divinity School faculty and their wives—and it was wives, women faculty being rarities on campus—formed the core of a kitchen brigade that made and distributed food, but other faculty participated as well, and some paid dearly when they were denied tenure or were otherwise made unwelcome in their departments. Among our most stalwart supporters were campus ministers like Helen Crotwell, whose apartment in the Methodist Student Center had always been a place of nurture and refuge, while she herself was a role model, especially for women students.

What came to be known as the Vigil wasn't the first Duke sit-in. Thirty-five members of the Black Student Association had held a study-in at the administration building five months earlier to press officials to ban university use of segregated facilities, but the Duke Vigil was one of the earliest of the mass student protests that circled the globe in the following weeks. During May and June, hundreds of thousands of students clashed with police at schools from Milan to Miami, from Santiago to Vancouver, from Dakar to Auckland, from Ankara to Bangkok to Tokyo.

Those with the most conflict, like Berkeley and Columbia, received copious media coverage. I was one of a committee charged with organizing press coverage of the Vigil, but only locals were interested. One who did take notice was Jesse Helms, then a commentator for a Raleigh, North Carolina, television station, who called us "clutter on the lawn." We tried hard to persuade national media that a major university at a standstill, with two thousand mostly white, privileged students sitting outside day and night, despite rainy spring weather, in the shadow of one of the country's most imposing cathedrals, was a pretty good story. I think my first impulses toward a career in journalism stem from my frustration with responses like that of the CBS television producer who told me to phone back if there was any violence. Even when the head of General Motors, who chaired Duke's board of trustees, was maneuvered into crossing his arms and holding hands while singing "We Shall Overcome" under an umbrella, it was a nonstory.

But the Vigil changed things. Duke's nonacademic employees' union was recognized, workers' salaries were raised from $1.15 or less per hour to the federal minimum of $1.60, and Duke officials did withdraw from the seg-

segated country club. More than three-quarters of the Vigil participants had
never taken part in a demonstration before, and countless subsequent research
papers and retrospective articles have documented that lives were altered, often
in profound ways. For many of us, including Duke's first black professor,
Samuel DuBois Cook, the Vigil was a continuation of the intermingling of
the spiritual and the political. Thirty years later he called the event "sacred"
—"one of those supreme and unforgettable mountaintop experiences in which
the "Word was made flesh."

Staying with Reed until he graduated offered the chance to become more
involved in Durham. The Ys had been supportive of an effort that took seriously the challenge from SNCC and other black groups for whites to organize in their own communities. Led by former Duke student Harry Boyte,
who had been active in organizing support for the university's nonacademic
employees, whose father had been an aide to Dr. King, and who married Sara
Evans, the group called ACT encouraged residents of poor Durham neighborhoods to form associations that could press for reforms. The ultimate goal
was collective action by poor people across the color line, and in some scattered but important ways that eventually happened.

For me, the year was a gift. Although many Duke graduates found it
difficult to sustain the euphoria and community spirit of the days of protest,
I found myself in a real world that demanded my best efforts and provided
community of another kind. Edgemont folks were my childhood familiars:
mill hands, churchgoers, sawmill workers, whose cadences were as easy on
my ears as a lullaby. It was encouraging to see the long days of conversation
and meetings begin, slowly, to yield small victories, like a stop sign at a dangerous crossing. When Reed graduated and we were accepted into a program
that would take us abroad, I felt guilty to be leaving a project that clearly
needed a long-term commitment.

The Frontier Internship in Mission was another project run by Margaret Flory's office on behalf of the Presbyterians, the Methodists, and the
United Church of Christ. Every year the program sent a couple of dozen
young Americans on international assignments for two years, and it was often thought of as a church Peace Corps. But unlike Peace Corps volunteers,
Frontier Interns were seen less as providing assistance, though that was a component of the project, than as potential leaven in the loaf of American society. Radical Vietnam veterans had begun a campaign to "bring the war back
home." As Frontier Interns, our mission was to bring the world back home.

Our orientation took place in Stony Point, New York, coinciding with the music festival in nearby Woodstock. Although bemused by the evolving iconic status of the festival, we were too caught up in our own stories to wish we were there. Fresh from campuses around the country, most of us were eager to continue the search for effective strategies to address the issues of poverty, war, and racial and gender equity that had preoccupied us. A succession of international visitors joined our discussions, sharing their expertise and prodding us to deeper thinking. We interns, too, offered our experiences to each other through both structured and informal programs. My clearest memory is the awe I felt when elmira Kendricks Nazombe—another of those formidably articulate women from the Methodist Student Movement and an urban planner—conducted a group exercise that neatly tied together all the complex, interlayered concerns with which I had struggled as a community organizer. Like Reed and me, elmira and her husband, Jim Thacker, were headed for Africa, and two years later when Reed and I were expelled from South Africa, it was at Jim and elmira's Nairobi home, in the middle of a Kenyan housing project, that we found sanctuary.

We had been assigned to the South African Methodist Church, where we ran multiracial youth courses in a daring program conceived by Alex Boraine, who later became Archbishop Tutu's deputy at South Africa's Truth and Reconciliation Commission. During the intervals between courses, we traveled the country, quietly investigating U.S. corporate and government ties to the white regime on behalf of U.S. churches. But when the World Council of Churches made grants to the African National Congress and other outlawed political organizations, South African authorities retaliated by kicking out foreign church workers, including us. So it was our "cover," rather than our clandestine research, that ended the project. Nevertheless, we had collected enough data, partly through interviews with the local heads of over two dozen of the largest U.S. companies, to publish the first comprehensive survey of the American role in sustaining apartheid. The book compiling that information, issued by a U.S. church publisher, Friendship Press, became a basis for the church shareholder resolutions that began the divestment campaigns of the 1970s and 1980s.

So we *had* managed to bring the world back home, and for that we were grateful. But we did more. We got to know South Africans and their struggles more intimately than we could have imagined, and our lives would be vastly different. In our first week we met Steve Biko and Vuye Mahshalaba, both medical students and leaders of the newly formed South African Students' Organization (SASO). Although relatively few people today know that a woman was one of SASO's founders and original executive officers, Vuye played an important role for the rest of her life, living and practicing medicine in a township, before dying suddenly of a heart condition. Attending her funeral twenty-five years later, Reed and I were reunited with dozens of friends from our Frontier Intern years, including the head of the South African UCM, now a judge heading the court that adjudicates politically sensitive land issues.

For the remainder of our internship, Reed and I worked and played and sang with the remarkable SASO leaders—part of our own student generation—who exhibited no fear at all in a situation carefully constructed to quell the strongest spirits. Because we had access to transportation, we were often pressed into service, driving people to meetings and conferences—and so we were privileged to watch as the confident air of defiance spread from person to person to person.

When we were expelled, we headed to Kenya, after a stop in Zambia where we traded research on U.S. investment in South Africa with a young, exiled economist, Thabo Mbeki, who in a new era succeeded Nelson Mandela as South Africa's president. Our official hosts in Nairobi were Bethuel Kipligat and Jose Chipenda, a Kenyan and an Angolan working with the regional office of the World Student Christian Federation. They commissioned us, along with elmira, to help produce issues of the WSCF magazine, and so helped facilitate our movement into journalism. Jose taught me to process photographs, and it was in his Nairobi attic that I first experienced the wonder of an image gradually appearing on blank paper in a tray of developing fluid.

Through Jose's wife, Eva, I learned more about African women and their struggles. A designer and a fabric artist who was working with the Kenyan YWCA to develop cottage industries for women in Nairobi's slums, Eva had often felt sidelined as a woman herself. But she had had the daring and initiative to escape from Portugal, Angola's colonial ruler, in a fishing boat overnight with two small children, when the regime in Lisbon wanted to use her to capture Jose. It is her legacy, and that of so many other women whose perseverance and courage are beyond imagining, that urges all of us to greater efforts, wherever we live our lives. The final words of Eva's book, *The Visitor: An African Woman's Story of Travel and Discovery,* published by the World Council of Churches, are "There is hope!"

For the last three decades, I have tried to help keep that hope alive, strengthened by the examples of women like Eva and Ella and Margaret and Ruth and Vuye and so many others. Through the nonprofit Africa News Service, begun in 1973 with a grant from Charles Cobb of the UCC Commission on Racial Justice, and continuing with AllAfrica Global Media and its

Internet service allafrica.com, which has become one of the largest content sites on the web and a source of revenue for more than ninety participating African media organizations, my colleagues and I have joined with our African counterparts to help give Africa a voice in the global marketplace of ideas. My two dozen co-workers at AllAfrica—among whom is Charles Cobb's son Charlie, a former SNCC organizer turned journalist—reflect the rich diversity of the world as it could be: African, European, Asian, Arab, Christian, Jewish and Muslim, and black and white and Native American, speaking some twenty languages. As shaky as any such enterprise is in a time of plummeting economic opportunities, we have been able to come this far because we stand on the shoulders of giants.

A few years ago Reed and I returned to the South African countryside, near Durban, where the Methodist minister Athol Jennings heads the youth leadership training program we had worked on together more than a quarter century earlier. At a commissioning ceremony for young church workers from all over southern Africa, a local minister enjoined the group to have the perseverance of Job and the assurance of the Psalmist.

> Because of the multitude of oppressions people cry out . . .
> where is God my maker who gives strength in the night?
> Job 35:9, 10

> The Lord will command his lovingkindness in the
> daytime, and in the night his song will be with me.
> Psalm 42:8

The lessons of my experience tell me this. Have faith that change is possible. Imagine a new world. Sing songs in the night. Never forget that courage, like fear, is contagious. Pass it on.

M. Sheila McCurdy

~~~~~~~

$\mathcal{M}$y involvement in the civil rights movement did not begin with a conscious decision to join the struggle for freedom in the South. As the daughter of a Methodist minister in the Alabama–West Florida Conference, I attended a Methodist college, majoring in religion and philosophy, and suddenly found myself overwhelmed by the evil reality of my world. My responses to the injustice around me came slowly, after much prayer and personal struggle. I still wanted to be the respected daughter and student, but was faced with choices that would often exclude me from the security I had once known.

When I entered Huntingdon College in Montgomery, Alabama, in 1962, the bus boycott had been successfully completed and the civil rights movement was making radical demands on a resistant South. During my first year at college, students were not allowed to use the city buses because of the fear of violence. The fear seemed ungrounded, as I never heard of anyone being injured on a city bus. This was one of many rules that demonstrated the fear of a society faced with the demands of change.

In response to the integration of the city library and park, the Montgomery City Council removed all chairs from the public library and benches from the park. Blacks and whites would not be allowed to sit next to each other. I never heard a stated reason explaining why the animals were removed from the zoo. We would laugh at the insanity of our environment as we took our folding chairs to the library, but our laughter was often a mask for our uneasiness. We were being confronted with the absurdity of our segregated society and were faced with its evil results for both the black and the white communities.

Near the end of my freshman year in college, I heard that Martin Luther King, Jr., was going to preach in a small church near my college. I had heard a lot about him, including many negative things that I read in the Montgomery papers. I knew no one who had heard him speak and had never read any of his writings. At this time, Dr. King had moved from Montgomery to Atlanta and was coming back to visit Dexter Avenue Baptist Church, the church he had served as pastor during the bus boycott. I decided that I had to hear him speak, that I had to know who this man was and what he had to say. Churches were segregated in Montgomery, and I was frightened at stepping over the barriers that had been so carefully erected in my midst. A new rule had been passed in my college that students were not allowed to go to places of "tension or demonstration," under the penalty of expulsion. I felt pretty certain that this ruling included Dexter Avenue Baptist Church. Therefore I decided to inform the president of my college of my decision to go to hear Dr. King preach the next evening. He asked me to reconsider my decision and assured me that I would risk being expelled if I went. Women students were required to sign out, stating our destination, when we left campus. It never occurred to me to simply disobey the rule, by lying about where I was going or not signing out at all.

I entered the doors of Dexter Avenue Baptist Church the next evening, terrified. All of the taboos of my childhood in a segregated society were there, and yet, as I began to sing the words of "We Shall Overcome" for the first time, a strange calmness overcame my fears. I experienced the presence of God in a powerful way as I joined hands with the people on either side of me and sang the words, "We are not afraid today." Dr. King announced that the police and their dogs had surrounded the church and that he knew we were afraid—but that we would just keep singing until we were not afraid. I was amazed that my own sense of powerlessness began to be replaced by strength within that gathered community. Then Dr. King began to preach, and I began to see the vision that he so powerfully proclaimed. As I heard his prophetic words, I knew that my life would never be the same again. When I reflect on that evening, I realize that it was a conversion experience, a time in which I experienced the liberating spirit of the God of Exodus in a new way. My understanding of the church as the community of the faithful would be deeply strengthened as I experienced the courage and commitment of countless persons in the civil rights movement.

When I arrived back on campus that evening, I was met by an angry mob of male students, some KKK members and in robes. They were placing a cross in front of my dorm window, which they later burned. As I got out of the car, the college president appeared. He walked me to the dorm and told me that the state troopers had called him as I arrived at Dexter Avenue and asked if they should arrest me or bring me back to campus. He told them that he knew that I was there and to leave me alone; undoubtedly word also spread to the Klan. He told me to stay in my room and he would see me the next morning. I was not expelled the next morning, but was told that my behavior had not been appropriate for a southern lady, and therefore I could no longer expect to be protected when on campus. I was warned of the terrible things that happened to women who chose not to be ladies and was told not to go out alone after dark.

The foundation of my world began to crumble that day, and yet the possibilities of a new day were opening to me. Several close friends were very supportive, often accompanying me to various obligations for the remainder of my college years. I was pushed, shoved, and abused verbally, but not physically injured. When I later read Lillian Smith's book *Killers of the Dream*, I understood that my experience was not unique. Smith explained the relationship of a "southern lady" to a "good Negro." They were each allowed certain privileges if they stayed in their place, but faced severe consequences in this closed society if they chose to challenge that place. The possible results included lynching or rape.

During the next few months, I began to hear about the work done by the Montgomery Improvement Association, one of the major organizations evolving from the Montgomery bus boycott. Through its meetings, I became aware of the voter registration projects in Alabama and the weekly vigils being held on the steps of the churches in Montgomery and other southern cities. Almost all white churches were steadfastly refusing to allow blacks to enter their doors for worship. Thus black and white students were going in groups to selected churches in various southern cities and asking to be allowed to worship. The churches responded by assigning men of their congregations the task of physically refusing to allow the students to enter their doors.

My first experience confronting the segregated churches in the South made a lasting impression. While attending a Mississippi Methodist Student Movement conference, I stood on the steps of a Methodist church in Jackson, Mississippi, side by side with another student my age, Howard Spencer, who was black and also the child of a Methodist minister. As we were refused entrance to the church and were pushed and knocked down the steps, we could hear the congregation singing the Doxology. Suddenly, the institution that had nourished me since birth became a dramatic symbol of the oppression inflicted upon others. After thirty-five years I am still sobered by the pain of that reality. A few months later I arose with other Methodist students, black and white, and went to the Easter sunrise service at the Atlanta stadium in Atlanta, Georgia. We were, of course, refused entrance. Some in our group were injured by rocks and bottles, but most of us knelt quietly in prayer. I can remember the tears streaming down my face as I listened to the "Hallelujah Chorus" in the background and watched a friend wipe the blood from a black student's head. My understanding of Good Friday and Easter took on a new meaning that day. I was beginning to see the church as the body of Christ in the world.

Most of my early involvement was in response to direct communication from students working in the South or with black students on campuses nearby. The networks of black and white southern students were often formed through mutual contacts in the National Methodist Student Movement or National Student Christian Federation. We rarely participated in demonstrations or activities in our own community, but connected with activities in other cities. Alabama was a police state. We understood that we were being followed by state troopers. It would have been impossible for me to stay in school and participate in a demonstration in Montgomery. We were committed to staying in our colleges, keeping open dialogue with students on our campuses, and trying to build bridges between black and white campuses.

During my second year in college, George Wallace ran for reelection as governor of Alabama on an aggressively racist platform. He actually ran under the umbrella of his wife's name, as it was illegal for him to serve a third term. Twenty to thirty students on my campus joined together to work against Wallace's reelection and for his more moderate opponent, Richmond Flowers. We worked very hard for several months and then were forbidden further participation by our college. Two students from Alabama State, a black college in Montgomery, had been stabbed while passing out leaflets. The Flowers campaign headquarters was bombed several times by the Ku Klux Klan. Finally the campaign staff asked volunteers to stop coming to the office. They could not guarantee their safety. I also remember being told that Richmond Flowers had to get all of his literature printed in another state. Printers in Alabama had been warned of the consequences of printing anti-Wallace literature. The fear and violence quickly forced most volunteers into silence and inaction. The risks were too great.

Each action in which I participated was a radicalizing experience. In trying to participate in the election process, we were confronted with the reality of the police state in which we lived. As we tried to worship with friends, both black and white, we understood that the closed doors of our segregated society included the church's doors. It was a painful, confusing time. I can remember listening to Bob Dylan's "The Times, They Are a-Changin'" and struggling with the demands that these times were making on my life.

My junior year in college, I was elected president of the Alabama Methodist Student Movement. The summer prior to that school year, I had attended a two-week conference sponsored by the National Methodist Student Movement at the Ecumenical Institute in Chicago. I was confronted with the demands of the gospel through the prophetic words of Rev. Joe Matthews. We studied community organization with Saul Alinsky and civil disobedience with Jesse Jackson. The day before I left Chicago to return to Montgomery, Joe Matthews looked at me, and said, "You've heard what we've been saying here and you are afraid of where it will take you." I agreed with him and would often remember his challenge in the next few years as I struggled with the decision ahead. I was no longer afraid of the hellfire of Alabama revivals, but I was frightened of being unfaithful to the struggle for justice and freedom to which I had been called. The theology of the Ecumenical Institute helped me to build bridges between my fundamentalist background and the social revolution around me.

Most of my work the next year would be directed toward establishing communication between black and white students in Alabama colleges and universities. After difficult negotiations with the bishop and church leadership of the Alabama–West Florida Conference, the first integrated conference of the Alabama Methodist Student Movement was held in the spring of 1965. We were told that the final reason for our being allowed to have the MSM conference at a Methodist campground was that the powers that be were afraid that someone might get killed if we held it outside the church, as we had threatened. Unlike the conference structure of the Methodist Church in Alabama, where the black churches were separate from the white churches, the Methodist Student Movement included both black and white colleges. There had been no acknowledgment of this by previous state officers. As president, I traveled to local MSMs on various campuses. Traveling to black colleges was difficult, but not impossible. At least one other white student went with me, and for safety reasons we met on campus only, with a minister present. I found that I could use some of the political skills that I had been learning to my advantage. Intricate networks developed for our protection. When I left my campus, I would call Charles Rinker, the national Methodist Student Movement president at Drew Theological School in Madison, New Jersey, and tell him where I was going and when I should arrive. On arriving at my destination, I would call to confirm my arrival. If my departure and arrival were not within the correct time period, people would be contacted to look for me.

During this year, I began attending a small Methodist church in Montgomery whose minister, Dr. Charles Prestwood, became my dear friend and a constant inspiration. I would also keep Dr. Prestwood apprised of my activities and consult with him on the best methods for achieving my goals. I was once expelled for refusing to stand in honor of George Wallace when he spoke at a required convocation in my school. I called Dr. Prestwood and said that I had just been told that I had been expelled. He instructed me not to pack my bags and to wait until I heard from him. I was reinstated that evening. Dr. Prestwood had spent most of the day on the phone with various people from the Methodist office in New York, who had finally convinced the college that as a Methodist school, it had to adhere to basic guidelines concerning a student's right of conscience. Recalling these events seems almost unreal, and yet it was the reality of life in Alabama at the time.

Dr. Prestwood lived a few blocks from the college, and I used to babysit his daughters two afternoons a week. One day I walked to his house and discovered that the Ku Klux Klan was surrounding it. I quickly walked back to school and called him and asked if I should try to come. He laughed and said, "No, we will not be going out this afternoon." Dr. Prestwood finally had to leave Alabama in order to continue his work and provide for his family, as did many other courageous people in the South. They found themselves locked out of their careers and unable to provide their children a secure environment. The South lost many of its more creative, perceptive citizens during those years and destroyed the lives of many who chose to stay.

During my work in the Methodist Student Movement and conference, I got to know students who were field staff members of the Student Nonviolent Coordinating Committee. The witness of Sam Shirah and Bob Zellner was especially important to me. They were both sons of Methodist ministers in the Alabama–West Florida Conference. Bob had also gone to Huntingdon, but had graduated before I arrived. Sam and I served on the conference youth council of Methodist Youth Fellowship. For years he had been a role model for me, giving me books to read that we would later discuss. At Sam's suggestion, I read all the books by James Baldwin and Richard Wright—*Black Like Me* and many others. He also introduced me to *motive* magazine, which became a catalyst for my spiritual growth and political commitment.

During my junior year in college, I attended a SNCC conference in Atlanta. That weekend we listened to stories of the workers in rural Alabama, Mississippi, and Georgia, and sang freedom songs with the SNCC Freedom

Singers. I will always remember that on my arrival, Stokely Carmichael was waiting to greet me. He had heard that a white Alabama student from Montgomery had registered for the conference. He was sensitive to my fears and introduced me to others and invited me to eat meals with him. In the middle of the conference, the SNCC office in Atlanta was bombed, injuring two volunteers. I was frightened but strengthened in my commitment. Later that year, when I had lost several scholarships from my college because of my questionable character, SNCC offered me scholarship assistance. I did not have to accept that offer, because the Board of Missions in New York had helped replace my lost funding.

Faced with the threat of a loss of funding, both from the Methodist Church and the federal government, Huntingdon decided to integrate my junior year. It fulfilled this demand by admitting one black young woman, Patricia Guy. She would not live on campus and would only attend day classes. Huntingdon was a small campus with one cafeteria. On the first day of school when Pat walked into the cafeteria for lunch, everyone stopped talking and stared at her. She looked so fragile and frightened as she sat down by herself at an empty table. No one sat with her or at any table nearby. I had decided to stand back, feeling that other students who were freshmen would break that barrier. I did not want to force Pat to be identified with me, as I was already so isolated. This continued for three days, and on the fourth day, I could no longer stand it. I told my roommate that I was going over to sit with Pat and she agreed to go with me. We became close friends during that year and the next. Pat would share our dorm room during the day, as a place to rest and keep her books. She was a quiet person of great strength, and won the admiration of many students and professors during her time at Huntingdon. She continued to be the only black student my junior and senior year. One day Pat walked with several of us to the laundromat near our campus. While we waited for our clothes, we went to the ice cream shop next door, as usual. When we sat down at a table, the waitress came over with the manager behind her and said, "Is this one of those sit-ins?" I said, "No, we just want some ice cream." She came back in a minute and said, "We just wanted to be sure this wasn't one of those sit-ins. What kind of ice cream do you want?" On the way back to school we laughed about integrating the ice cream parlor. Even though we could often laugh together and enjoy the quiet moments we sometimes shared, the time was marked more by tragedy and fear.

Near the end of my junior year, the march from Selma to Montgomery occurred. For months before the march, I met continually with black and white students, most often separately, trying to keep communication open between the black and white communities. I decided not to go to Selma, feeling that I could be more effective in Montgomery. Dr. Prestwood met with me often, helping me to look for alternatives that would allow me to keep a foot in both the black and the white communities. I was a child of the Alabama–West Florida Conference and my roots there did provide me some leverage. I also personally loved many of the racists whom I was trying to confront, as did Dr. Prestwood.

Certainly my greatest struggle was with my father. My mother had died when I was thirteen, and her calm, loving presence was sorely missed. As I became more and more involved in the civil rights movement, I became more and more estranged from my family. My old circle of friends, too, got smaller and smaller. One of my most painful memories is when my high-school boyfriend came to visit my college after returning from duty in Vietnam. He had been my first true love, but now he angrily confronted me with his knowledge that I had become "a nigger lover." I knew that underneath his anger lay his own fears and pain. Here he was on my territory, where I was preparing to graduate from college. He had no idea what to do with his own life, and he had been deeply wounded by his experiences in Vietnam. His racism, however, was real and stood in opposition to everything I believed. I longed to hold him and be held by him, even as I felt repulsed by his very being. I never saw him again after that day, but I can still feel the wounds of his hatred.

During the week of the march, Dr. Prestwood traveled back and forth between Selma and Montgomery. I shared his pain as he told me about being in the hospital room when Jonathan Daniels, the Unitarian minister beaten in Selma, died. We cried together and grieved over the brokenness in our community and the hatred and violence that was destroying all of our lives. I was continually strengthened in my struggle for faithfulness by his sermons and the example of his life. During that week, I also met with several staff and officers of the national Methodist Student Movement who had come to Montgomery. They were supportive of our local efforts in raising consciousness and building bridges within our broken community.

The day the march entered Montgomery, some students from Huntingdon were preparing to join the marchers. Early that morning, we were escorted to a classroom where we would be held for most of the day. When the march was over, we were allowed to go back to our rooms. When I reflect on that day, it seems amazing that we all sat there all day with none of us trying to physically push our way out. Yet that possibility never occurred to any of us. It was hard to be a revolutionary when we still said "Yes ma'am" and "No sir" to anyone over thirty. It was possible for me to risk my own safety, but to be rude or openly defy my elders was not in my worldview.

Dr. King understood the southerner, black and white, when he taught us the methods of nonviolence. Confronting our oppressors on our knees not only was a political strategy, but enabled many of us to have the courage to face the injustice in our midst. As we prayed together, we were empowered by the presence of God. In the years ahead I would often find it difficult to march near those on the more radical fringes of the movement, because their language seemed to reflect hatred, rather than love. In those days I would find the words of Che Guevara comforting, "Let me say, with the risk of appearing ridiculous, that the true revolutionary is guided by great feelings of love."

My network with other white southern students became much stronger after the Selma to Montgomery March. Our day of captivity was community building for those of us at Huntingdon. During my senior year, we would try to use that base to more effectively confront the racism around us. Our steps were small but pushing us in new directions. By the middle of my senior year, I began to think about where I needed to respond to this struggle for justice after college. I had always wanted to go to seminary, but began to feel more strongly each day that this was not a faithful response for me to make at this time of crisis in my community and nation. I was offered a position as a field staff member of the Southern Students Organizing Committee (SSOC). This organization had become a supportive place for southern white students to network, and I had worked closely with its members that past year. Again Dr. Prestwood supported me as I struggled to make this decision. He encouraged me to get some experience outside the South, and he shared with me the importance of his seminary days in Boston, where he was a classmate of Dr. King. I felt the limitations of my worldview and yet wanted to work in the civil rights movement. I finally decided to join the US–2 program through the Methodist Church and was assigned as a community organizer to the inner city of Newark, New Jersey. It was a good decision that would push me to new levels of faith, as I worked day by day alongside the welfare mothers that I had been sent to assist. My grounding in the civil rights movement in the South would be central to my continuing development on my faith journey. My eyes were opened to the vision of God's promise of Shalom through the words of the prophets and the lives of the people of God on those dusty roads of Alabama.

One of the reasons that I chose Newark, New Jersey, as my placement as a US–2 was because of the work that I knew the Students for a Democratic

Society were doing there. My assignment was in no way related directly to the SDS project, however. It was simply in the same community in which SDS was organizing. I was assigned to Trinity United Methodist Church in the South Ward of the inner city, where SDS had formed the Newark Community Union Project. Shortly after arriving, I went down to their office to network with the other organizers and the community, but I was not immediately accepted by SDS organizers. I remember Tom Hayden's shock at my sudden appearance in a dress (I didn't have movement clothes) and my deep southern accent. He looked at me and said, "Where in the hell did you come from?" to which I replied, "Montgomery." Nevertheless, I learned a lot from Tom and other SDS organizers during those two years, valuing their work and feeling valued in return. I quickly began to focus primarily in the area of welfare rights and assisted several welfare mothers who were primary organizers in that area. SDS had done a good job of organizing the community and sharing information that helped people understand their rights. They had published a book on welfare rights for the community's information. As welfare organizers, we would represent recipients at the welfare office as well as in other areas of need where they faced legal questions. We also did a great deal to expose slumlords and slum conditions and to try to prevent the welfare offices from placing people in below-standard buildings. We found one particularly effective means to get a slum landlord's attention. We would fill a van with concerned members of the community and drive to the landlord's home, usually in a nice suburb, and demonstrate in his neighborhood with signs that said "No Rent for Rats."

I became very close friends with several of the community welfare organizers and grew especially close to Julie, the eight-year-old daughter of one of the mothers. When she was not in school, she was my companion. In the spring of 1967, Julie had to go to the hospital to have her tonsils removed. She came back home after the surgery, seeming fine, but then had to be rushed back to the hospital. Julie was hemorrhaging. I went with her mom to the hospital and asked for immediate care. The nurse said that Julie's mother must complete the welfare medical forms before Julie could be admitted. So as Julie continued bleeding, I tried to assist her mom in filling out the forms. Before we could finish, Julie died in the corridor of the hospital without one doctor examining her. All she needed was a simple tracheotomy to save her life, but since she was on welfare she had to wait. That day I realized that racism killed little girls not only in Birmingham but throughout the United States on a daily basis. My consciousness as a woman was being awakened by the struggle of welfare mothers trying to raise their children with dignity in the midst of hatred and exploitation.

Late in the spring of 1967, the Newark Community Union Project organized a boycott of Jack's Meat Market. Several months of research revealed that Jack was involved in an intricate system of exploitation. He often did not label his food items and would charge different people different prices, always charging welfare recipients who were buying on credit a greater price. Jack had gotten social workers to refer their clients to his store. While they were waiting to be accepted on welfare, he would give them credit, and by the time they got their first check, they owed him a huge portion of it. The caseworker would insist that he be paid, and then the cycle would begin again.

In response to the investigation, we organized picket lines in front of the market. During my time as a US–2, I often traveled to suburban churches to speak and to network for community needs. A delegation of United Methodist Women came to observe my work as the picket was occurring. I explained the situation and then went back to join the picket line. Just as the women were about to leave, the police arrived and began to throw us picketers in police cars. A huge group of community people started screaming and followed us to the fifth precinct station. The United Methodist Women came along, too, and offered to try to bail me out, but I explained that I could not leave unless we all could leave. They went back to their church and raised money to help support a food co-op that was organized as an alternative to Jack's Meat Market.

The church to which I had been assigned, however, was not as supportive. They felt that I was working with the wrong kind of people, and I was asked to leave. My work with SDS had not met with the approval of Trinity's pastor. The US–2 program reassigned me as a field staff worker for the University Christian Movement so that I could continue my two-year assignment.

On July 12, 1967, the tensions between the police and the black community in Newark climaxed, thus beginning the Newark "rebellion." We never considered these actions a "mindless riot," but an honest rebellion against injustice. One more time the people witnessed police brutality and responded with anger. During the first two days, I was not afraid and was out on the street talking to people. But on the third day, the state troopers and National Guard arrived and the city was under siege. State troopers rode up and down the street firing their guns. A nine-year-old boy was shot while taking out the garbage. A mother was shot in the eye while she stood in her kitchen preparing dinner for her family. I remember sitting under the table to eat, trying to protect ourselves from the troopers' bullets. This week of siege changed our lives. The police state not only was in Alabama, but was a reality for the oppressed of this country. Our vision of social justice began to be blurred by despair and the pain of those around us. In the fall of 1967, I was investigated by the Senate Intelligence Investigating Committee for inciting the riots, along with other community organizers. We, rather than the police or other oppressive agents in the community, became the target of the investigation. Our government was radicalizing us daily.

Much of the Newark community was destroyed and has never been revitalized. The Vietnam War was taking its toll on the poverty program and the youth of the nation. Our consciousness as women was beginning to form. My first consciousness-raising group was made up of community and SDS women in Newark. We were ridiculed by most of the male SDS organizers and began to understand the limits of their ability to see us as equals. We were beginning to feel the connection between the oppression of women and the oppression of minorities and third world people. The male SDS workers felt that our issues were trivial compared with the pressing problems of the world. We still shared many goals and commitments, but there was an uneasiness in our midst. My last months in Newark, I was deeply touched by the opportunity to meet and talk with men and women from North Vietnam. Their strength and courage were empowering.

The death of Dr. King in April 1968 was devastating and brought on a time of deep sorrow and despair. During this time I began to struggle with where God was calling me, as the US–2 program was near completion. Vietnam had broadened my commitment to a global struggle for justice, and I began to search out possibilities for international service. I was encouraged by my supervisors and friends from the University Christian Movement to apply to the Frontier Intern program. At this time I was engaged to a young African American man who was completing a two-year term as a Vista Volunteer in Harlem. We each applied to the Frontier Intern program and, as a backup, to the Peace Corps. My Peace Corps application came back with a rejection—I had not passed government clearance. We were married that summer, and my relationship with my father and most of my extended family was deeply strained. My father told me never to come home again. For years after my marriage, my letters to family members were returned unopened.

My husband and I entered the Frontier Intern program and were assigned to the Caribbean Student Christian Movement, to assist its members in connecting English- and Spanish-speaking student groups while developing a deeper understanding of their common needs and goals. We would spend the first year in Jamaica and the second year in Trinidad, Puerto Rico, and Mexico. My understanding of the church as the community of the faithful was deeply strengthened during those two years. We were privileged to study with Paulo Freire and to meet on a continuing basis with students deeply involved in the liberation struggles of their countries. As we prayed and worked together, we were confronted with the demands and possibilities of the gospel. I can remember sitting around a circle at the end of a conference in Mexico holding hands and experiencing the beauty of our common struggle for humanness.

The future of some of our members was very unclear. Some might be jailed or killed after returning home. We prayed for a friend missing in Argentina and understood what it means to be the body of Christ in the world. We were connected to one another in the joys and sorrows of our separate countries' journeys toward liberation. The movement toward liberation in Chile brought us all closer to the demand for justice and freedom. Several years later we would understand that the overthrow of Salvador Allende and the repression of our brothers and sisters there darkened the possibility of liberty for all.

One of the great gifts of the Frontier Intern program was its ability to facilitate communication between the interns all over the world. We sent regular reports to New York that were then forwarded to interns in other countries. This gave us a sense of personal connection to the liberation struggle worldwide. We became global people, making connections to justice issues that would inform our thinking for life. I am so thankful for the vision and faithfulness of the church leaders who provided the youth of the church with such a rich opportunity to develop in faith and knowledge as world citizens. On returning to the United States, we were assigned to do research for the North American Committee on Latin America (NACLA). I still find NACLA's publications some of the most helpful in keeping informed on the Caribbean and Latin America. It was a long journey from Montgomery, Alabama, to Kingston, Jamaica, but one grounded in the courage of a faithful remnant pursuing the promise of justice and freedom for all. What a blessing to have interacted with so many of their lives.

Through the liberation struggle of my sisters and brothers in the African American community in the United States and in Latin America and the Caribbean, I began to understand more clearly the relationship between sexism and racism. Only as we recognized the depth of oppression in the structure of patriarchy could we begin the process of liberation based on mutuality. Women's consciousness-raising groups offered many North American women their first opportunity to begin this process. As we cried together and shared our stories, we celebrated our sisterhood. As we were strengthened in community, we were able to move forward together, empowered in our struggle for liberation. Our work often began in our own homes and within the organizations in which we volunteered. As we began to feel connected to other women's struggles in this country and throughout the world, we could no longer remain silent in the face of any woman's dehumanization. When American soldiers raped women in Vietnam, we shared the suffering and understood the connection to our own inability to walk alone in the streets of our communities. As we saw the countless faces of women and children dying of starvation in Africa, we knew that the great majority of the poor and hungry in our own country were women and their children. We began to understand that an increase in military spending directly affected the quality of the education offered to our children. We began to recognize that a world based on justice and freedom could only be possible when our girl children and boy children would receive the same possibilities for humanness in their development toward adulthood.

As we were sensitized to the destructive force of patriarchy in our society, we became aware of those same forces at work in the structure of our church. My first memory of confronting this was with other Frontier Intern women. We formed a women's caucus and explored our uneasiness with some of the male interns. They seemed never to listen when we spoke, or else they paused for us to speak and then continued the conversation, ignoring what we had said. The caucus provided the first opportunity most of us had to explore our feelings about this situation. It was 1967, and women were just beginning to gather to support one another and insist that their voices be heard within the church structure.

Living in New York City from 1970 to 1973 provided me with a wonderful opportunity for submersion in the women's movement. As a member of the New York Radical Feminists, I participated in a consciousness-raising group, demonstrations, and decision making by consensus at the Women's Center. As an activist, I became more in touch with my feelings and began to allow myself to feel the pain of the brokenness with my family.

After our son was born in 1973, my husband and I decided to move to Columbia, Maryland—with its ideals of multiculturalism and its symbol of the People's Tree, a beautiful sculpture that welcomes all people into an inclusive community. This is where we wanted to raise our interracial children. I immediately became very involved in the local women's center, several peace and justice groups, and a community activist church.

Since my children's birth, I have often experienced the world through their eyes—the immense joy and the deep pain. When racism and sexism shatter their world, I can hardly breathe. At age three, my son came inside crying and said, "Mom, they said I can't play because I'm black." I held him close and then explained that that was called "racism." If someone didn't like him because of the color of his skin, they were racist. However, if they would not play with him because he was a boy that would be called sexism and they would be sexist. We talked about this a lot, and he confronted his friends when necessary. Several years later, I was holding his baby sister in my arms and holding him by the hand, when a man in the mall began to point and curse at me. My son stopped, looked at the man, and then asked, "Now mom, is that racist or sexist?" I knew then that he was strong enough to handle the pain that he would surely face.

Both of my children often asked to go see their granddaddy. They were close to cousins in Virginia who visited their grandfather often. I continued to ask my dad to allow us to come home and he continued to refuse. To answer my children's many questions, I tried to explain that there were many racists in Alabama, and Grandaddy didn't want us to come. One day my son had drawn a picture at school showing him fishing with his granddad (which of course he had never done). As he showed it to me, he started to cry, and said, "Mommy, if Alabama is racist, why doesn't Grandaddy move?" Several years later, he would ask me the real question, "Mom, is Grandaddy racist?" My daughter seldom asked the questions, but was always very close to her brother, absorbing the pain. They were also very aware of my own pain, even as I tried to make everything all right.

Both of my children grew up in the playroom at the women's center in Columbia and knew all the songs of "Free to Be You and Me." Both had male and female and black and white anatomically correct dolls, plus blocks and trucks, but no guns. My children have been the source of my greatest joy and my greatest pain. I wanted them to have the possibility of living in a world free of racism and sexism, but have only been able to support them in their own struggles for love, justice, and equality.

I began seminary in 1984, culminating a long journey that had begun when I was a child in Alabama parsonages. That was where I first experienced love, acceptance, and the ideal of inclusiveness: "Jesus loves the little children, all the children of the world, red and yellow, black and white, they are precious in his sight, Jesus loves the little children of the world." It was also there in the church, in my Methodist college, and from my Methodist minister father that I first faced the realities of exclusion, racism, and sexism.

Women were simply not allowed to enter the ministerial track in my college. The classes were not open to us, nor was ordination a possibility. It never occurred to me to challenge this. I simply looked for other means in which to serve God in our world.

Central to the exclusion of women in the life and ministry of the church was the idolatry of a male God. The use of exclusive language often made it difficult for us to experience the good news of God's all-inclusive love. As an adult, my own spiritual journey was strengthened by my participation in a church that understood the importance of inclusive language. After I had left this church to take my first appointment as an associate pastor, my ten-year-old daughter confronted me with the task ahead. On the way home from church after the first Sunday, she said, "Mom, they think God's a man in that church. Isn't that silly?" I was pleased that she recognized the inappropriateness of the language but saddened at the reality that faced her and all the children in our churches who would hear God referred to only as "He."

My many years in the women's movement have empowered me for my life as a clergywoman. My grounding in a church that supported and challenged me to struggle for justice has given me strength in my journey to be faithful. The Methodist Student Movement, University Christian Movement, and the World Student Christian Federation surrounded many of us with an opportunity to be agents for social change within the institutional church. I am painfully aware that my own two young adult children, Dedrick and Kendra, have not experienced that same reality. As they studied at Union Theological Seminary, they continued to feel more and more alienated from the United Methodist Church. As interracial children, they experienced racism, sexism, and heterosexism in the local churches I have served. Not until the late 1980s was our family allowed to go to my father's and other relatives' homes in Alabama and attend the United Methodist church that he pastored. After I was ordained deacon in 1988, my father finally agreed to invite my children and me to come home. It's been a painful, slow, but beautifully healing process for us all. Dedrick and Kendra continue to experience the church as an exclusive institution. Yet they both chose to go to seminary and today struggle with their own place in the justice issues calling them to ministry.

The Methodist Federation for Social Action (MFSA) continues to be a supportive community for those of us within the United Methodist Church who struggle to confront ourselves, our church, and our society with the demanding justice issues before us. I recently served a term as co-president and work with many persons who also received their theological grounding in the student Christian movements of the 1960s. As women, many of us were empowered for ministry when that was still only a remote possibility in the local church. Each time I face conflict as the first woman clergy of a local church, I am grateful for that faithful remnant that I experienced in the 1960s, 1970s, 1980s, and 1990s. I continue to enjoy the privilege of being connected to faithful and courageous persons who are committed to a church that is inclusive, just, and visionary. The importance of community was central to the early student movements and has enabled me to search for support groups for nurture and for challenge. MFSA provides one of those possibilities, as does a weekly clergy group in which I participate.

My faith journey began in a Methodist parsonage and today continues from that space. I now realize that the struggle for justice is a lifetime commitment, and yet it is absolutely what is required of me. It makes me hopeful to know that the Methodist Student Movement is beginning again. I hope it can renew some of its past vision and courage for justice to challenge and support the church of the new millennium. The liberation movement continues to find new voices and catalyst groups. When I hear the Word through my children's hip-hop music, the homeless man at my front door, or the children in our church nursery school, I know that the resurrection has occurred and is occurring and that the revolution continues—even now.

CHAPTER 9

Alice Hageman

Sometime in the mid–1970s, early in my pastorate at Church of the Covenant in Boston's Back Bay, I preached a fourth of July sermon entitled, "I pledge allegiance . . . " In exploring the meaning of loyalty oaths—those affirmed by persons joining the church, those required by the federal government during the McCarthy era, those exacted by feudal lords over their subjects—I wanted to test the limits of our understanding of patriotism. In doing so, I invited the congregation to consider an issue with which I had struggled for many years: the source and focus of our primary loyalty. I knew that I defined myself as an American Christian rather than as a Christian American, that if pressed, my loyalties were as a citizen of the household of God more than of the United States of America. I also knew that even that description was inadequate; I have parted company with the majority in my denomination on several important issues, and am comforted by church doctrine which says that "God alone is Lord of the conscience."

During France's war with Algeria in the late 1950s and early l960s, Albert Camus wrote, "I should like to be able to love my country and still love justice." During the United States' war with Vietnam, Sister Mary Corita, IHM, transferred that phrase onto a red, white, and blue silk-screened poster, a copy of which hung in my living room for many years. In my young adulthood I learned that loving justice was not synonymous with loving my country. I continue to struggle to understand how, and whether, even after 9/11/01, it is possible for a United States Christian to love both country and justice.

I was born into a middle-class family in central New Jersey. My Dutch forebears helped settle the area in the mid-eighteenth century. My family was active in the Dutch Reformed Church for generations, until my parents moved to a community where the Presbyterian Church was the closest alternative.

Our family motto is "Hurl thunderbolts at evil," reflecting the past presence of clergy and lawyers.

My father, Maurice Herman Hageman, was born in 1899 and died in 1963, three weeks after the assassination of John F. Kennedy. His family's resources were modest: his father was the bookkeeper in a lumberyard, his stepmother a stitcher in a tent factory. His mother had died when he was five. His stepmother, who doted on her son, my father's half-brother, kept her distance from this stepson who still fondly remembered his mother. He received a church scholarship to Rutgers, to support him in study for the ordained ministry. His family was unable to provide financial support for his educational goals; on the contrary, since the eighth grade he had worked before and after school to pay his parents room and board.

A severe case of pneumonia forced my father to leave college, and he never returned to his studies. He then became a salesman, selling books in the Smoky Mountains, where he went to strengthen his lungs, and selling gas stoves for Public Service during the Depression. In the late 1930s he took over an insurance business in Hightstown, my hometown. Too old to be drafted, he served in the National Guard during World War II. Daddy was active in Presbyterian men's organizations at various levels, and in the 1950s served a year as the first lay moderator of Monmouth (N.J.) Presbytery. His insurance business expanded to include real estate in the mid-1940s. In his first successful venture, he and a partner created a mini-Levittown development in central New Jersey in which returning GIs could purchase a home for virtually no down payment and $50 per month. When he died we received letters from people who had bought those homes, expressing their appreciation and saying they would never otherwise have been able to own their own home.

My mother, Lillian Mae Little Hageman, was born in 1905 and died in 1996. The daughter and granddaughter of blacksmiths, she was the first in her family to attend college, a teacher training school. When she married my father, she was an elementary school teacher earning $1,500 per year, and for the first eight years of the marriage, she was the more stable source of the family income. Although Mother, like other middle-class women of that era, stopped work outside the house when I was born, she took increasing responsibility for managing my father's office. She also maintained an active volunteer life. In addition to the PTA, she was a central figure in the local congregation's women's association and promoted interest in missions in our congregation.

Although somewhat diverse religiously—Presbyterian, Baptist, Methodist,

Roman Catholic, Jewish—Hightstown residents were predominantly white. Most of the African Americans in our area were, or had been, migrant workers who came to help harvest the area potato farms, then remained north. There was a large enough community to form a separate church and an informally segregated neighborhood a few blocks from my home. Precursors of the civil rights movement were largely confined to local challenges such as the integration of swimming pools or the town's teen canteen. It pains me to confess that, although I was active in my church youth group and the canteen, I did not participate with those seeking to effect such modest change, but rather acquiesced to arguments that such changes would disrupt our community.

The cold war was in its most frigid phase during the 1950s. The only people I knew who really questioned the cold war mentality were the students from Roosevelt, one of the four sending districts to Hightstown High School. I discounted their opinions, since "everyone" knew their parents were "reds." Several of their families were even said to subscribe to the *Daily Worker*, the newspaper of the Communist Party U.S.A.

Roosevelt, originally the "Jersey Homesteads," was a planned WPA community to which people from the Lower East Side of Manhattan had migrated in the 1940s. Its population had little in common with the populations of Hightstown, a modest small town of five thousand; Cranbury, the even smaller upper-middle-class adjacent town; or East Windsor Township, the surrounding rural area where people continued to work farms. By graduation time, the upper-middle-class kids had transferred to private schools, en route to elite colleges; and the lower-class kids had dropped out, blocked by economic limitations and occasional unplanned pregnancies.

Despite a semester in Washington, D.C., where I studied issues related to the Middle East, I retained a largely U.S.-centered view of the world during my four years at the College of Wooster in Ohio. That perspective began to shift during the summer of 1958 when, as a college graduate, I joined thousands of other young Americans wandering through Europe. That summer I also spent a month in a World Council of Churches (WCC) work camp in Battersea, London, with some twenty-five other young adults. We helped reconstruct a community hall in an urban Anglican parish and explored what brought us together as Christians across barriers of language, nation, and race. That first taste of international ecumenical life whetted my appetite for more.

During the winter of 1959 I learned of a Presbyterian fellowship program that offered a relationship with the John Knox House (Foyer John Knox) in Geneva and a stipend of $1,500. I applied without much further thought. It just felt right. I was completing my first year in the Master of Religious Education (MRE) program at Union Theological Seminary in Manhattan. During that year I had done field education in the East Harlem Protestant Parish, where I learned firsthand about the interrelation of race, gender, and class, of study and worship. I was unsure whether I wanted to continue in seminary, and even if I continued, I didn't know what I wanted to do with the education. A year's hiatus would give me time to think through my near-term future. When I was notified that I had been awarded the fellowship, I immediately called home to share the good news.

"What do you want to do that for?" asked my father. Stunned by his cool response, I stammered out some incoherent words, and the conversation came to an abrupt end. In light of their roles as pillars of our community and local congregation, my parents' reaction to my phone call took me by surprise. They had been enthusiastic about my travel the previous summer; I thought they would share my excitement about this opportunity for broader exposure to the world church. Even after the phone conversation with my parents, I had little question about whether I would accept the fellowship. Nevertheless, I was relieved when my parents called back the next day to say that, although they didn't understand my enthusiasm, they would support me in my decision. And they did, to the extent that they and my younger brother joined me in Europe during the summer of 1960 to travel for several weeks.

By the time I left for Geneva I had already benefited from the influence of three women who were to be my lifelong mentors, role models, and friends. Margaret Flory, the staff person in the office of Student World Relations of the Presbyterian Church nationally, had arranged for my participation in the 1958 work camp. She later initiated the Frontier Intern program, under whose auspices I eventually went to Paris. Veronique Laufer, originally from Lausanne, Switzerland, was the staff person of the Youth Department of the WCC assigned to visit my 1958 work camp. During the 1960s she was the associate general secretary of the CIMADE (Comité Inter Mouvement Auprès des Evacués), a French Protestant movement active in resistance to the German occupation of France during World War II that continued work with refugee and immigrant aid after the war. She was also my closest friend in Paris. Letty Russell, one of the first dozen women ordained in the Presbyterian Church, had been ordained and installed as pastor of Church of the Ascension in the East Harlem Protestant Parish in 1958, the year I entered seminary. Each of these women passed along to me her insight and vision, patiently encouraged me to develop my skills, and helped shape my perception of the world, the church, and the vocational opportunities open to me.

*I*n Geneva I made my first, stumbling forays into an other-than-English-speaking world. I studied French, theology, and psychology (auditing a course by Jean Piaget) at the University of Geneva and audited a course for theological students at the Ecumenical Institute at Bossey. The Bossey theme that year was the theology of the laity, an issue on which I had written my senior independent study thesis at Wooster. I was "big sister" to a group of junior year abroad students sent by Margaret Flory's office. I participated in the local student Christian movement (Association Chrétien des Étudiants, or ACE), and I took meals with the international and ecumenical community gathered at the Foyer John Knox.

The World Student Christian Federation was preparing for a major international teaching conference on the Life and Mission of the Church in Strasbourg, France, in July 1960. To enhance my experience of international ecumenical organizations in Geneva, I volunteered to help prepare for the conference and then attended it as a steward. I remember vividly an intense interchange between a student from Cuba and Karl Barth, the esteemed author of a many-volumed church dogmatics, regarding whether one could be a Christian in a socialist country. Barth had written a much-discussed article stating that perhaps a socialist country could be a more fertile field for Christian teaching than a capitalist country. It was already clear that Marxism had a strong influence on the Cuban leadership, and the Cuban questioner was troubled by this conflict.

At that time it had not occurred to me that it was possible to be a Christian in a socialist country—at least, it had not occurred to me that it was possible to be a Christian who supported socialist goals. Certainly I was not aware of anyone at the College of Wooster who had had any kind words for the changes in Eastern Europe. At Union I had taken a course on Christianity and Communism with Reinhold Niebuhr, John Bennett, and Searle Bates. Although their dialogue challenged some of my preconceptions, the issues had remained theoretical. The interchange between Barth and the Cuban student opened for me a whole new way of looking at, and thinking about, the world.

*B*y the time I returned from Geneva I had decided to switch to the Bachelor of Divinity program. Although I left in limbo the issue of whether I would be ordained, I had decided I would not pursue the MRE degree, which I perceived to be of lesser status. Nor did I have much interest in becoming a director of Christian education in a suburban church. I decided to follow the curriculum for the program that trained students for leadership in the churches. I noted, but did not really analyze, the fact that women made up only some 10 percent of my approximately ninety-member B.D. class. By and large, the men assumed they would be ordained, whatever their work. No one, women or men, really thought we women would be ordained or serve as pastors in churches. That assumption was not unfounded. I was not ordained until thirteen years after my graduation from seminary. In all, only three of the women in my entering class were ever ordained.

*A*lthough the December 1959 Athens, Ohio, Ecumenical Student Conference on Christian World Mission took place while I was in Geneva, its work had a major impact on my life. Within weeks after the conference ended, Margaret Flory presented a proposal for the Frontier Internship in Mission (FIM) program to a committee dealing with conference follow-up. The committee responded positively, and the first Frontier Intern was appointed in June 1960. Twelve persons, some of whom were Union Seminary friends, were appointed as the first class of interns in 1961. Within a few years, thanks largely to the efforts of Ruth Harris, United Methodist staff for student work, the United Methodists and United Church of Christ joined the Presbyterians as sponsors.

The FIM program had three major tenets. The first, *study for involvement*, reflected the ideas of "Christian presence," of being present in a place to listen and learn, before initiating any kind of activity. It was practiced, for example, in Europe in the CIMADE, where I had done internships during 1960 in Coudekerque in northern France and in Marseilles. A second tenet, *subsistence living*, was later characterized as economic discipline. And finally, *a community of mission* meant that interns reported to one another rather than to the mission boards that provided their financial support. FIM explored engaging in mission in ways that contrasted with the more traditional patterns of the mission boards. It also reflected the parallel development of the Peace Corps, whose first volunteers were trained in the summer of 1961, and whose patterns placed in question the more traditional modus operandi of the U.S. government's program Aid for International Development (AID).

The idea of frontiers identified by issue rather than by national boundary appealed to me, as did the possibility of engaging in another international and ecumenical experience. Since I did not have much more vocational clarity when I completed seminary in 1962 than I had when I set off for Geneva three years earlier, I decided to apply. I asked to be sent to a French-speaking country. I assumed I would go to Africa. I was sent to Paris, assigned the frontier of the "emerging international community," and placed with the World Student Christian Federation as its representative at UNESCO.

Like other organizations in the United Nations family, UNESCO is constituted by member states, but also has consultative status with numerous nongovernmental organizations (NGOs). During my three years in Paris I participated in innumerable meetings with other NGOs on topics of common interest, such as ways in which NGOs could assist with literacy programs. At the time Cuba had just completed its campaign for universal literacy, and some representatives of that justly famed effort shared their experiences with our working group. I participated with a group of international civil servants based in Paris as they attempted to discern the relationship between their faith and their work. They very graciously welcomed into their group this young North American, fresh out of seminary. Although they understood my work as an NGO representative, they were mystified by the FIM aspect of my assignment.

Working in relation to an international organization brought me into close contact with people from many countries. Some of these were diplomats from Eastern European countries. My human curiosity overcame my ideological biases. I wanted to know what these people, who had always been portrayed as subhuman, were like, and whether they really were quasi-monsters prepared to seize any opportunity to brainwash an unprepared westerner. I met some very wonderful people, and some less wonderful people, from Eastern Europe during this period. I discovered that communists were not necessarily the ogres I had been led to believe; on the contrary, many of them shared my hopes and aspirations for a society that would be more just and attend to basic needs for food, housing, clothing, medical care, and education. In fact, some of those from "behind the iron curtain" seemed more humane than some people I knew in the United States whose main concern was how to make more money.

During my three years in Paris I also spent time on WSCF activities. I traveled to some kind of international activity approximately once a month. Three such trips stand out.

In January 1963, the infamously cold month when all of Europe shivered, I attended a WSCF staff meeting in Brighton, England. Although I remember little of the purpose of the meeting, I remember vividly a conversation with Milan Opočenský, then Europe secretary of the WSCF, subsequently executive of the World Alliance of Reformed Churches. I warily engaged in conversations with Opočenský about conditions in Czechoslovakia, his home-land. He was forthright about some of the limitations with which he and others in his country lived. We walked up and down near the sea wall, our conver-sation so animated that we ignored the cold and wind. As our conversation progressed and we became more trusting of each other, Milan began to chal-lenge some of my assumptions. What made me think that the United States acted with disinterest? Why was the United States willing to support dicta-torships in other parts of the world? Given the resources of my country, why wasn't more attention given to housing, education, health care? I tried to de-fend my country, and by extension myself and the view of history I had learned. I will never forget Milan's conclusion—after I had made some middle-American anticommunist statements—that I had been brainwashed. Me? I had been brainwashed in the United States of America, home of the free and land of the brave, site of all that was good, better, and best about democracy? I was indignant, outraged, as I denied any such possibility.

Little by little, during succeeding months, I learned to listen to and look at the world through the eyes and ears of Europeans, east and west. I met people from Africa, Asia, and Latin America, who had still different perspec-tives from those of the Europeans. I began to concede that Eastern European countries had no monopoly on manipulating the perceptions and affections of their citizenry. It was a painful awakening, one to be further intensified during the Vietnam War.

A second life-changing trip took place in the late summer and early fall of 1963, when I attended a consultation in Geneva between the Prague-based International Union of Students (IUS) and the WSCF. Such gatherings were rare, because there was little opportunity at that time for students in Western Europe and the United States to exchange views with students in Eastern European "communist" countries. The cold war was at its height, and conversation through what was termed the iron curtain was viewed as suspicious.

At that IUS-WSCF consultation I met and initiated a lifelong friend-ship with Carmen Barrosso and Luz Marina Ortiz, both of them Cubans studying in Montpelier on WCC fellowships. Luz Marina is now a psycholo-gist in Cuba. Carmen, still a resident of Cuba, has in recent years been work-ing at the United Nations headquarters in New York as a translator, with the support of the Cuban Mission to the UN. Our paths were to cross again in Europe and, subsequently, many times in Cuba.

In July 1964, I made a third life-changing trip, as the WSCF represen-tative to the assembly of the Prague-based Christian Peace Conference (CPC).

The CPC had been created in the late 1950s to foster communication between Christians of Eastern and Western Europe. Participants in the CPC accepted the working hypothesis that it was possible both to be a faithful Christian and to support certain goals within a socialist society. Although by then I was willing to accept that theoretical premise, I still felt somewhat uneasy actually venturing on my own into a communist country. The experience was much more benign than I had imagined. My fears were unwarranted. Even when I stayed an extra week with the friend of a Czech friend in Paris and had to register with the local police—a reminder that I was in a setting very different from the one to which I was accustomed—the hospitality of my Czech hosts assured me I was among friends.

The single event at the 1964 CPC assembly with the most lasting impact on my life was a luncheon that brought together U.S. and Cuban participants. There we had an opportunity to discuss our perspectives on our respective nations as well as the issues separating our two countries, so near yet by that time so very far away. Batista had left Cuba on New Year's Eve 1958, and Fidel Castro and his followers had come to power in early 1959. A series of standoffs followed, as the United States attempted to maintain most aspects of the economic and political status quo ante while the revolutionaries were determined to forge new patterns. This struggle culminated in the United States' severing diplomatic relations in January 1961. The U.S.-supported invasion at the Bay of Pigs took place on April 17 of that year, followed two weeks later, on May 1, by Castro's declaration that Cuba was a socialist republic. The ultimate standoff, between the United States and the Soviet Union during the 1962 missile crisis, froze positions on every side. After that, the Treasury Department imposed a ban on travel by U.S. citizens to Cuba. By 1964 it was almost as difficult for Americans to obtain direct news about Cuba as about China, on the other side of the world. At this 1964 luncheon I met Adolfo Ham, Dora Valentín, and Sergio Arce. Ham was at the time executive of the Ecumenical Council in Cuba. Arce, who had abandoned his graduate studies at Princeton Theological Seminary to return to Cuba following the revolution, was professor of theology at, and later president of, the ecumenical seminary in Matanzas. Valentín, Arce's wife, then at home with two children, later became the seminary's administrator and another of my mentors. Ham gave me his card and told me to look him up if I ever came to Cuba. I saved the card and retrieved it when, five years later, I made my first trip.

When I returned to the United States in the summer of 1965, I was determined to go back to Paris one day to work as a civil servant at UNESCO.

But during my three-year absence from the country my father had died, the civil rights movement had broken out, and U.S. involvement in Vietnam was increasing. Although I flirted with the idea of returning to Paris for an indefinite period, in my heart I knew that for family, civic, religious, and personal reasons, I needed to live in the United States again, at least for a while.

*A*fter a summer with my mother and brother in New Jersey, I returned to Manhattan and rented an apartment in East Harlem, on the fifth floor of a tenement on 105th Street. Letty Russell lived on the sixth floor and my college roommate, Jane Thompson, on the fourth floor of the same building, giving me ample opportunity to talk through my dilemmas of work, vocation, and location with trusted friends.

Although I quickly resolved the question of where I would live, I still faced the issue of what work I would do. It had to have something to do with international issues. Finally, with the support of Margaret Flory and several others, I put together a project working with international students and international issues, that ultimately was lodged in the Ecumenical Foundation for Higher Education in Metropolitan New York. I was given office space at Two Washington Square North, a religious activities building at New York University.

Sometime in early 1966, Aubrey Brown, a former Peace Corps volunteer (PCV) in Nigeria and graduate student at Columbia, invited me to participate in a group of returned volunteers. He and his graduate student friends, primarily former PCVs, were planning to bring together returned volunteers to make known their experiences in third world countries and to figure out ways to counter the increasing U.S. involvement in military activities in the Vietnam War. In retrospect, our assumptions were very naive: if we made enough information available to government officials and the general public, U.S. policy would change. We sent notices to every former volunteer whose name and address we could find, whether PCV or FI or an alumna/us of Yale in China, Operation Crossroads Africa, the American Friends Service Committee, or some other academic or voluntary organization. The group met formally for the first time in December 1966 for an organizing meeting and soon after chose its name, the Committee of Returned Volunteers (CRV).

As the Vietnam War continued to escalate, my attention was increasingly absorbed with antiwar activity and specifically with the CRV. Its members shared, and virtually took over, my office space. Many CRV members were graduate students, and had the fortuitous combination of firsthand experience and some academic training related to various countries of Asia,

Africa, and South America. We did research and prepared position papers on several parts of the world, particularly Southeast Asia and Latin America. We participated in the major rallies and demonstrations in New York and Washington, which became increasingly frequent. We wrote a position paper on Vietnam, published in *Ramparts* in1967, which, while stating a slightly left-of-liberal consensus, served to stimulate interest in developing similar groups around the country. By 1968 there were CRV chapters in several cities, including Boston, Washington, Chicago, Madison, and the Bay Area. Several CRV members were graduate students at Columbia and took a major role in events at Fayerweather Hall, one of the buildings occupied during the spring of 1968. Many of us supporters were in and out of the university buildings during that period. On the night of the "bust," when the NYPD was called in to clear the campus, those of us with no Columbia affiliation stood on the sidewalk and watched while our friends were herded into paddy wagons and driven away.

In August, a sizable group of us joined the people in the streets at the Democratic Convention in Chicago. We were sitting on Michigan Avenue in front of the Hilton when the police charged, and we scattered to the four winds. I had my first experience with tear gas there, and learned that those of us who wear contact lenses suffer an extra dose of pain from the gas.

We were also part of the small march that the comedian and civil rights activist Dick Gregory attempted to lead to the convention site from the park across from the Hilton. The situation was volatile. Although a majority of those participating were by then veterans of many demonstrations, others had little or no street experience. I asked a teen-aged boy standing near me whether he had ever been in a demonstration before. No, he answered, he'd watched what happened the night before on television, and he had come into the city to be part of what was going on—probably motivated in roughly equal parts by curiosity and outrage. We were forced to turn back when we came to a section of the street where, hemmed in by buildings on either side, we met a line of armed personnel carriers and National Guardsmen, fixed bayonets protruding from their guns, who blocked our way forward.

*I*n the spring of 1969 the CRV was invited to send two delegations of twenty each to Cuba, and I applied to go. By this time the Cuban Revolution was ten years old. Since the break in diplomatic relations, the U.S. government had engaged in a relentless effort to isolate and undermine Cuban society. The travel ban remained in effect, and travel to Cuba as a U.S. citizen potentially meant the loss of one's passport and of the right to travel outside the

United States. This trip represented my most decisive break with the world in which I had grown up. It also led to some of my most profound ecumenical experiences.

While the selection criteria for those who would make this trip were being debated and the selection process was under way, I was terminated from my campus ministry position, along with three of the other four ecumenical campus ministry staff. Those of us who lost our jobs had all supported dissident students the previous year and been outspoken in our opposition to the war in Vietnam. My letter of termination ironically informed me that the board's action reflected no negative judgment on either my work or my person. They had just decided they wanted a "clean sweep" and a "fresh start." The Ecumenical Foundation some years later went out of existence, and its treasurer, Robert Preuss, who had been one of the staff's harshest critics, was jailed for misuse of United Methodist pension funds to support some failed personal financial ventures.

After much internal questioning, and after relinquishing any hope of ever obtaining State Department clearance to work in UNESCO or any similar agency, I prepared for my first visit to Cuba. I think I used the balance remaining in my Ecumenical Foundation travel budget to underwrite my trip.

"What will people think of us?" my brother objected, echoing my father's puzzled and anxious question a decade earlier when told of my fellowship to Geneva, when I told him and my mother of my plans to go to Cuba. My initial response was, You don't have to tell anyone; "people" will never know I went. Only much later did I hear the anxiety and fear of the unknown that accompanied the question—an anxiety and fear that, truth be told, I shared. However, I carried my defiance of U.S. policy toward Cuba as a badge of honor and did not see it as an emblem of shame, although I knew there would be reverberations from this trip for years to come. "How will we get in touch with you?" worried my mother, a valid concern, since direct communication between the United States and Cuba was so difficult as to be virtually impossible. Although we were able to set up ways to communicate in the event of an emergency, by and large we had no contact with our families from the time we left the United States until we returned eight weeks later.

Our orientation session took place in Austin, Texas. Since one could not enter Cuba directly from the United States, we had to go on to Mexico City for our flight. As we boarded the buses that took us to the airport in Dallas, an FBI agent stood outside taking our pictures. Once we arrived in Mexico City, customs officials disappeared with our passports, while other

Mexican officials typed our answers to extensive questions onto forms. We were lined up in groups of three and photographed. We assumed the photos, our passports, and the forms were made available to U.S. personnel located inside the airport. After an extensive wait they finally stamped our passports "Mexico, D.F., Jun 20, 1969, Cuba." Only then did they allow us to board the Cubana flight to Havana. Except for the material found in my FBI file, the Mexican stamp is the only official record I have of the trip.

For three weeks we traveled throughout the western portion of the island: Havana, Matanzas, Varadero, Santa Clara, Pinar del Rio. We visited the literacy museum, which told the story of the 1961 campaign, during which anyone above the age of eleven who could read went into the countryside to teach those who could not. We went to a sugar mill, a cattle artificial insemination center, a psychiatric hospital, schools, hospitals, community centers, women's groups, and block committees called "committees for the defense of the revolution." We visited the Isle of Pines, renamed the Isle of Youth, the location of what appeared to be a perpetual summer camp for students from third world countries, except that the program was lots of work and study, and not much leisure. I was especially moved by our visit to Playa Giron, the Bay of Pigs, the site of the U.S.-sponsored invasion in 1961, which the Cubans characterize as the first defeat of imperialism in the Western Hemisphere, and during which many Cubans died.

From the beginning we objected to what we viewed as an agenda for tourists. We pointed out that we were all returned volunteers, and we wanted to do some kind of volunteer work in Cuba, too, in which we would be more directly connected to the Cuban people and make some material contribution to the revolution. Finally we were given work weeding and fertilizing banana plants (at who knows how much risk to the plants!). Later we worked on a coffee plantation. Of course, we were not nearly as efficient as the Cubans beside whom we worked, but at least we felt we were being more active participants.

The *comedor*, or dining hall, at the coffee plantation had a large mural that I can still picture. Inscribed under a tropical scene were the words: "LA REVOLUCION DE LA MUJER ES MAS GRANDE QUE LA PROPIA REVOLUCION." The woman's revolution is greater than the revolution itself. This was a graphic statement, in an unexpected place, of what I was finally beginning to realize. The government had given special attention to the role of women and provided retraining for women who had earned their living as prostitutes and maids. Other women were encouraged to enter the work force for the first time. Even with societal support, women were finding that they had signed up for a double shift—one outside the home, the other inside the home, maintaining family and household. The women in our CRV group had already begun to consider our own roles as women before we left the United States, and were meeting in women's caucuses. Our conversations in Cuba, however, let us look from a new perspective at gender issues as they affected our own lives.

We Cubans and North Americans also had vigorous discussion of the use of violence to achieve revolutionary goals. Many of us were committed to nonviolent means, however confrontational. Some of our Cuban hosts pushed us, hard, to think about whether such means were effective. Although sympathetic to the kind of desperation that leads one to resort to violence to confront injustice, I was unable to shift my perspective. I did not join those, who like the Weathermen later that year were calling for more violent action in the United States. Although I am still critical of violent means used to whatever ends, I suspect my stance may be as much a product of temperament and early conditioning as any reasoned ideological position.

After we had followed the itinerary of the planned portion of our trip, we then faced the problem of how to get back to the United States. Although we could leave from Mexico, we could not return through Mexico without authorization of the State Department which, for reasons of principle, we did not request and likely would not have received if we had. So our options were either to fly to Spain and then return to the United States or wait for a sugar freighter bound for Canada. The only problem with the freighter option was that they had no regularly scheduled sailing; we just had to wait until a ship was available.

During the days spent waiting for a freighter to dock, I reconnected with several people I had met in Europe in the early 1960s—Adolfo Ham, Carmen Barrosso, Luz Marina Ortiz, Dora Valentín, Sergio Arce. I also made new friends within the Cuban churches. I learned more about these churches, children of U.S. Protestantism cut adrift by the Cuban Revolution. I began to collect manuscripts on religious life in Cuba, which were later published in English as *Religion in Cuba Today: New Church in a New Society.*

Finally a ship docked in Havana harbor bearing a cargo of Peruvian fishmeal loaded in East Germany. (Because of the U.S. embargo, the cargo couldn't be carried directly from Peru to Cuba.) Once the fishmeal was unloaded, we boarded and sailed around the eastern end of the island. We who wanted work to do finally had our wish granted. It was our task, using a very strong disinfectant that wreaked havoc on gloveless hands and bare feet, to scrub all vestiges of the fishmeal out of the hold. When we reached Camaguey port, a public health inspector evaluated our efforts. The ship passed! A new cargo of raw sugar bound for Canada poured in. Then we headed west, past the U.S. base in Guantanamo Bay, then north to St. John, New Brunswick. From there we would return to the United States by bus from Montreal. There were approximately forty passengers on the freighter—the CRV delegation constituted half, the rest were more radical activists, dominated by the Weathermen. (Several months later, two of these Weathermen, Diana Oughton and Ted Gold, were killed in a 1970 townhouse explosion in Greenwich Village in a bomb-making effort gone awry.) The Cuban crew assigned the women to eat in the officer's mess, the men in the crew mess. The decibel level of the political discussions on board ship was often very high.

During the twelve-day trip back I pondered the "iron curtain" blocking any exchange of persons and information between the United States and Cuba, and the situation at home to which we were returning. I felt under siege in our conversations, lacking courage, or will, or conviction, to adopt a more militant position. I knew that my positions were shaped more by the theological convictions that had led me to East Harlem, Eastern Europe, and now Cuba than by ideological considerations. I was among those who argued against participating in the Days of Rage that fall—as I later declined to follow my closest friends into the Revolutionary Communist Party.

I had no employment to which to return. Progressive persons from several mission agencies shared my concern about our isolation from our Cuban brothers and sisters and helped fund a project that became the Cuba Resource Center (CRC). We sought to facilitate exchanges of information and persons between the United States and Cuba. During the two years I served as CRC staff, we produced several publications, initiated a newsletter, and organized three ecumenical trips to Cuba. In 1971, at the close of my tenure, I made my second trip to Cuba, this time with a group of church-related people. The CRC continued its work until 1979, two years after travel restrictions were lifted by the Carter administration and people began to move back and forth relatively freely. Unfortunately, the Reagan administration reimposed travel restrictions in 1982, and they have been maintained by each succeeding administration. In recent years the restrictions were codified by the U.S. Congress through the Helms-Burton Act.

One of the unexpected results of my 1969 trip to Cuba was the initiation of my FBI file. I made my Freedom of Information Act request in 1980 and obtained a file of more than ninety pages, most of it blacked out for "national security reasons." I learned that the FBI had researched my personal and family history in 1969. They found nothing suspicious about anyone else in my solidly Republican family, but they followed my movements closely through 1972 and my first year in Boston. It was sobering to learn of the effort and resources they had expended on tracking my movements.

Though no longer employed by the Ecumenical Foundation, I maintained connections with the campus ministry world after I returned from Cuba. In the spring of 1970 several of us importuned United Ministries in Higher Education to make funds available to support a campus ministry women's caucus. This group, which continued for several years and sponsored a newsletter and regular gatherings, was a forerunner of the WSCF Women's Project in North America, a story that Jan Griesinger tells in greater detail.

I moved to Boston in 1971 with a one-year Danforth campus ministry grant. The next year, while I was making plans to return to New York, I experienced one of those providential moments of convergence. Out of nowhere, I received offers of housing and work that kept me in Boston, where I remain. I was invited to apply for a year-long appointment in women's studies at Harvard Divinity School; from that experience came the book *Sexist Religion and Women in the Church: No More Silence*. I was invited to join a team ministry at Church of the Covenant in downtown Boston; I remained for fourteen years. I was offered a cheap and spacious apartment in the Jamaica Plain section of Boston; I still live in J.P., half a mile from my original apartment.

I struggled with the issue of whether to be ordained. Although I had seen Letty Russell functioning in a pastorate in 1958, the expectation then was that women would be directors of Christian education, or marry ministers, not *be* ministers. When I was finally ordained in 1975, Letty preached at my ordination. At that point I sought ordination because I was in a parish, the person primarily responsible for the liturgy, and I could not tolerate being liturgist without being able to celebrate the sacraments. I gradually realized that, notwithstanding the rhetoric about the theology of the laity, most male seminary graduates who worked in the church managed to overcome any principled reservations they might have had about ordination. Only the women were scared off. The current generation of women appears to be successfully removing that roadblock.

In 1974 I entered law school. After graduation I worked in a community law practice for twelve years. I was an assistant bar counsel of the Board of Bar Overseers of the Supreme Judicial Court of Massachusetts from 1989 until the fall of 2001. In this job I prosecuted lawyers for professional misconduct. The position required me to deal with many unhappy and often troubled people, whether lawyer, client, or bystander.

I have traveled to Cuba fifteen times since 1969 and have authored or coauthored several articles for anthologies about Christianity and Marxism in Cuba, and women in Cuba. I have continued to participate in denominational and ecumenical activities. I am currently a parish associate at Fourth Presbyterian Church in South Boston, the moderator of the permanent judicial commission of the Presbytery of Boston, and a U.S. Trustee for the World Student Christian Federation, with particular responsibility for follow-up among "senior friends" during the federation's second century.

*I*f ever I had questioned whether I defined myself as an American Christian or a Christian American, that question was resolved in 1969. Notwithstanding the opposition of my own government, my primary allegiances were to my commitments as a Christian to people with whom I shared religious and ethical commitments and to active engagement in the ongoing struggle to respond to God's call to do justly and love mercy. I am interested to see how these will play out in this final third of my life.

In thinking about the years described above, I return repeatedly to the close of W. H. Auden's prose poem, "For the Time Being."

> He is the Way.
> Follow Him through the Land of Unlikeness.
> You will see rare beasts, and have unique adventures.

The "rare beasts" and "unique adventures" that have graced my life are many. I come to this part of my life with a sense of profound gratitude, coupled with a profound disappointment that the current generation must face again, in different guise, so many of the issues with which we previously struggled.

CHAPTER 10

Jan Griesinger

In my freshman year at DePauw University, in 1960, I decided to write my English term paper on the topic "Being a Minister's Wife." My English professor thought it was a very strange topic. I was writing in part about my local church pastor's wife and how difficult it was for her to balance all the demands made on her. But I think I was writing myself a future—the only one I could imagine. No one had really asked me as a child, "What are you going to be when you grow up?" There was no need to ask, because women in my class and race—white, suburban, middle class—had only one future: husband and children.

I was the only woman in my graduating class at DePauw, a United Methodist college in Greencastle, Indiana, to major in religion. I was the only woman who entered the sermon-writing contest open to college students. In both situations, I felt odd. Certainly I had no name to put on the experience of being a minority of one, of feeling that male professors and students were nervous about my presence, that they saw my entering the sermon contest as a kind of joke. I knew I was being teased in class in a way different from my male colleagues. I believe now it was a form of flirting. Why did I persevere? Apparently I had come to see my future as working in and for the church. I liked the academic challenge of philosophy and theology. I think my competitive streak, nurtured in many card games growing up, led me to want to play this game, too. I had tried to play sandlot softball with the boys but was forever consigned to right field.

Church was an important activity in my family—a suburban Chicago family with two parents, three sisters, and a brother. We all went to Sunday school, Sunday worship, potlucks, and special activities. My parents took on leadership positions—typical ones, of course: my father on the church finance committee, my mother in the women's organization. When a director of Christian Education came to our church in 1959, when I was seventeen, I found myself very interested in what she was doing, and I began to entertain some possibility of a job like that for myself. But apparently the concept of "minister's wife" had a much longer tenure in my consciousness.

Although I was in the Honors program in the Philosophy and Religion Department, I told my advisor midway through my senior year that I didn't see any reason to finish my thesis, because I was planning to get married. Bless his heart, he listened to me and reminded me that I had a good mind and that I should finish the work because I had the capability. I was lucky to have this man as a substitute for my regular advisor, who was on sabbatical that year and who I fear would have supported my idea of quitting.

I was active in my campus ministry, the United Campus Christian Fellowship (UCCF), which was based at the local Presbyterian church and staffed by the pastor, Rev. Dennis Shoemaker. Like the other women in the group, I took a turn coordinating the Sunday evening meals but otherwise stayed in the shadow of the older, wiser male students, who far outnumbered the women. The men were largely philosophy and religion majors, too, and the debates were heady. We used WSCF study books such as Alexander Schmemann's *For the Life of the World*. I attended an important national UCCF conference in Beloit, Wisconsin, in the summer of 1962. Yet whatever leadership skills I might have had were neither spotted, utilized, nor encouraged.

Despite my freshman paper and my caution to my advisor, I can't remember having any particular interest in getting married. My family expected that I would go to college. After that, there apparently were no expectations. I doubt they pressured me to get married. But it was in the air, in the molecules, so pervasive an expectation that it overrode any conscious decision making. There were a few women at my college who went on to seminary, and I knew I wanted to go too. Nevertheless, after I graduated I married a Southern Baptist schoolteacher I had met in Green Lake, Wisconsin, at the national American Baptist conference grounds, where we both served on the summer staff. We went to live in his hometown, which was how things were done at that time, and I began work as a director of Christian Education at Christ Church, United Church of Christ, in Ft. Thomas, Kentucky, a Cincinnati suburb. Since there was no seminary in the immediate area, I poured myself into my work and then into denominational activities.

United Church of Christ clergy, events, and national conferences became my window to the world outside my suburb and my marriage. The Ohio Conference of the UCC served as the setting where I could hear debate on social issues of the day. Thank God for those folks in our conference who

knew there was a war happening in Vietnam. They brought a resolution opposing the war to the Ohio Conference annual meeting in June 1966. I don't
recall knowing anything about the war at that time, but my clergy colleagues
and friends were involved, and they pulled me into the conversation and the
excitement of bringing an important issue to the floor. Being female brought
me the task of typing the resolution as it was drafted by the men around me.
I was a good girl and played my part. I was still in right field, but at least I
was in the most interesting game being played at the time that I knew of.

A crisis within my marriage prompted me to flee my Christian Education position. I was already perceived as too liberal for some leaders in the
congregation, so my days appeared numbered anyhow. Seminary was still
beckoning me, as it had been since I finished college. I began in March 1967,
commuting forty-five miles each way from my suburban Cincinnati apartment to United Theological Seminary, a United Methodist seminary, in Dayton, Ohio. I had no idea, however, what I would do with my seminary
education.

During my first week of seminary, several students reported on a conference about the war in Vietnam they had attended in Washington, D.C.,
sponsored by Clergy and Laity Concerned. I was intensely interested in their
report and identified them as students I wanted to spend time with. They were
all male, of course. I joined First Reformed Church, United Church of Christ
(UCC), an integrated activist congregation, and spent the summer of 1967
helping with Bible school and day camp. In addition, I was finishing a term
on the University of Cincinnati campus ministry board, and I met people there
who steered me into involvement with Vietnam Summer in 1967. This was a
national effort among peace activists to go door to door talking with people
about the war. The Vietnam Summer group in Cincinnati met regularly and
provided strategies and materials. In the evenings, I knocked on my neighbors' doors in my suburb, pretty much alone. I recall being nervous but sum-
moning courage, knowing that this was the right thing to do. I don't believe
I had great success, but many of the other activists who were working on
more friendly turf were impressed that a nice suburban housewife like me
would take on this work.

At the end of the summer, at age twenty-five, I was chosen co-chair of
a new organization, Cincinnati Action for Peace. Over Labor Day weekend,
I attended the National Conference for New Politics in Chicago, an attempted
coalition between the civil rights and peace movements, with Martin Luther
King, Jr., as the keynote speaker. Later that year, I was arrested at a draft
resistance sit-in. It was my first experience of civil disobedience and arrest.

I don't think I knew one other person being arrested that day. I can't say what drew me to be involved. Other activists have used language like being "drawn in" or "being led." I can only say that I felt I couldn't *not* do it. It was the right thing to do. It was also exciting, pushing the edge of respectability, I suppose. And it was a new game with different rules, far less competitive.

I had gone downtown to the Cincinnati federal building on that very cold December day wearing my nice wool pleated skirt and stockings. This was my everyday work and school outfit, and I guess it didn't occur to me to wear anything different. I remember the arresting officer giving me the chance to get up and leave. He said something like, "What's a nice girl like you doing with a bunch of weirdos like this?" The others at the sit-in were mostly students from Antioch College and a few from Hebrew Union Seminary, and they were at least dressed for the occasion in jeans. We were hauled away and imprisoned in an ancient jail underneath the old courthouse. Many of us were packed into a single cell. We sang and kept ourselves entertained. Soon it dawned on me, and I think on most of the other women, that we had entered another world, one where we had absolutely no control and could expect no special attention. Requests to be let out to go to the bathroom or to take medication were ignored. No one could tell us what was going to happen or when. And no, we could not make any phone calls.

We waited all day and eventually were taken upstairs for our court hearing. Several of the more experienced activists had decided ahead of time to be noncooperators. They did not walk into the court room. They did not give their names. And they were not treated well. The judge decided arbitrarily to triple the usual bond for trespassing for all of us. The Antioch students had come prepared to pay $30, or 10 percent of the bond, and get out, but the bond was set at $900 and we were to pay the whole amount. All of us were taken to the Cincinnati workhouse, an even more ancient prison, where the reality of our action really began to sink in.

I was one of the fortunate few allowed a phone call that evening. My friends in Cincinnati Action for Peace, longtime Communist Party activists, put their home and property up to serve as my bond, and I was freed to go home and spend the night in my own bed. My husband was not impressed. His parents were even less so when they read my name on the front page of the newspaper the next morning. My decision to take some of our savings to bail out two other women who had no college or family connections was the beginning of the end of a not-so-great marriage. We were divorced the following year, and I moved to the seminary in Dayton. Shortly after that I began an eight-year relationship with a fellow seminarian though we never married.

I continued to try to organize seminary students to participate in local antiwar demonstrations and draft resistance actions. At that time, many male students found a haven in the seminary, since their enrollment got them an automatic draft deferment. Therefore the war didn't affect them personally. Despite the ever-present media hype to the contrary, not all students in the 1960s were out in the streets. I know: I was trying, with minimal success, to get them out there. At most, only 10 percent of the student body ever became active in the antiwar movement. Nonetheless, I felt compelled to keep organizing and drew strength from other movement activists, mostly outside the church. There were few women in the leadership.

My privileged background had given me a good education. I had learned to think and write critically, to question the assumptions of the mainstream, to speak well in "standard" English. I added to that knowledge lessons in how to organize projects, march for peace and justice, and work to oppose racism. I went with a carload of male seminarians to march in Memphis, Tennessee, three days after Dr. King was assassinated in April 1968. I marched in Washington, D.C., several times, protesting the Vietnam War. I felt I was getting my real education in the streets, at demonstrations, writing for and distributing an underground newspaper, attending community meetings where strategies were debated, and at other events outside the seminary's ivy-covered walls.

Yet my own life as a white woman didn't take on a clear shape and meaning until the women's liberation movement came into my life. Organized religion was not the seedbed for this movement in my experience. Although I was an organizer at my seminary, I had no contact with any national student Christian or seminarian movements. The national University Christian Movement had dissolved by this time, and I knew of no national Christian student events to give me a sense of connection. My teachers and supporters were other antiwar and community activists. Many of those who were younger than I had dropped out of college "for the movement." Most of those who were older were longtime Quakers, Unitarians, or members of the ACLU. I did not know any women clergy or church leaders, or any women who spoke out about the situation of women's lives. For me, it was the arrival of feminism that captured my imagination and made me a convert. The feminist movement was contagious and propelled me back into church-affiliated organizations to reach other women with the good news of liberation to the captives.

Dayton Women's Liberation came into being in September 1969, my last semester in seminary. A seminary friend's wife dragged me to the first

meeting. She had attended an underground (alternative) newspaper conference in the summer and had heard about this new thing called "women's liberation." I was pretty suspicious and didn't really want to go. I felt I could
already do whatever I wanted, and that so many other things, like war and
racism, were more important than worrying about the situation of women.
There were about twelve women at that first meeting, mostly in our twenties
and thirties. We were a mixture of antiwar activists, members of the League
of Women Voters, housewives, and others urged to attend by friends.

We began to meet weekly in a private home two blocks from the seminary campus. By the second or third meeting, I was very excited, as were
the others, about sharing the stories of our lives and our political perspectives. We reflected on what had happened to us or been prohibited to us
because we were women, discussed how to change the male-dominated movements from which we had come, and strategized about how to reach women
who didn't realize they were oppressed—any more than we had, just a short
time earlier. So many pieces of my own life that had not made sense began
to appear as part of a pattern that was so much bigger than I: never being
encouraged to have a career, being treated as a strange animal in college and
seminary classes, feeling pressured to marry, never getting to be out front as
a leader. I felt truly saved: from isolation, from always feeling "other."

We were unsure what we were doing and unsupported by the men in
our lives, as well as most of the women. We spent endless hours raising our
own consciousnesses, trying to get a fix on how our shared experiences
formed a pattern and how to integrate that knowledge into our political work.
We went from the political to the personal and always back to the political.
As unsure as we were, we started new consciousness-raising groups; spoke
at schools, colleges, churches, and community meetings; organized abortion
rights demonstrations; put out a newsletter; created a consciousness-raising slide
show and dramatic program; and evaluated elementary and high school text-
books for sexism. Women were hungry for what we had to say, and Dayton
Women's Liberation grew very rapidly. Women joined the new consciousness-
raising groups that we started every month. They came to meetings, wrote
for the newsletter, went along to observe, and eventually began speaking at
our public presentations. They were young and middle aged. Few were in their
fifties or older. None were factory workers. Almost none were women of color.

Feminists, in my world, included the hundreds of women involved in
Dayton Women's Liberation, a few women at my seminary who never joined
an organization but were beginning to see and hear what was going on around

them, and women such as Robin Morgan and Germaine Greer, who were brought in to speak on the Phil Donahue show, which then originated from Dayton. I met other feminists when I traveled to women's liberation conferences in Lexington, Kentucky, and Durham, North Carolina. Women friends I had met through United Church of Christ national events were also reading and talking about these new ideas. The movement later to be called "feminist" was happening everywhere in the early 1970s as far as I could see, along with tremendous resistance to it.

We were alive with the Spirit. Something had happened that changed our worldview, our priorities, our lives. It seemed momentous and prompted us to act boldly for change. Women were oppressed. This was wrong. It was a matter of life and death to many women facing abortion, rape, battering, and severely limited or meaningless lives. So of course we had to act. Now. Regardless of what might be said about us. And things were immediately said about us. Strangely, they are the same things still being said about us: lesbians, manhaters, too ugly to get a man, and so on.

The labor movement and the civil rights movements had blazed the trail. These movements taught me about the nature of power in this country and made clear who was calling the shots and who was benefiting. But white women, especially those like me who were raised with privilege and college educations, had long been seduced by the freedom and security that relationships with white men provided. We had no idea we were oppressed. We didn't realize what the "problem that had no name" (Betty Friedan, *The Feminine Mystique*) was. We had the raw life experience, but we had no political or analytical framework or even words to understand what was happening to us. Nor did we know that we were oppressing other people, despite our increasing consciousness about racism.

There were 8 women at my seminary in a student body of 175. The lone woman faculty member (teaching Christian Education, of course) was away on sabbatical my final year and missed all my excitement about women's liberation. In the spring of 1970, I graduated as the only woman Master of Divinity in my class, wondering what on earth I could do for a living.

I had met Rev. Elinor Galusha at a UCC conference for graduating seminarians a few months earlier and had heard her speak about her work with the Boston chapter of the Clergy Consultation Service on Abortion. This was a national organization begun in 1967 by Protestant clergy and Jewish rabbis to talk with women who had "problem pregnancies," as they were called then, and refer them, if requested, to doctors who were doing abortions. They made referrals to places like Montreal, Quebec; Rapid City, South Dakota; and Mexico City. Abortions were not legal in any state at that time.

A light went on, and I saw a direction for my life that could bring my faith, my seminary degree, my politics, and my feminism together. I met with leaders of the Clergy Consultation Service on Abortion from other cities in Ohio and talked with my Dayton Women's Liberation sisters about how this organization might meet the need we were discovering for information on and access to abortion. I was able to negotiate a very part-time job with the Dayton Area Campus Ministry organizing this specialized counseling service. This temporary job constituted enough of a "call to ministry" that I was able to get ordained within a few months. Several white male UCC pastors served as my advocates, or it never would have happened. There were no women at all on the decision-making committees.

About a year after my ordination, a new opportunity opened that further allowed me to bring my feminist politics and my church experience together. My campus ministry boss's wife gave me one of the first newsletters ever produced by the Women's Campus Ministry Caucus, a national, ecumenical Protestant organization that was barely off the ground. The newsletter contained a notice for the position of coordinator of the Women's Project for the North American Region World Student Christian Federation. The person hired was expected to be involved in a grassroots feminist organization and would not need to move to a national WSCF office in New York City. Charlotte Bunch, former president of the U.S. Methodist Student Movement and UCM, who advocated for and succeeded in creating the position intended this stipulation as a critique of those who worked in national or international church bureaucracies, were not doing any local organizing, and were thus too far removed from action on the streets.

I applied and was hired, and found myself involved in the national student Christian movement network for the first time at age twenty-nine. I was not that familiar with the World Student Christian Federation, but the idea of working nationally and internationally to bring the good news of women's liberation into the church and student Christian movements was very exciting to me. My job with the WSCF enabled me to use skills I had learned in my formal education and in movement activism to reach out to students and women.

Part of my job was to find other women in campus ministry as I traveled around the country on WSCF business. I provided support to women across the country, especially in isolated places, through personal phone calls and letters. This was a wonderful opportunity for me personally, as it put me in contact with women who were putting their feminism to work on campuses: students, secretaries, wives, board members, part-time and full-time campus ministers. In whatever way they were connected to campus ministry, we wanted to bring them together in a network. There were very few ordained women campus ministers. Our feminist politics took grave offense at separating the women who did the work without titles or status from the few women who were ordained or had titles.

Early leaders in establishing the Women's Campus Ministry Caucus included Judy Davis, Helen Ewer, Alice Hageman, Ellen Kirby, Lynn Rhodes, and Virginia Wadsley. and. Several of those who were based in New York City had taken aggressive action in 1970 to demand funds for an organization to benefit women. They went uninvited to the national, ecumenical United Ministries in Higher Education offices, made their case, and were eventually granted $30,000. These funds were stretched over four years, making it possible for women to attend meetings once or twice a year. We held these meetings in different locations across the United States in order to reach women who would not think of traveling across the country or had no resources to do so.

From the same $30,000 we gave seed money to women's projects sprouting up on campuses through the efforts of women serving in campus ministry. Some of those projects included the Valley Women's Center in Northampton, Massachusetts, the Center for Women's Affairs at the Graduate Theological Union, a women's conference at Prentiss Institute in rural Mississippi, the republication of *The Women's Bible* by the Seattle Coalition Task Force on Women and Religion, and a women's group begun by the campus minister in Menominee, Wisconsin. We rotated newsletter production around the country so that each woman would learn how to produce a newsletter and would give it a local flavor and perspective. In the era before desktop publishing, mimeograph production was most common. Content and style varied tremendously, but most issues were readable, and our feminist politics of shared power were being lived out.

We held our own conferences just prior to each conference of the National Campus Ministry Association to meet one another and discuss how to change our denominations and our campus ministries. We shared our stories: the way men in campus ministry were treating us, the way male church leaders were ignoring us, the way the men we lived with were threatened, the sexism we endured at national campus ministry conferences, the way our jobs were so part time or tenuous or even unpaid, the way we risked our livelihood by being feminist activists. These stories helped us make sense out of our isolated experiences as women leaders in the church. And we examined the politics of sexism, racism, imperialism, and heterosexism in order to move from the personal to a systemic analysis of our experience.

We laughed and prayed and danced and shared bread and wine. We indeed reimagined the sexist traditions we had inherited and created liturgies that offered a celebration of our survival. I recall several specific occasions of great joy. We were meeting in Atlanta and went out one evening to visit the Underground entertainment area. I love to dance and made sure to organize an evening out to do just that. We ended up at a club, dancing wildly, in pairs of women, to some 1920s Charleston music. We weren't about to let anybody turn us around. A closing worship service during our meeting in Minneapolis was equally meaningful, if more sober. We pondered the rich realities of sisterhood and rejoiced that when we were among our sisters, we received bread, not a stone. I felt an incredible sense of privilege: I worked for a living (by this time $400 a month!) finding women like me, giving and getting support, and building a network for change. And I got to travel as a feminist evangelist.

My work with the WSCF added global dimensions to our conversations. A key part of my job was assembling materials on women from around the globe. The first edition of what later became WSCF Book vol. III, 2/3, *Women in the Struggle for Liberation*, was collected in 1972 with assistance from Helen Ewer and Chris Hynes in the Boston area. There were few networks available then to locate articles, especially since our criterion was that the material must be written by women who were natives of the countries they were writing about. We didn't trust men writing about us, and we knew enough not to trust the accuracy of Americans writing about Tanzanians. We scrounged from every source we could think of and received material from both secular and church-related women's networks.

We managed to gather forty-five different articles, and we grouped them according to the regions of the WSCF: Africa, Asia, Europe, Latin America, Middle East, and North America. We were very excited to know that this uprising of women not only was happening in the United States, but was indeed worldwide. Knowledge of what these women authors were writing about gave us good ammunition for those leftist men who tried to tell us that women's liberation was just a white, bourgeois thing. This material was typed and pasted up by hand, then collated and stapled on my living room floor.

I personally carried about fifty of these packets in my backpack to the WSCF General Assembly in Addis Ababa, Ethiopia, in December 1972, where I spoke to the plenary as part of the North American Region panel. I compared women's oppression to the oppression of colonialism. (I wonder whether I would be so bold to do this today.) When I consulted Charlotte Bunch about doing this, she warned me that it would be unpopular, but encouraged me to do what I felt I should. I realized that a white woman from the United States making this comparison was in a precarious position. Except for positive comments from a few feminists attending as delegates from Europe, my presentation met with responses that ranged from stony silence to disbelief to open hostility. Several men confronted me with great anger. I was nervous, but I told them I would need to speak to women from their countries before I could believe their insistence that women were not oppressed where they came from.

Over the next three years, I continued working for WSCF North America, spreading the gospel of feminism and liberation theology as well as a commitment to antiracism, anti-imperialism, and antimilitarism. Our colleagues in WSCF offices around the globe were providing us with excellent theological reflections on their own struggles for justice amid corruption and dictatorship. I struggled with our North American regional committee, which was overwhelmingly male during those years. We complained, cajoled, and hounded the men to send women representatives to the meetings. We tried to get them to see that their old boy networks, which gave them the opportunity to travel to national and international meetings, were doing nothing for women or people of color. The names we suggested to be leaders of events were not names these men knew. Since they all knew the same circle of male presenters, their suggestions always won out. They didn't get it and couldn't understand where in the world our anger was coming from.

The Women's Campus Ministry Caucus became Women in Campus Ministry by 1973 and in 1980 became Campus Ministry Women, with a broader base. We lobbied our male colleagues to make sure women were present and visible as speakers at national conferences and in staff positions. We tried to get more women hired. We tried to get more women ordained. We tried to get feminist faculty into the seminaries and feminist theology into seminary curricula. We tried to get WSCF internationally to encourage and empower women. It was both exhilarating and frustrating work. I loved it and was sustained by complaining to my Dayton Women's Liberation friends continually about sexism in the church.

It is hard to imagine how little a feminist perspective was understood at that time. Now, even if people don't agree with it, they are aware that such a perspective exists and have some clue about what it is. I remember a small group of men and women at a national campus ministry conference in Colorado in the mid–1970s. Our women's movement had come far enough that our insistence on sharing stories was beginning to have an impact on events. When people in our group were asked to go around and share their stories, one of the male campus ministers said that he didn't have a story. He had simply graduated from college, gone to seminary, and begun work as a minister. I recall being terribly angry at this stark example of white, male privilege, neither understood nor acknowledged.

Change was happening. Women were attending such events in larger numbers, but the resistance was very strong, even among liberal men who wanted to be our allies but just didn't get it. I was enraged and saddened when a woman colleague in Cleveland was fired from her campus ministry job for being an outspoken feminist, a not-very-out lesbian, and an organizer of campus feminist groups and programs on women's spirituality. I remember a woman colleague at the University of Illinois who was fired because her women's spirituality programs were labeled as witchcraft. At a Lutheran Campus Ministry conference I attended in the mid-1970s, the keynote speaker opened with a series of sexist jokes and then outlined what he said were his theological presuppositions. Within a few hours of his presentation, I sent him a written challenge, noting the unstated antiwomen presuppositions he had laid bare in his introductory jokes, in addition to those stated theological presuppositions he had outlined formally. I expressed how angry this made me and how demeaning it was to women. A day or so later I was admonished by my boss, who said, "We are trying to cultivate relationships with the Lutherans, and you know they are conservative. Why would you confront one of their conference presenters and confirm their suspicions that the WSCF is a radical organization?" This scenario was to be repeated often, especially at campus ministers' conferences.

Feminism in those early days was heady, demanding and uncompromising. We knew we were up against deep-seated beliefs and prejudices that required more than the ladylike politeness we WASP girls were brought up with. We were inspired, on fire for the truth, tired of acting nice, and determined to turn the heavy wheel of history that had ground up so many women before us. I saw my task as a feminist to name and challenge sexism, especially among self-identified liberals like campus ministers who believed themselves to be on the cutting edge of the church. What always seemed to be at issue was my manner or style of opposition or confrontation, rather than the issue at hand. Admitting that sexism was present and struggling together to make change seemed to be out of the question. Is this not a classic situation that students and activists have always faced: being seen as challenging, rejecting authority, uppity, not properly respectful, unsophisticated, too direct, not tactful enough, too emotional, or limited in perspective because of our age, sex, race, sexual orientation?

In the process of struggling and empowering others, I was, of course, getting an incredible education: in Canadian–American politics from the Canadian Student Christian Movement, in the realities of contemporary American racism from people of color and white activists among us, in imperialism and the terrorism of death squads from Korean and Brazilian and Filipino WSCF activists. I was learning to organize, to make a diffuse national organization function across the miles, to share the wealth of access to travel and international visitors. As my hope for America and its church institutions dimmed, I was increasingly inspired by Christians in South Africa, Lebanon, and Cuba. This, in turn, made me understand that they were counting on the vigilance of activists in the United States to keep them from being killed. Brazilian leaders from the WSCF in Latin America talked about being in prison and managing to sing and celebrate communion (without the bread and wine) while torture was closing in on them. I was awestruck. Could the Christian faith really be a resource of hope and courage in the face of death?

This new sense of the liberating power of Christianity contradicted my feeling that white American Protestantism seemed fixated in the past, having accommodated to power and privilege. Protestant churches by and large avoided involvement in the human rights and antiwar movements, continued their racist attitudes and practices, and were fearful of anything that seemed like change. I found I was not nourished or challenged there, except in the presence of justice-seeking colleagues who hovered around the fringes of church institutions. The changes taking place in American politics during the 1960s and 1970s, if not yet in the church, gave us a sense of ourselves as American radicals who were bravely standing up to great power. This sense of historical importance often blinded us to our own naïveté and protected status. Although we were committed to bringing together people from very different places, we didn't have much multiracial, multicultural experience.

I found myself deeply conflicted over an event that took place in 1974. A woman from the Korean Student Christian Federation (KSCF) was traveling across the United States for the WSCF. I drove her to the national student YWCA conference in Oklahoma, where she spoke openly about the struggle of the KSCF for democracy, the street demonstrations they were taking part in, the arrests and the danger they faced. Out of my own lack of experience and my privilege, I had neglected to explain in introducing her that her presence with us could in fact be dangerous to her and to her family back home. When I did so a few hours later and asked that people tell her story but not use her name, I ran into a firestorm. I was accused of manipulating her, maybe luring her against her better judgment to speak publicly. I was accused, particularly by African American women in attendance, of operating in a racist way by "using" this woman to further some agenda of my own. The Korean student was very confused about what was going on, and I struggled to make sense of it all.

The complexities of racism, sexism, and American dominance came together in a way difficult to untangle. Within a short time, I came to believe several things. First, I was very sorry I had not introduced her in a way that put her speaking to us in context. I should have explained the KSCF's political understanding that American imperialism was destroying their economy and their democracy, and that many of them could not get out of the country to tell the story. It was their hope that if Americans understood why Korean students were in the streets, we would become allies. Second, I was aware that racist and sexist stereotypes had conspired in this situation to make women think that a shy, soft-spoken Asian woman was not her own person, and to imagine that she herself didn't know the risks she was taking, that she was not fully in charge of the decision to speak publicly. I saw how prejudice infects the psyches of the oppressed. Third, I was forced to confront the conviction of African American students that white women were not to be trusted. My behavior had given away my own biases and lack of understanding. I am grateful that they were willing to challenge me. I certainly expected white men to learn something when I confronted them. Being confronted by people of color was both personally unsettling and very important in my own education. I have carried the belief that anger and conflict are prime venues for learning. In the 1990s, this approach seems to be glibly discredited in favor of a belief in kinder, gentler, nicer (whiter?), safe small groups of "people like us."

I got further into conflictual politics when Campus Ministry Women began to seek additional, substantial funding from two foundations that were making grants to campus ministry programs: the Danforth and the Lilly foundations. It was the first lesson for most of us in what happens when a small feminist organization seeks support in the mainstream. The patriarchs who controlled these funds were not comfortable with feminism or with the antiinstitutional, shared leadership by consensus we chose for our business affairs. We weren't incorporated or tax exempt yet, although we did do this eventually to become more "legitimate" in their eyes. We hadn't gone to the right schools and didn't have any men on our board. We didn't even have a board! The foundations didn't know us personally and couldn't get any of the old boys in their network to vouch for us. They did, however, know some women in campus ministry who were not feminists, and they hired them as consultants to find out who we were and to advise them on how to proceed. Patriarchal power maintenance tactic number one: Hire safe women who are accountable only to the men who hire them.

After a number of meetings and phone calls, the Danforth Foundation convened a larger consultation of Jewish, Catholic, mainline, and evangelical Protestant women. Campus Ministry Women had been largely Protestant, and this seemed too narrow to the foundations. Many of the Catholic women knew each other through the Catholic Campus Ministry Association. We were coming together in an interfaith dialogue for the first time and had had no chance to share the differing perspectives of our religious traditions. In addition to getting acquainted by sharing stories and hearing speakers at this three-day consultation, we were pressed by the foundation's agenda of forming a national organization that would be acceptable to foundation fathers. We had just met and were not yet ready to get married. The Protestant women, who were more involved in grassroots feminist movements, soon felt distracted from our feminist agenda by the institutional complexities and by women who were trying to play the game by the rules. Power maintenance tactic number two: Bring people together with widely differing experiences, try to get them to operate on the basis of the least common denominator, and get them to fight among themselves.

We did in fact form an organization and a steering committee. We incorporated as a nonprofit corporation. We applied for tax exemption. We wrote grants. And we were turned down. Power maintenance tactic number three: Lead them on, take up their time, and then drop them. We continued as a small, underfunded group of women in campus ministry, predominantly Protestant but with a significant Catholic presence. Many women paid a high price for our efforts: being terminated from positions; leaving positions when the sexism became intolerable, as did a woman staff member in the national office of United Ministries in Higher Education; having great difficulty finding jobs, as I did after my WSCF project was terminated.

By 1975 it became clear that there was little ongoing denominational support for the WSCF Women's Project. I was on my own to continue the project. The funds that had been committed were directed to other things. Women were not much of a priority. We had little entrée into the male networks at 475 Riverside Drive, the New York City address of the national offices of many denominations. This was my first experience at fund-raising, and I did it with very little confidence and almost no success. Our male allies either were not behind the Women's Project or were not willing to make it a high priority. Our women's network was being eroded by the efforts to gain foundation funding, and we did not yet have women executives in leadership positions in national church structures.

So the project disappeared and I was unemployed. I was saved once again by the women's campus ministry network. Women I had met at Campus Ministry Women conferences urged me to apply for a job in campus ministry and paved the way for my interview in 1976. I was hired as a codirector of United Campus Ministry at Ohio University, where I have served for twenty-six years. In 1977 I came out as a lesbian, and since that time I have been very active locally and nationally in the United Church of Christ as an organizer and spokesperson for lesbian, gay, bisexual, and transgender people. In 1979, I cofounded an international women's community and outdoor feminist education center called the Susan B. Anthony Memorial UnRest Home Women's Land Trust with my partner of many years, Mary M. Morgan.

I believe that Charlotte Bunch's vision in establishing the WSCF North America Women's Project—that women needed to articulate their own experience, challenge the churches to work for justice, and join together as key participants in struggles for liberation—gave birth to many lasting accomplishments. The strong feminist network among women in church leadership today was fostered in a significant way through the women in the campus ministry movement. We serve in every part of our denominational structures and are making a difference in church policy, because of what we learned in Campus Ministry Women. We have a long-established network and can count on each other for support. We have not, however, been successful in stemming the tide of vanishing funds. Few of us work full time in campus ministry. Many positions have been discontinued altogether, and some are part time.

I continue to see myself as an activist, demonstrating, I hope, not only a feminist perspective but an international antiracist, anticapitalist commitment. The competitive game I learned from men on my neighborhood softball field and in my college and seminary classrooms gave way to collaborative work and skill-sharing with women. My work in campus ministry has included work with local women's collectives, cofounding a battered women's shelter, and cofounding groups like the Free South Africa group, the Coalition to Overcome Racism, the Middle East Peace Coalition, the Central America Solidarity Committee, and the Gay, Lesbian or Bisexual Employees at Ohio University. In addition to doing the administrative and fund-raising work necessary in campus ministry, I have chosen to work closely with students who want to change the world—including a student group called Swarm of Dykes—and through volunteer work and educational trips to encourage more mainstream students to see the dynamics of power and oppression in this country. In December 1999 I took a group of students to Cuba, hosted by the Cuban Student Christian Movement, a local WSCF affiliate. In 1993 and 2002 I took a group on a tour of historic sites of the civil rights movement.

I love doing this work. I get energy from working with people for systemic change in church and society. I have formed wonderful friendships on picket lines, at rallies, and on bus trips to Washington, D.C. I believe the Christian faith has resources for the long-haul liberation struggle, as feminist, civil rights, and gay and lesbian church movements and gatherings have demonstrated. African American spirituals, inclusive-language hymns, new music by gay composers, music from Asian, Native American, and Hispanic traditions— all of these nourish my spiritual life. I am privileged to live and work with others who celebrate that faith.

CHAPTER 11

Eleanor Scott Meyers

I do not know if I was born angry, but I doubt it. Too many of my baby pictures show me looking chubby and happy. And my overall sense of my life is that it has been overwhelmingly happy, privileged, and filled with contentment and satisfaction. Pretty good list.

Nevertheless, I have been angry, noticeably so. Anger has been creative for my life and I trust it has been so for others, as well. Without women's anger there probably would have been no social movements. I believe my anger and that of my sisters in the movements of this time kept us alert, committed, learning, and active. We learned to care about each other and ourselves while caring about the world we wanted, not only for ourselves, but for our children—all children to come. Our anger was—and is—a faithful journey.

My mother did not teach me to be angry. Dorothy Ann Davis Meyers was a smart woman, an intellectual who happened to live in a small Kansas town about an hour outside of Kansas City, Missouri. Her dad was a high school teacher and her mother, a housewife. She wanted to marry and have children (especially a daughter) someday, but she always had a life of the mind, nurtured by her father and by their life within the church.

Granddaddy Davis was a thinker. He moved slowly. When I was young I thought it was because he was old and fragile; later I came to understand that it was because he was taking the time to think. He taught the men's class at the local Christian Church (Disciples of Christ) in Merriam, Kansas. I remember how, on Sunday morning during Sunday school, his class sat in the back two pews of the church, and he stood in the middle of the third from the back pew, with a stack of books in front of him, and spoke to them in his steady, gentle voice.

Years later when I was in my teens, it was my mother, his daughter, who taught the adult Sunday school class at the larger, newer Christian Church in Mission, Kansas. She stood at the front of the church with a small lectern, and the place was always packed. Sometimes more people came to hear her lesson than came to listen to the sermon. Even though I was not in the room, I knew what the topics were because I watched her work all week at her desk reading Paul Tillich, Dietrich Bonhoeffer, and the Niebuhrs. The issues were the meaning of faith, the calling to be a Christian in the world, the social gospel, the relationship between politics and religion, the mission of the church in history, the future of religion, the definition of sin, the call for justice found in the Bible, loving your neighbor, and many more. I remember my mother saying that she went to church because it was the best place to do politics. As I got older I began to understand more fully what she meant.

Mother believed that the way into issues was to read for knowledge and understanding and then to act. She frequently took me with her when she was invited to give a talk. On one occasion, following her speech, several of the women from the audience gathered around her to continue the conversation informally. When she noticed me standing nearby watching, she called me over and introduced me. One of the women asked Mother if she was teaching me to cook. It might seem like a simple thing, but that question and my mother's response have turned out to be a very important moment in my life. I can remember the tone of her voice as well as her words: "I am teaching Eleanor to read. If she can read she can do anything."

My father was a carpenter, a builder with his own small business. He was a strong supporter of my mother and her work in the church and community. He worked more to help others than he did to earn a living. If my mother had not had the business sense to bring to their "team," we would probably not have had the middle-class economic well-being that we enjoyed by the time I was in high school. Dad was an artist with people and with his hands; he could fix anything from the broken toaster to the roof with a tree fallen across it, and he could design and build a new house. Or operate on the cat for worms. I came home from grade school one day to find Dad sitting on the back sidewalk with my cat. Dad had found a lump in Calico's neck. His diagnosis: worms. He had been to the pharmacy to buy ether and had me hold it under her nose and count to five. I did not feel at all certain about this but got caught up in the amazement of watching my father figure out what to do: to sterilize his knife in the flame, decide where to make the cut, take out the worms (he was right!), and sew the cat's neck up again with Mother's needle and thread.

There are three things that I remember as basic to my early development: family, the importance of the church, and the value of education—along with the willingness (even necessity) to break the rules from time to time. My parents were always willing to take a new path. The fact that they could envision something new was key to my development, for I learned by watching them discern what was important to them. In the early 1950s, blacks were not allowed to stay in motels or eat in good restaurants in Johnson County. I learned about this when our church brought a well-known gospel singer and speaker to town. Her name was Rosa Page Welch. My mother told me she was one of the most wonderful and gifted women of the church in this country, and yet she would not be welcomed in local establishments. And she would be our guest for overnight and a big Sunday dinner following worship.

Mother was right; Ms. Welch was terrific in the pulpit and in our home. I loved her immediately. But the day was not without incident. My mother's parents, who lived just around the corner, always ate Sunday dinner with us. Early that morning as we were all getting ready for church, my grandmother called to say that they would "skip" dinner since we had a guest. My mother was furious. "Mother, you WILL eat dinner with us just like every other Sunday noon. I will not serve the meal until you arrive, so be here on time!" Mother continued to fume as she prepared the roast so it would cook while we were at the service.

When we got home after worship, my brother and I sat and visited with Rosa while Mother and Dad completed work on the meal. My mother had helped me to see this day as a very special privilege for our family. I remember my grandmother's face when she arrived from church and took her place at the table. She was present but not very comfortable with her knees under the same table as our special guest's.

As theologians have pointed out, it is not we who have the church; it is the church, and the gospel, that have hold of us. This has been my experience, for as I have worked to compose my life, I have wanted to run from this church that has taught me to love my neighbor while people of the church, including members of my family, have ostracized persons of color and anyone a bit different from themselves. When I was a young mother in the early 1960s, frustrated with all the racism and sexism within the churches and thinking the best thing for me and my children was to leave the church, my mother admonished me: "I stayed in the church for you, not for myself, all these years, and you need to do the same for your children." I believe that she actually stayed for herself because she could not do otherwise, and in staying active where she was often a solo voice in matters of her concern, she did provide an important venue for my education.

Education was the theme of our lives, and Mother was in charge. She orchestrated church and also vacations: by the time my brother and I graduated from high school we had been in all but one of the forty-eight states, including inside the capitol building of each state, and we had learned about the state's history and the people who made it. Mother saw to it that we went to good schools and eventually got a college education. She was not pleased with my college choice but agreed to it, and so I went off to a small church-related college in Oklahoma to study Christian Education. That major lasted only two and a half weeks, as the classes were so dull and boring that I went to my advisor and told him I had to get a new major or leave. He helped get me into the School of Education.

These were the only options I knew for women in the late 1950s: teaching or Christian Education. I was female, had never known a woman to be a preacher, and the only women I had seen working in the church were directors of Christian Education. But my mind and heart were ready for something more than what the kindly professor of Christian Education had in mind for her female students in 1958. My preparation as an educator would serve me well, however, in the years ahead as I became first a public schoolteacher and eventually a campus minister, church pastor, seminary professor, and academic administrator. My life has been about teaching, and teaching has fit me well.

In 1960, at age twenty, I was married in Mission, Kansas, in our family's congregation, Countryside Christian Church. By 1978 I was a single parent, a seminary graduate, and an ordained minister. Between these two dates, an era of new social movements radically changed my future as a young woman and as a professional person, as it also altered the future of the social institutions that had been at the center of my early life. In retrospect, I see how very much my early life had been part of the preparation for these social developments, and how my life and work across these fifteen years were very much a part of these major social movements. At the time, however, I was not very aware that the steps I was taking were all that unusual. The paths I chose to walk just seemed the way ahead for any responsible, thoughtful woman in the place that I happened to be located.

My first teaching assignment was in the public schools in Tallahassee, Florida, where my husband and I were both graduate students at Florida State University. The move into the Deep South just after our wedding was an eye opener to me and a lesson in racism, my own and that of others. It was an entirely different thing to be an "activist" in Tallahassee than to be one in Kansas City. Simple acts like drinking from the "colored only" public water fountains were easy, I found, but not very effective in moving the decades of slavery, ostracism, and poverty. Nothing else was simple.

I will never forget the morning when three young black men walked up the sidewalk to the front door of the sanctuary of our local congregation. Worship was just beginning. There was a stir within the audience, as people could see the men out the side windows. Several of "our men" gathered at the back and went outside, closing the doors behind them. I went to the back of the hall myself and watched as the church men met and talked with the black men, who in a few minutes turned around and walked away. Worship proceeded as usual and nothing was said. I asked one of the men who had gone out to tell me what had happened. "We merely told them we were a closed community and that they were not welcome," he said. That did not sound like the appropriate way to describe the church to which I thought I belonged, I said. I was angry, and yet I had no idea what to do.

Within a few years, we moved to the North and my "southern chapter" was closed, but not before two events took place. First, some of the local church-run schools were ordered by their church hierarchies to integrate, and my segregated public school sixth grade class was suddenly filled with new students whose parents had pulled them out of the religious schools. I was, at the time, in the midst of a fight against the censorship of school library books. Books about blacks were under attack by a segment of the community. One particular book that I read aloud to my class each year, *Amos Moses, Free Man*, was a beautiful story about a freed slave. Some parents felt this book unfit for their children and wanted it banned. The struggles associated with the desegregation movement were being felt everywhere in the Tallahassee schools.

This was also a time of serious military buildup in Florida, in reaction to Castro, the Bay of Pigs, and the Cuban missile crisis. Even a busy young mother, full-time schoolteacher, and graduate student could not miss these developments, as the convoys of military machinery and personnel traveling through the city would close east-west traffic for hours at a time. As schoolteachers, we were instructed to have our students crawl under their desks to protect themselves from bombs, and we carried out elaborate school bus drills for getting our students back home in case of an atomic attack. My family was assigned space in a bomb shelter on the university campus. There was enough food and water, we were told, for two weeks—along with disposable diapers! I was not fooled. I knew that if atomic bombs were dropped, I would never get there and neither would my children, who were with a sitter on the other side of town.

In these early years, I was quite distant from any new developments regarding women's rights. I faced my first, but significant, personal struggle as a woman all by myself. As I completed my undergraduate degree in the School of Education, I applied for the master's degree program in Administration and Supervision. I had visions of becoming a school principal. I received a letter, however, stating that my request for admission had been denied. I could not believe it, and I certainly did not understand the decision. Feeling I had at least the right to an explanation, I called and asked for an appointment with the person who had signed the letter. I asked him to tell me why I had been denied entrance to this graduate program, and I handed him a copy of my transcript, noting my 4.0 record.

"Oh," he smiled, "it has nothing to do with your lack of academic promise. You have a wonderful undergraduate record. It is because you are a woman. We do not admit women students to the graduate program in Administration."

To him, that appeared to be a satisfactory answer. But my puzzlement was growing, along with my anger.

"May I please have a copy of the university's policy stating that you do not admit women to this program?" I asked. "I have a lawyer I would like to show it to." I will never know how the idea of saying this came to me; it was just there at that moment. My family had never turned to lawyers for anything, and I did not know a single lawyer. But I knew this rule was crazy and unfair and needed to be challenged.

"No, it is not written down anywhere; it is not really an official policy," he said, getting a bit uncomfortable. "You might say that it is an ethical issue for us, because we know that women will never be appointed principals or supervisors in the state of Florida."

I was dumbfounded. "Did it ever occur to you," I said, as I leaned toward him across his desk, "that, first of all, I might not remain in Florida all my life, or, for that matter, that perhaps things might change, even in Florida?"

Silence.

"You will hear from me," I said, as I left the room. He did not even get up from his chair. Within the week, before I had figured out what to do next, I received a letter of admission to the program and that summer became its first woman graduate student. A simple, individual contest, easily won and without any fanfare. I do not know if they changed their informal rule about this issue or whether they just let me in. I did not see myself as an actor in a larger movement of women to gain basic rights; not yet.

I had not really connected this experience to other issues that were all around me and which, in hindsight, shout out to me about women's rights. The list seems long and ponderous from this "other side." I was following a husband, making up my life around his priorities; I was pregnant partly because my husband did not enjoy the male birth control option (the condom); and I was earning the primary income. When his major professor moved, we followed him, leaving behind my graduate work. When it became too expensive for both of us to do graduate work, I was the obvious one to drop out. He was—everyone said—the one who would need to have the degree and the professional career "to provide for his family." That plan lasted about ten years.

Getting pregnant was, in the early 1960s, just what happened to women, and when you were pregnant and things went well, you had a baby, period. Women were easy victims in the matter. I was told by a doctor who I later found out "loved" for his patients to have babies, that I would never get pregnant, but that if there was any chance, it was now. This startled me. I did eventually want to have children, but at the moment I was the breadwinner in the family as well as a graduate student. I felt torn, but decided to stop using my "rubber ring" as protection, thinking that it wasn't that I had been so smart for the first year of marriage, only infertile. Wrong. Within thirty days I was pregnant and back in the dear doctor's office in tears. He was not pleased—about the tears. "You should be happy and thankful," he said.

Almost to the day two years later, I was in my (new) doctor's office, having just delivered a second child. "I love these kids," I told him, "but this has got to stop. Tell me what to do." He gave me a prescription for the new "pill." I felt tremendous relief, and yet across the next few months or so, the level of tension I felt rose to new heights. I mentioned this to the doctor during a routine checkup, and he gave me a prescription for Valium. I was, after all, he said, a very busy young woman with two young ones in diapers. I slowly began to schedule my day around those four-hour spaces between doses of "my calming pill." One morning I fell apart in the middle of a huge grocery store, pushing two carts full of potatoes, canned goods and children. Behind on my schedule and still at the grocery when it was time for my pill, I grabbed one kid under each arm, leaving the full carts behind, and flew out of there, kids screaming, in a rage. Dashing to the apartment, I dropped the kids on the floor in the front room and went to the bathroom medicine cabinet, took out the Valium and threw all of them in the toilet, followed very quickly by the contraceptive pills. And I flushed it! With my coat still on, I went to the phone, called the gynecologist's office, and merely said to the receptionist, "Please tell the doctor that Mrs. Burchill is on her way."

When we arrived at the doctor's office, no one was pleased. But it was clear that I would be seen or else sit there with my two screaming children all day. They put me into a room in back. Finally the doctor came in and I told him I had just taken my last contraceptive pill and my last Valium, and that now he was going to have to do something, as I was not going to get pregnant again. He offered to insert an IUD (intrauterine device or "loop"). I said he would have to do the procedure immediately and he agreed. By the time my husband was home again, I was calm and renewed, having fully rearranged my former medicated life. At the same time, I swore that I would join in some effort to help legalize a woman's right to choose the time (or whether) to have a baby, and that I would become an advocate for male contraception efforts.

We left Tallahassee for Cleveland in late November of 1963. During the move, President Kennedy was assassinated in Dallas. By January, as we were settling into our new surroundings, President Johnson declared his War on Poverty, and the Civil Rights Act of 1964 was being crafted. We took an apartment in what was called a "transition" neighborhood, where about half the residents were black. Our neighborhood association, which I joined, worked to build an integrated neighborhood and to halt the "white flight" that was taking place as black families moved into the area. We joined the neighborhood church, which was still all white. The church was developing work groups for rehab efforts in the Hough area, the all-black ghetto, which was not far away. With two small children, I was unable to work (the cost for child care for two in diapers was almost exactly what I could make as an elementary schoolteacher) and we did not have enough money for me to continue my graduate work, so I volunteered for a work group.

I found a neighborhood center in Hough where I could leave my children as I participated with the work crew. They were the only nonblack kids in the center. Since I had no funds to help support the center, I bartered my teaching skills and set up classes for local mothers on topics they arranged: cooking, sewing, knitting, and hat-making. This was my first opportunity to be in friendship with women of color. During the days I was on the work crew, I used the skills learned at the elbow of my father, scraping and painting, restoring woodwork and floors, and basic plumbing. I can reset a toilet with the best of them.

The most important lesson I learned during my relationships with the people and the structures of the Hough area came on Thanksgiving Day in 1964, when my younger brother was killed in his Navy plane. The war in Southeast Asia was building, and his squadron was in Alaska en route to the war. From Cleveland, the war seemed very far away and the poverty of the ghetto so close. It was all a puzzle to me until that day, when the pieces, driven by my grief and anger over my brother's death, began to come together. I remember a growing suspicion that there was an important relationship between the war in Vietnam, the economic structures of our country, the racism of the church and the society at large, and the poverty of the Hough area. My brother's senseless death was a last straw; anger now became a defining part of my everyday life.

Two formative events took place my final year in Cleveland. Martin Luther King, Jr., met with our small group of community volunteers. We had lunch together in a church basement. He spoke to us about his dreams for our life together in this country and in this world. I was in awe of his words and his way of being. His ability to focus his anger in constructive ways impressed me, and I committed myself to do the same. The church continued to be my touchstone for thinking and action and continued to nourish my sense of hope in the waning days of my naïveté about the world in which I lived.

The civil rights struggle, the war in Vietnam, and the journey home to Kansas City to bury my brother were still fresh in my mind when, in the summer of 1968, my family moved back "home" to Lawrence, Kansas, where my husband got his first job. The children were beginning school, and I looked for part-time work in the schools. Another teacher and I both had young children and did not want to work full time, so we suggested that we share the position open for a sixth-grade teacher. The administrators would not even read our proposal.

Once again the community became my work. I became engaged in local politics and in the McGovern presidential campaign, as well as in the local church. My volunteer work centered on issues involving institutional racism, education about the war in Southeast Asia, and women's rights. I worked with Planned Parenthood and as a phone counselor for an underground medical clinic for those in need of safe, but illegal, abortion. All of these efforts brought me in touch with campus ministry at the university. Under the direction of one of the local campus ministry centers, I took the training to become a draft counselor.

With my children both in school, I became a graduate student again at the University of Kansas (KU) in the fall of 1969. A key issue on the campus and across the nation during this time was the war in Vietnam. Being a graduate student placed me right in the middle of the antiwar demonstrations on the campus, frequently accompanied by my children. During the 1969–

70 academic year things were hot on the KU campus, as they were over much of the United States. Students, along with faculty and campus ministry staff, succeeded in closing down the campus, stopping business as usual, and holding teach-in opportunities on the issues raised by the war.

I volunteered with a small local committee encouraging the Lawrence business community to boycott companies that continued to practice racist hiring procedures. Through that committee, I became closely connected with the work of the Student YWCA-YMCA on the university campus. One day the director of the Student Y, who had become a real colleague, asked if I would be interested in applying for her job as executive director of the KU-Y. She was moving away. She said the organization was faltering, lacking both funds and students, and a lot of rebuilding was needed, but she believed in the Student Y program and wanted it to continue. She felt I had the skills and the commitment to help make that happen.

I agreed to meet with the few members of the student board and found them determined not to let the KU-Y die. I arranged to visit with Tom Moore, who had been the longtime director of a once flourishing campus organization. Through Tom's vision for the Student Y movement, in which he had spent his entire professional career, I caught the deep spirit of the KU-Y and its history. I was not really looking for a job, but decided that if the students were willing for me to work part time, I would work with them. This decision would give me a base for my community efforts and a set of colleagues in the twenty-six campus ministers present in the university community at that time.

It was at the Campus Ministers' Association meeting in the spring of 1972, as I looked around that table of seminary-trained and ordained, male campus ministers, that I "found" myself in a very important way. If I had been a man, I realized, I would by now be a seminary graduate, ordained, and active in the ministry. I knew suddenly, on that day, that my life as a community activist and teacher had always been about ministry and that it likely always would be.

Since our arrival in Lawrence, we had become active in the First Christian Church (Disciples of Christ). I had agreed to chair the Christian Education Committee until, as part of a hiring process for a new Christian Education director, I was told by the other members of the search committee that we would not read the file of an applicant who had disclosed in her cover letter that she was going to marry a black man in a few months. I was outraged. I took the position that we were not talking about hiring her, only that her portfolio should be read just like any other applicant's, and that the decision of whom to hire should be based on our stated criteria, not on anyone's marital status. I was unable to gain their support for even a first reading, and this outcome deeply concerned me. I knew, of course, that the church was a racist institution, but I had thought that things were changing. Naive, again.

In addition, I had been offering, in response to requests in the church bulletin, to be a lay reader for morning worship. No one ever called me to pick up on my offers. Finally I decided it was obvious that women were not allowed to be lay readers, and I asked the minister about that. "Oh," he said, "there is no rule about who the lay readers are. The women just do not want to do it."

"I do," I offered, and was still never asked.

My public outcry at these structures and processes, along with my connections within the campus ministry networks in the town, led to invitations to be interviewed on various radio and TV programs or by newspaper reporters. Colleagues pointed out that I had been assigned the role of Lawrence's "angry housewife and community worker." I was angry at the limited roles allotted to women in the church, in the professional and business world, in the university, in the family. I was angry about racism. I was angry about a lot of things. And I was becoming better and better informed and increasingly articulate about my anger. I was reading voraciously in theology—especially in political theology and social ethics, new works by black authors, and, as works by and about women appeared, in feminist literature. I helped to organize reading groups among my women friends, taking up Mary Daly's *Beyond God the Father*, along with others that were to become classics of the women's movement of that time.

I was feeling increasingly uncomfortable in my local church. I was angry, but I also believed in the need for the church as a base from which to develop one's faith journey and to act in concert with others. My mother's lessons were still with me in a strong way. My congregation was liberal enough to provide some faith-related and perhaps intellectual support, but it was conservative to the point of inaction. I wanted and needed more. Together with other campus minister colleagues I helped initiate the development of what we eventually called a "house church." We knew there were many of us within the congregations in town who were feeling this alienation and yet valued the church. A group of our families made a covenant not to leave our local congregations, but to add another layer of church by coming together on a regular basis to share in worship, study, social involvement in community issues, and family celebrations.

For about seven years we "lived" actively within a house church community of between four to ten families in Lawrence. So that we could continue to participate in our regular church communities, we did not meet on Sunday mornings, but we met almost weekly in our own homes to share food, prayer, dance, ourselves, our thinking, our giving, and our actions on behalf of community social efforts. It was a very good experience of church—one my children and I will never forget. We were women, men, children together without prescribed roles, teaching and learning from one another something very new about the walk of one who would seek to live in harmony with all people and the Creator.

At the same time, some of my work in conjunction with the KU-Y began to bring young women, graduate and undergraduate—as well as community women—to my small office in the Student Union. They began to ask me to help them form women's consciousness-raising groups. These young women wanted to talk about sexuality, educational choices, professional choices, having children, not having children, relationships with men, friendship, marriage, relationships with women, abortion, self-help clinics for new forms of well-being for women and new ways of taking control over giving birth, and on and on. It was a deeply spiritual journey and a privilege to be asked and allowed to learn along with them during this time of ferment among young women. We read together, but most of all we told our stories and listened to one another and learned and spoke and "heard" our way into new lives and new ways of being.

I had been involved in the community Planned Parenthood group that maintained a network for women in need of a local doctor who was willing to do abortions, still illegal at that time. As the executive director of the KU-Y, I became part of the staff at the university and continued my efforts in conjunction with the Dean of Women's office—especially the establishment of a Rape Crisis Center. Following the *Roe v. Wade* decision in January of 1973 that legalized abortion, we developed an official Problem Pregnancy Network within the Dean of Women's office. As a phone counselor for women concerned about the issues of pregnancy, sexuality, and abortion, I helped my women colleagues on the university staff to see how religion and a woman's faith created dilemmas for those trying to make choices about pregnancy under difficult situations: following rape, after unprotected sex, or when the mother or fetus was ill. At first they would refer women with religious issues to me—I was, after all, the campus minister. It did not take us long to realize that for almost everyone, pregnancy, adoption, and abortion *were* religious and faith issues.

My work among women on the campus and in the community led to the formation of a small group of us who decided to provide safe housing for victims of domestic violence. At first women in need of such support were housed in some of our homes. We developed, and worked to maintain, a highly professional volunteer community of women who could respond on the phone to emergency calls. Our training program was extensive. In 1975, we were able to locate and renovate an older home in Lawrence for the purpose of housing what we came to call the Women's Transitional Care Center. A decade later, when, as a faculty member at Union Theological Seminary in New York City, I was asked to develop with Dr. Beverly Harrison a course on the theological, social, ethical, and pastoral issues in domestic violence for ministerial students, I learned from a book on the battered women's movement that we in Lawrence had established one of the first safe houses in the United States.

Nationally the Student YWCA was involved in its most important effort against racism, following passage of civil rights legislation. The One Imperative adopted in 1970 by the National Student YWCA, with support from the National YWCA, was the elimination of racism. This was work to which the students in the KU-Y were fully committed. On the initiative of an early KU-Y program, the University of Kansas had, decades before, become the first state university to provide on-campus integrated student housing. We had an important legacy behind our work on the One Imperative, and we struggled forward in various ways to make a contribution in this new era at KU. There was also a tremendous amount of energy on the campus for antiwar efforts, and we in the Student Y worked to tie the issue of the war to the issue of racism, guided by Dr. King's understanding of the interaction between our national political economy, the war, and the perpetuation of racism in this country.

It was about this time, in 1972, that a letter arrived at the KU-Y from Jan Griesinger, a campus minister in Ohio who, while working for the World Student Christian Federation on a part-time basis, was trying to locate other women in campus ministry across the United States. Hungry for women colleagues, I filled out her questionnaire. A few months later she sent another letter. The national board of United Ministries in Higher Education had given Jan a $30,000 grant to help bring together some of the women she had located in her survey. Would I be interested in attending? Did I need financial assistance? Yes and yes. I was paid $3,000 a year to work at the KU-Y, and I was responsible for raising every penny of that salary and all program funds. We had no travel budget for the executive director, and I wanted to bring along with me one of the women students on our board who showed interest in the ministry.

That first gathering of women who worked in campus ministry was a miracle to me. Sisters in the ministry! Companions on a journey for which there was no road map but certainly many barriers. We talked about our lives, about our campus settings and the work there, about our sense of ourselves as ministers, and about our experiences of alienation within our local churches. We talked about the future for women in the church and determined to forge new paths. We had no idea where we were headed.

Once we were together we began organizing. We established ourselves as Women in Campus Ministry (WICM) and worked to garner further support from the national church structures for our little organization. We attached our national gatherings to the front end of the National Campus Ministry Association's annual meetings and eventually came to call ourselves Campus Ministry Women (CMW). The dollars we had were few, but our commitment was large and so was our potential. Campus ministry was one of the only doors through which Protestant women were, at the time, able to enter the active ministry. We joined with our Catholic sisters in their struggle to initiate the movement toward the ordination of women. Within the Protestant stream, many of us belonged to communions that had historically invited women to ordination but just never to the leadership of ministry as a professional vocation.

At first there were so few of us in WICM that everyone had to take a job. I was asked to be our representative on the WSCF North American Regional Committee. The NARC had been supportive of Jan's first efforts to locate women campus ministers, and we wanted to stay in touch with them, to support their efforts and to continue to help build strength among formal church structures for the ministry of women within the churches, and, especially at this time, on the campuses. As part of the NARC, I came into contact with representative leaders from other student movements in North America: the Lutherans, Methodists, and Student YWCA in the United States, along with the remnants of those who had been involved in the national, collaborative student Christian movements, including the University Christian Movement in this country.

The Canadian representatives on the NARC, from student movement groups active in Canada, brought wonderful insights and a history of active involvement in social issues of the day. Through my work as a member of the NARC I became aware of the international student Christian movement and the WSCF itself, and my horizon began to broaden. Not only did my understanding of Christianity and the ministry develop in new ways, but also my understanding of the interconnectedness of people and issues all over the world. The NARC was, for me, a teaching and learning laboratory in political economy and the work of faith, a move toward boldness, and a way to engage my anger creatively with others who were walking similar paths.

It did not take me too long to discover the challenges of maintaining momentum within a student program or movement, where the constituency was in frequent rotation as students graduated. Much of the early vitality of the national student movements had disintegrated by the early 1970s. Small, highly independent groups here and there continued the struggle for various social justice issues, but even after my exposure to the NARC, it was difficult to locate them and make connections. The Student Y movement on the KU campus was a small setting, low on resources. We worked to establish relationships with various campus and local or regional social action groups that we were aware of, including some collaborative work on women's issues with the Student YWCA at the University of Missouri at Columbia. Through the Dean of Women's office on our own campus, we worked to develop women's groups and contribute to their programs for women. We took road trips to connect with other women and their conversations, including trips to Grailville in Ohio, a center where women with connections to religious traditions were gathering to work on their lives in a supportive environment. We brought Peggy Way and Mary Daly to the campus to learn from them about new and different possibilities for our lives as women. Our work on women's issues through the early 1970s gained us more attention and more participation across the KU campus than any of our other programs.

Partly as a result of our extensive work on women's issues, I received invitations to preach, always about the controversies surrounding women and the growing women's movement. One spring I was asked to preach in a small, nearby Kansas town. Some of the players in the movement to repeal *Roe v. Wade* and a women's right to choice regarding pregnancy had moved into the state and were stirring up trouble in these smaller communities. My colleagues in the Dean of Women's office were concerned about my safety, as threats had been made against my life. The unnamed voices on the phone strongly suggested that I not show up in their town. I called and talked with the local pastor. He was horrified to learn of these threats, but was glad to know that I was still planning to attend. My children and husband accompanied me, as they always did, and it was just another day on the preaching road for me. There were folks in the audience who were not pleased, but I was used to that. We did not overstay our visit, however, but left immediately following the worship service and the traditional handshaking at the door.

At the Student Y, we continued to build coalitions with other activists on and around the campus. In conjunction with a few faculty members in the Department of Social Welfare, we established a program to provide an "Urban Plunge." Every few months, we in the Student Y took idealistic young men and women from the social welfare classes into the urban ghetto of Kansas City for a long, eye-opening, and, for many of them, life-changing weekend. We also provided the leadership to organize against the proposal to reinstate the death penalty in the state of Kansas. The KU-Y was one of the first groups in the country, we were told, to hold a mock impeachment trial for President Nixon, long before Watergate became a national issue. We worked to build relationships with local Native American tribal leaders who were attempting to reclaim land promised to them in treaties. We became colleagues with the new student organization for gay and lesbian concerns, the Black Caucus, and the Hispanic Student Organization. On the basis of the wide and varying interests of the students who came to form the KU-Y board, we developed programmatic interests in a number of areas. What a time of learning this was for me! And all the time, we remained focused on the issue of racism, which we saw everywhere we looked.

While both the job and the KU-Y itself grew, I also yearned for a community of scholars with whom to talk about these issues, and so I began to think about seminary. I applied for a Danforth scholarship, describing my increasing discomfort with the growing "human potential movement." I thought that perhaps when one was encouraged to look so intently within one's self, the work of building relationships and connecting with the wider social issues that were obviously before us might, in fact, be lost. I wanted to study and ask this and other questions within the context of a seminary. Danforth said yes and I became a Danforth Fellow at Yale Divinity School in New Haven. Early in my seminary experience I realized that my first vocation, that of teacher, was really still my vocation, but that I needed to tie this calling with my now clear understanding of being called to the ministry. This meant teaching in a seminary, and that meant I needed a Ph.D. I had taken a two-semester sabbatical from my work at the KU-Y to attend seminary full time on my Danforth scholarship and complete a master's degree. Now, with the decision that I would eventually seek further graduate work, I returned full time to the KU-Y.

*I*n the spring of 1977, I was approached by a group of women from the Kansas City area asking me if I would allow my name to be put before the regional committee that oversaw ordination within my church. "You have all the credentials for ordination," they pointed out to me, "and we need women to test the system." At that time I was clear that I had not attended seminary with the notion of being ordained. First of all, it did not seem a logical possibility for a woman. Second, I was not sure that I would have the opportunity to build a career in the ordained ministry. I enjoyed my work on the campus—for which I did not need to be ordained—and had decided to begin work on the Ph.D. in order to prepare for seminary teaching one day. With the support of this group of women, however, and knowing of the rising political issues surrounding ordination, I agreed to enter the process.

With tremendous support from Kansas City Women's Theological Collective and other colleagues from around the country, I survived what was frequently an unfriendly experience of the church's political process and was ordained in March of 1978 in my former home church in Mission, Kansas. One horrible and grace-filled moment brought this experience all together for me. The congregation had a new, rather conservative pastor, which was quite a surprise since the church of my youth had been such a progressive one. He and some of his supporters among the elders (all male) were engaged with me in the ordination interview that was standard practice once the regional Committee on the Ministry had authorized my ordination. The obviously unfriendly elders were grilling me. Finally someone asked, "What do you believe about the Virgin Birth?"

I was so astounded by all these questions, and this one in particular, because within the traditions of the Christian Church (Disciples of Christ) there are no such test questions about one's faith. For Disciples, faith had always been an open, rational, self-determined journey with no particular creed or belief held within the church on any one issue. Hence a question such as this was unexpected and inappropriate. My response was far too rational for those newer elders present. I said that I believed the story of the virgin birth was an important "story" or "legend" of the Bible that held great importance for some and not so much importance for others, and that for me, it was not a central issue of my faith. The new pastor, his face turning red, lifted his wilted Bible high into the air and, shaking it at me, shouted, "Well, then I have only one question: Is this fact or is this fancy?"

I thought it was all over—the ordination service planned for the following week was not going to happen, and certainly not in this congregation, ever. But the preacher's question did not, in my mind, deserve a response. Silence reigned for a moment. Then gently and without a word, one of the long-standing leaders of the congregation got up and came to stand behind me. Putting his hands on my shoulders and looking around the circle of men, he said calmly, "If there are any other questions about Eleanor's theology, I would like for you to address them to me. I was her Sunday school teacher during her high school years and am willing to answer any further questions you might have today." A moment of sheer beauty and the meeting was adjourned.

I was ordained the following week after a full-blown struggle among the leadership of that congregation. And what a celebration! The church was packed to standing room only. The laying on of hands was rich in meaning for me. Politics took the back seat on that day as the movement of faith and my sense of call came full center. In the years that followed, I would continue my work in campus ministry through national leadership of a WSCF program on campuses in the United States on "Education for Change," and I would become a local church pastor at the First Congregational Church in Madison, Wisconsin, as I completed my doctoral studies in sociology at the University of Wisconsin–Madison. Following the completion of my degree, I was off to New York City and Union Theological Seminary and an unfolding career in academic administration and teaching within seminary education. And I would eventually become the first woman president of Pacific School of Religion in Berkeley. Across the years, as I followed my vocation and stayed in touch with my women colleagues in the ministry, I watched with great joy and deep satisfaction as we moved into areas of church leadership and the ministry. The lessons we had learned and shared with others during years of preparation for and work within the student movements of the 1960s and 1970s were very fertile ones.

It cannot be said that we, as a nation or as a church, have overcome sexism, racism, militarism, homophobia, or any of the other issues that so captured our attention during those years, but our involvement in these movements as women—along with our supportive male colleagues—has, I believe, changed the face of organized religion and, more important, its possible futures. Women can no longer, will no longer, be left out. We will still be forced aside from time to time, are still often unwanted in halls of former male privilege, but we will not be denied our voice and our presence. And when we speak, we will continue to speak from the hearts and minds of those who knew marginalization, a lesson we took with us into the social movements of that era and for all time to come. And yes, many of us are still angry, but we continue to laugh and smile a lot, as we always have, when we are together.

CHAPTER 12

Nancy D. Richardson

~~~~~~~~~~~~~

$\mathcal{W}$hen the police drove black stu-
dents shouting "Duke is racist!" out of the Administration Building at Duke
University in the spring of 1968, I knew that something significant had happened, not only for those students and for Duke University, but for me. It
was some time later, at a National Student YWCA meeting, that I began to
realize what that something was, and it has taken years of reflection and action for me to understand what a transformative experience that incident was
for me. It came at the midpoint of my experience in the student Christian
movement; I had entered college in 1958, become involved in the Student
YWCA in my first year, and continued to work in campus ministry until 1977.
This event turned out to be a pivotal point that not only laid the foundation for
my professional future, but gave me the tools with which to analyze my past.

I was an unlikely candidate for getting involved in campus politics. I
had been raised in a fairly sheltered working-class community, was active in
the Southern Baptist Church, and was the first member of my family to go
to college. My father was a carpenter who became a draftsman's apprentice
with the Appalachian Electric Power company just prior to Pearl Harbor and,
as a result, was never called to serve in the armed forces because he was working in a job considered essential to the war effort. My mother was a pieceworker in a garment factory, later a nurse's aide, and by the time I was in
college, was working as a sales clerk in a department store. Obeying the rules,
staying out of trouble, working hard, getting an education, earning a living
were "norms" that were assumed, more than explicitly taught, in my family.
Family life was deeply rooted in the church, which reinforced these values.
No one would have expected me to challenge any of these norms, least of all
the "staying out of trouble" one, and, interestingly enough, they were right.
When I began to get in "trouble"—that is, "break the rules"—it was not defiance but naïveté that led the way.

Perhaps I inherited this naïvete from my father. When the Supreme Court handed down the *Brown v. Board of Education* decision, I had just entered high school in Salem, Virginia, and wondered what the decision meant. I have clear memories of reading about it in the newspaper and hearing my father say, "Well, that's only fair. I wonder why somebody didn't think of it before." That comment revealed more than a little naïveté. This is not to suggest an absence of racism in my upbringing; certainly such everyday lessons as the segregated schools, buses, water fountains, waiting rooms at train stations, as well as the more subtle assumptions of family and church, were powerful teachers. Living in the segregated South, I had little contact with black people and knew none by name until I entered Westhampton College, the women's undergraduate college of the University of Richmond, in 1958.

The civil rights movement was taking shape across the South, but given my lessons on "obeying the rules" and the political naïveté of my upbringing, I encountered it only from a distance. Yet its effects quickly began to seep into my education through my affiliation with the Student YWCA. Every student at Westhampton College was a member of the YWCA by virtue of student activities fees, and YWCA elections, like student government elections, were campuswide. In my first year I was asked by my orientation counselor, who was an officer in the Y, to join the Y Cabinet as the "Mimeograph Chairman," my mimeographing skills having been honed through volunteer work at my church. As a member of the YWCA Cabinet, I had an opportunity to participate in Southern Regional Student YWCA meetings. These gatherings were held either in Y-owned facilities or on black college campuses, the only places in the South in those days in which integrated gatherings could be held. I don't remember when I first attended one of these meetings, but I do remember that they were a context in which I was challenged and inspired by YWCA staff such as Ella Baker and students, both black and white, who were involved in desegregation efforts and who told stories of being arrested and jailed. Hearing their stories of defiance and courage was both frightening and moving to me. Nevertheless, when I first got in trouble with regard to race, I was motivated by neither defiance nor courage. Indeed, it happened because I was so conscientiously trying to follow, not challenge, the rules, unaware that the college's "race rules" were unwritten.

In the spring of my sophomore year, I was appointed Vespers Chairman (*sic*), responsible for planning the weekly Y-sponsored Vespers services for the following year. With the help of my campus minister, Betty Jean (B.J.) Seymour, I contacted most of the same speakers who had spoken the previous year, including a local black pastor. Vespers speakers were routinely

invited to have dinner in the college dining hall before the service, the unwritten rule, of course, being that the black speaker was not to be invited.
Being a conscientious rule-follower, politically naive, and something of a literalist, when the instructions for planning Vespers said to invite the speakers
to dinner, I invited all the speakers. It was not until the week that he was
scheduled to speak that I knew I was in trouble: I had stepped across a line
that I had not even known was there. B.J. Seymour confronted me with the
problem. She had been told by the treasurer of the university, whose office
supervised the dining halls, that it was inappropriate for this particular speaker
to eat in the Westhampton dining room. I did not want to disinvite him (probably, I must admit, for reasons of manners more than politics), and both B.J.
and my dean supported me. However, it was the central administration of the
university that had the power to make the decision. Finally, B.J. and the dean
negotiated a compromise: the Vespers speaker could eat in the dining room
provided that I could find seven "Westhampton ladies" who were willing to
eat at a table with him, and another who would be willing to serve as a waitress for his table. Both provisions were easily met, and the dinner became a
politicizing experience not only for me but for eight other white "ladies."

At the same time, I was beginning to learn the connection between faith
and politics through the Bible courses I was taking, especially a course in
the Hebrew prophets taught by B.J. Seymour. Hearing the prophets' calls for
justice to "roll down like waters" and learning to make connections between
the practices they were condemning and the political situation in the United
States, I began to see that what my father had called "only fair" was much
more complicated and demanding of me as a Christian. I was, however, still
a long way from translating that new-found relationship between faith and
justice into intentional and explicit action. Thus my second encounter with
"race rules" at my college was no more intentional than the first. In the spring
of 1962, I requested permission from the dean to be away from campus for a
weekend conference of the Southern Regional YWCA. She informed me that
when another Westhampton student had returned from a YW meeting a year
earlier, reporting that she had stayed in the home of the president of More-
house College, the president of the University of Richmond was scandalized
and decreed that no Westhampton student was to be permitted to attend a
conference at a black college again. My dean wanted to know whether the
Interdenominational Theological Center (ITC) in Atlanta, at which the conference was to be held, was a black college. I didn't know and asked both
B.J. Seymour and Philip Hart, the campus minister for Richmond College,
the men's undergraduate college in the university. They thought it was inte-

grated, but not black. So permission was granted. Upon my return, the dean asked about the conference and I said, "Guess what. It was a consortium of black colleges." Her reply: "I won't tell, if you don't." Years later, when I told this story to Jeanne Audrey Powers, she commented that much of campus ministry in the 1960s was, of necessity, "subversive activity." She said that while I didn't know what ITC was, my campus ministers probably did and "stretched the truth to enable you to do what was right. That was a subversive act that helped change your life."

I have thought a lot about Jeanne Audrey's comment. The OED says that subversion is to "overthrow a law, rule, system, condition." Certainly my experience as an undergraduate in the late 1950s and 1960s was one in which the laws and rules as I had known them were being overthrown, both literally and figuratively. The rules were being challenged directly by students and staff whom I knew through the Southern Regional YWCA and indirectly by campus ministers and teachers at Westhampton, whether by "stretching the truth" as Jeanne Audrey suggested or by creating spaces in which I could move out of the protective and "safe" notion that being Christian is about being nice. They helped me see that it is, rather, about doing justice.

These lessons followed me into Southeastern Baptist Seminary in Wake Forest, North Carolina. As a young person, I had decided that I wanted to go into what was called, in Southern Baptist circles, "full-time Christian service," so I entered college with the intention of going on to seminary. I had assumed that I would be engaged in some kind of church-based religious education, because ordination was not an option for women in the Southern Baptist Church and was not an idea that I ever entertained. However, through my work with B.J. Seymour and the YWCA, I was introduced to campus ministry as a vocational option for women. After teaching high school for a year to pay off some of my college debts, I entered Southeastern, which was, at the time, the most liberal of the Southern Baptist seminaries. In the second year of a three-year program, literally on a dare, I applied for a Danforth Fellowship in campus ministry. Much to my surprise, I received the fellowship and was assigned to be campus ministry intern at San Diego State College. This proved to be an internship in more explicit "subversive" activity. I worked with a Quaker who was the director of the campus YM-YWCA, which housed and gave moral and administrative support to all manner of civil rights and antiwar groups. The students involved in groups like SDS and other leftist groups introduced me to political perspectives I had never encountered before. And David Neptune, my supervisor, introduced me in his quiet way to a Quaker form of gentle but persistent "subversive" campus ministry. This internship in "subversive activity" proved to be a valuable resource in my next job, at Duke University.

Prior to leaving Southeastern Seminary for San Diego, I had decided not to return because the theological and political perspectives represented by the school had become increasingly intolerable. For example, several faculty members were fired for being too "liberal," and the president of the seminary had refused to allow the Student Interracial Ministry to hold a meeting on campus because Wake Forest "was not ready" for that many black students to come to town. The only black students at Southeastern at the time were, ironically, African converts to Christianity. So when I was offered a position the following September (1966), as associate to the chaplain at Duke University, I accepted it. My responsibilities included directing the student YWCA on the women's campus, which, during the time I was there, joined the student YMCA on the men's campus to form a joint YM-YWCA. While at Duke, I also completed my seminary program, receiving the M.Div. degree in 1970.

I have often thought of my life as being divided into three parts. The first runs through my second year in seminary, though the seeds for the transition to the second phase had been sown in my junior and senior years in college. By the time I reached Duke at age 26, I had turned a corner, thanks to the influence of my year at San Diego State. I became more active in civil rights and antiwar activity, both at Duke and nationally, as well as in community-based social service and social justice activities sponsored by the Duke YM and YWCAs. Nevertheless, I was not prepared for the effect that hearing black students shout "Duke is racist" would have on me. I knew these students. I had worked closely with them in the YM-YWCA and on community service projects and campus political issues. I knew they weren't lying, nor were they simply shouting meaningless epithets. Yet I had no idea what they meant. Duke was "integrated," I thought; they were there. Then how could they say Duke was racist? My college years during the civil rights movement had reinforced my family's teaching against racial discrimination and disproved the "outside agitator" theory of racial desegregation so prevalent in southern white communities and churches. I had learned that racial justice was not achieved by good intentions, that segregation and discrimination had left a legacy of exclusion and disempowerment that required direct action and concrete struggle to remedy, and that engaging in those efforts entailed substantial risk. Nevertheless, it was not until this event at Duke, in the weeks following the assassination of Martin Luther King, Jr., that I began to understand that desegregation did not solve the problem of racism. I supported the students' demands for changes such as more scholarships for black students, more intentional recruitment of black faculty, and a black studies program. However, I did not begin to understand what had happened that day until I attended a National Student YWCA conference two years later.

In the meantime, my political education continued as I was drawn— reluctantly—into the women's liberation movement. When Duke students like Tami Hultman began talking about being oppressed as women, I thought they had gone off the deep end. True, I had read Betty Friedan's *The Feminine Mystique*; indeed, while still in seminary at Southeastern, I had, at the invitation of Sara Evans and Charlotte Bunch, led a discussion of it at a Duke YWCA retreat. But that was about my mother, not me. And besides, I was the first person ever to go to college in my family and here I was employed at *Duke!* Surely I would not be here if I had been the victim of oppression or discrimination, and neither would these women. It was not until much later when I began to understand my class roots that I realized that Betty Friedan's book wasn't really about my mother either. Growing up on a farm and working as a pieceworker in a garment factory hardly qualified her for the "feminine mystique" moniker.

It was not until I heard a male colleague suggest that the issue of *motive* devoted to women should be burned that I decided I'd better pay attention to the students. I began to participate in consciousness-raising groups, learning more than I had ever imagined about what it means to be a woman in this world. It is difficult for me to recall the specifics of these lessons from this distance. I remember hearing other women's stories about understanding their bodies, about having their ideas recognized only when stated by their male colleagues, about images of women perpetuated by church and media. I remember recognizing that I had simply responded to these messages by believing that *I* was the problem—that I didn't look right and wasn't smart enough to be taken seriously, and that male leadership in church and society was ordained by God. What I remember most vividly is the feeling: the feeling of affirmation and connection to women and the realization that by finding the tools to see the world and my place in it in a different way, I was beginning to gain a self-confidence that I had never had before.

Certainly my involvement in the antiwar movement during my years at Duke was another important part of my political education. My antiwar activity took many forms, from draft counseling to participating in draft-card burning ceremonies to traveling to Washington, D.C., for antiwar protests. The most significant protest, for me, was the Mobilization against the War in 1968. There had been much talk about the potential for violence at this event. To counter that, several groups, including numerous church groups, were encouraging participation on the theory that it would be violent only if those who desired a peaceful protest stayed away. The Duke YM and YW had organized two busloads of people to go. I had decided to avoid telling my parents that I was going, knowing they would be worried, so I called them in the middle of the week before the event, hoping they would not call me while I was away. Unfortunately, they asked if I was going and when I said yes, my father threw a fit—calling William Sloan Coffin, Abraham Heschel, and Benjamin Spock (the scheduled speakers) communists. After the phone call, I wrote my parents a long letter and sent them the then-famous photo of a marine setting fire to a Vietnamese hut with the caption "We burned every hut!" I told them that if they didn't think I should be involved in protesting this, they had to take some responsibility for it, because what I had learned from them and from the church made it clear to me that this was immoral. In a letter that crossed mine in the mail, my father wrote and apologized and sent a check to pay what turned out to be a rather large phone bill. That incident proved significant not only for me but for my parents, especially for my father, who became outspoken in his small rural Southern Baptist church in Appomattox County, Virginia, not only against the war, but against racism and for women's ordination and women's right to choose.

Other political events at Duke that significantly shaped my political education were the Duke Vigil and the development of the University Christian Movement. The former, a massive student and faculty sit-in that gained national attention and support from people such as Pete Seeger and Joan Baez, both of whom visited the campus during the sit-in, was geared toward supporting the demands of Local 1199 Service Workers' union for decent wages. Because Duke was the largest employer in Durham at the time, the wages that Duke paid not only affected the workers at Duke, but set the standard for the area. The development of the University Christian Movement drew me into discussions about the very nature of education—who decides what we learn and whom does it benefit—that affect my life to this day. My engagement in these discussions became the basis for my graduate work many years later, which drew on the "education for liberation" work of Paulo Freire and the liberation feminist ethics of Beverly Harrison to develop a liberation feminist approach to education. Those discussions continue to shape my current work in many ways, including a course I teach regularly at Harvard Divinity School entitled "Education for Liberation."

It was significant for me that all of this political education at Duke took place in the Bible Belt, not because I was a biblical literalist, but because in that setting it was not just okay, but expected, that the theological implications of political struggles would be addressed. Political actions made claims about Christian responsibility and drew on the prophetic calls for justice. The strong connection between faith and justice in the student Christian movement made it possible for me to draw on my own faith roots while, at the same time, I moved beyond the narrow definitions that had shaped my early church experience. And it enabled me to work effectively in a ministry setting that was both challenging the norms of the dominant society and making claims based on values that that society claimed to hold dear. Duke was an essential turning point for me in this regard.

In the summer of 1969 I decided it was time for me to leave Duke, and by the spring of 1970 I had accepted an invitation to become the associate chaplain and director of the YM-YWCA at Oberlin College the following fall. In preparation for my new job, I attended the National Student YWCA meeting in Madison, Wisconsin. The meeting's focus was to prepare the students and staff of YWCAs on college campuses to act effectively on the YWCA's newly adopted One Imperative, to eliminate racism "wherever it exists and by any means necessary." There I met Sally Timmel and Anne Hope, who worked with white women to help us understand racism and our responsibility for eliminating it, and national YW staff members such as Elizabeth Jackson, Dorothy Height, and Valerie Russell, all of whom became mentors for me as antiracism became a primary focus of my work in the years to come.

The meeting was intense. While we were on campus, the Army Math Research Building at the University of Wisconsin was blown up by an antiwar protester, and the explosion was so powerful that it blew some of the windows out of the building in which the YW was holding its meetings. To say that this increased the intensity of our meeting would be an absurd understatement. Again, what I remember are images and feelings more than details. I remember Valerie Russell standing up and beginning to sing, "We Are Soldiers in the Army," a song of freedom and resistance, and a song that drew the women together in solidarity when anxiety and distrust could have torn us apart.

Although it would have been impossible for me to grow up in the South—with its "White" and "Colored" signs on everything from drinking fountains to waiting rooms at the train station—without knowing that I was white, the 1970 YWCA conference was the first time I was asked to think about what it means to be white. In the session in which this question was raised, white women and women of color were meeting in separate groups, much to my surprise: wasn't the goal, after all, to work together? Yet, when we were asked to complete sentences that began with "To me being white means . . . ," "To me being Black means . . . ," "Whites have been responsible for . . . ," "Blacks have been responsible for . . . ," I began to understand as never before how many unnamed assumptions I held about whiteness and how those assumptions shaped my perception of black people. Most basically, I had assumed that "white" is normative—in culture, education, and accomplishments—and that black is "other." I realized that I knew a lot about the accomplishments of white people and virtually nothing about the accomplishments of black people. This enabled me to see that it was not only the education of black people that had been damaged by racism, but my own education as well. I received a new set of lenses through which to look at that university and other institutions. These lenses enabled me to look beyond desegregation to institutional analysis of the complex ways racism operates.

In short, I began to understand that racism is a white problem, and that I as a white woman had a responsibility to use the power to which I had access toward eliminating racism. Although I was convinced of my responsibility in this regard, it was not immediately obvious to me at age thirty, just starting a rather low-status job in a small liberal arts college, what sort of power was mine to exercise. Nevertheless, I learned, at this conference, to identify those elements of power, however limited, I did possess by looking at those places in which I had the capacity to make decisions. Through the use of a "power inventory," we were asked what decisions we had direct or indirect power over, what opportunities we had to influence the decisions of others who had power, whom we knew who had power, and so on. We learned, that is, to break the notion of power down into manageable pieces. I suddenly realized that in my new job I would have a budget, would be hiring staff, could design programs, offer courses for which students could receive academic credit, and train volunteers. If, as I had learned, it was my responsibility to work with whites against racism, here was my opportunity to begin. It is unbelievable to me at this point that I was so audacious in my first semester at Oberlin—another example, perhaps, of my institutional naïveté: I organized a faculty training program on racism during the fall, a January Term project for students on racism in the curriculum, and a summer antiracism action program in five predominantly white suburban Boston communities for Oberlin students.

The National Student YWCA conference was clearly, at that late date of 1970, not the first opportunity I had had to learn all this. However, the lenses acquired at the conference, trained on the black students' protest on the Duke campus, enabled me to see what had been there to see for years.

This remains emblazoned on my consciousness as a moment of awakening that challenged my assumption that "racial justice" and "integration" were synonymous terms and pushed me to transform the pain and anger I felt on hearing student friends shout "Duke is racist!" into fuel for personal and so-cial change.

In the ensuing years, the memory of that awakening has helped me pay attention when similar possibilities for new understanding have presented themselves. After a very brief time at Oberlin College, I decided that I wanted to focus more directly on antiracism work in white communities. I moved to Boston to accept a campus ministry position with Boston-Cambridge Minis-tries in Higher Education and to do volunteer work with Community Change, Inc., the organization that had provided the leaders for the antiracism train-ing at the 1970 YWCA conference and the antiracism work I did with fac-ulty and students at Oberlin. This move to Boston marks the beginning of the third phase of my life.

In 1974 I was asked to help develop a summer program in theological education for women, to be based on the educational theories of Paulo Freire and sponsored by The Grail, an international movement of mostly Roman Catholic women that focuses on women, liberation, and religious search. That work, combined with the community organizing and antiracism work I was doing in Boston, continued to hone both my political and my theological un-derstandings of justice-making work. When I accepted a position as director of student life at Boston University School of Theology (BUSTH), it did not occur to me that I could not take these new-found principles with me. While employed at BUSTH, I also took advantage of a benefit available at the time to all employees of Boston University—free tuition—and entered a doctoral program in social ethics and education. For some reason, I seem to have been unable to shake the institutional naïveté, and so I almost immediately got in trouble for raising questions about some funds BUSTH had in a bank heavily involved in South Africa. Although I weathered (and won!) that battle, I was to pay for it and other objections I later raised to racist and sexist policies, especially employment practices, by being fired in the summer of 1981. Hap-pily for me, the firing happened just as I was completing the last course in my doctoral program.

Harvey Guthrie, dean of the Episcopal Divinity School, in a gesture of solidarity, I believe, offered me a part-time job coordinating its women's pro-grams for the 1981–82 year. Working only part time left me free to sue BU and prepare for my doctoral exams. The following year, I accepted an offer to become one of two co-directors for the newly forming Women's Theological

Center (WTC). Defining itself as an organization that was "at once Christian and Feminist," the WTC, from its inception, saw its work to be an antiracist, multiracial approach to justice for women. Thus the first two staff people were two co-directors, one black and one white, and a coordinating committee, later to become a board of directors, was to be at least one-third black, and later more broadly women of color. After ten years with the WTC, I decided that I had completed my work with the organization and needed to move on. The next year, I accepted a position as associate dean for ministry at Harvard Divinity School, a post I currently hold that has given me the opportunity to teach courses such as "Education for Liberation" and "Confronting Racism in Ministry."

At each of these changes in my professional life, I have found that the process of learning to be subversive—learning to overthrow laws, rules, systems, conditions that make for injustice, and to see that as the bedrock of Christian commitment—has shaped my life. It is at the core of my faith, is the fuel for my work, and is the legacy of the student Christian movement for me.

CHAPTER 13

Valerie Russell (1941–1997)

THE REPAIRER OF THE BREACH (ISAIAH 58:12)

LETTY M. RUSSELL

Editor's Note: Valerie Russell had hoped to participate in this project, but she was ill even as the idea was being born. Her importance to the broader narrative, however, cannot be overstated. We are grateful to Rev. Letty Russell for her evocation of Val.

*I*n 1970 I walked into the YWCA building at 600 Lexington Avenue in New York City and I knew that there was something afoot. There were signs about the One Imperative to thrust our collective power toward the elimination of racism wherever it existed and by any means necessary. There were invitations to be part of a Women's Resource Center program and strengthen our women power. There were purposeful staff moving in and out of Dorothy Height's office, which was working to help the National Board and all the member associations to implement the One Imperative. In the middle of this ferment was a young staff member named Valerie Russell. She had come out of the Student YWCA and the civil rights movement to work as Dorothy Height's assistant. Valerie made good use of her strong and dynamic mentor, who was also the head of the National Council of Negro Women. Having similar backgrounds, Val and I became kindred spirits: "the Russell sisters," serious about the work on racism and sexism and looking for the soul power that would help move these justice agendas.

I had come to work part time at the National YWCA as the religious consultant because I was very impressed with the work that the YWCA had been doing in affirming its role as a women's movement and in passing a new and more open Purpose, as well as adopting the One Imperative. When Edith Lerrigo, the executive director, asked me to take this position, it was the first time I had seen her since she had worked with me as a staff member in the New England student Christian movement twenty years earlier. I was excited to reconnect to my SCM roots and to make a continuing ecumenical contribution from a feminist/ liberation perspective.

I will never forget my first experience of Valerie Russell in action when I attended a National Board meeting. Valerie was in charge of training the board members in what institutional racism was all about as they began the difficult task of interpreting and implementing the One Imperative. As they expected, she divided the women in groups with a separate caucus for women of color. What was not expected was that she appointed two women of color to attend the white women's sessions because they needed observers to keep them honest! It took a lot of skill and persuasion on Val's part to calm the uproar from those white women, many of whom were very privileged, and to get them to acknowledge that white racism is not so easy to see, let alone to resist.

Valerie Russell's charisma was truly a gift for a woman who had chosen such a difficult task as working for justice and an end to white racism in ecumenical organizations. She was an accomplished group leader, guitarist, and singer. Together we worked on liturgies that lifted up that agenda. In 1972 we worked on a liturgy for the Y's National Convention, and Val was out there in the front of that huge gathering calling for a vision of a new world of peace and justice, and leading us in litanies and songs of freedom that echoed earlier civil rights marches. Later we were part of a demonstration and liturgy on the New Haven, Connecticut, green on behalf of women unjustly held under grand jury indictments. Val and her guitar carried the day with the gathered throng, and her voice for justice was heard once again.

Val and I knew that this was to be a long journey toward freedom. We needed to strategize about how to build support among women for a justice agenda in national ecumenical organizations, so that they were able to have their voices heard and find enough support so that they did not burn out. Together we created a group entitled the Ad Hoc Group on Racism, Sexism and Classism. This group still meets, for racism, sexism, classism, and homophobia are still very much with us. Inviting women from national denominational offices as well as the YWCA has made it possible to build yet another network of women, with women who like Ruth Harris combine faith and action in their daily work and ministry.

Valerie Russell's life was full of work to repair the breach between those who are divided from one another by structures of oppression. She went on to become the head of the City Mission Society of Boston, and then executive director of church and society in the United Church of Christ. Even a stroke could not stop her "repair work." She just named her electric wheelchair "Justice Jeep" and kept on keepin' on!

CHAPTER 14

Renetia Martin

~~~~~~~~~⌒

$\mathcal{M}$y life was crafted by community, and it was in the breath-giving lap of tight-spun, playful, earnest, and loving groups of human beings that I became a woman and a creator of community myself. My family came five generations ago from the South to California. The first substantial migration of black people to the state was to work in the shipyards during World War II, but by that time my grandmother was already well established in her house in the center of South Berkeley. I was the first-born daughter and granddaughter, and it seems I've always been doted on . . . in my imagination. I felt homely and unattractive as a child and yearned to be a princess. I pretended to be Herself: my version of Snow White.

Not long ago, I was negotiating the congested streets of my hometown, and I turned to my now husband and said, "I used to skate these streets, along Alcatraz between Shattuck and Sacramento." It was a healthy distance, but safe and serene in the old days. On each block lived at least one or two family members. Around every corner was a neighbor, friend, family member, or an acquaintance of my grandmother. I was enveloped by the sense of safety and protection, and never gave a thought to the possibility that my folks might worry about me.

My parents divorced early, and I lived with my mother, but I spent time with my father and stepmother and their children. Most of the women in my family worked in the home, but my mother worked in department stores as a clerk and gift-wrap specialist until she became a grocery checker at Safeway. All the family was poor, and she needed to work hard to get by. She rang up groceries until her body gave out. Major surgeries on her back, knees, and neck could not restore her, and along with her health, her relationship with me deteriorated as well. My mother had two other children from a traumatic second marriage, and much of the responsibility for our household fell upon me, since she worked long hours away from us. I cooked, cleaned, and babysat, and began to realize that I wanted a bigger life than that. My fidelity to my mother shows more in my determination to create healthy environments for working women than in our ragged contact with each other.

My mother's mother, Lena Osibin, was the core of my young life. She loved me as thoroughly as a human can, and I, in turn, loved her more than my own mother. She was my inspiration, my ally, and the person I could absolutely rely on. She was responsible, along with my paternal grandmother, for making sure my father got to see me after his divorce from my mother.

Grandmother Lena's impact was bolstered by my father, a career military man until the late 1980s. As I grew older, I grew closer and closer to him and his family, and they exerted a powerful influence on me. My father's demeanor and style remind me of Colin Powell: collected, grounded, together. He commanded respect, and he always impressed me. He encouraged, supported, and facilitated, but rarely gave directives. He was (and is) so smart. He skillfully framed his aspirations for us such that they emerged as part of our own decision-making process. From him I collected ambition and pride. Happily married for fifty-two years now, my father and stepmother have two sons whom I love deeply.

My relationship with my family during the 1960s was very healthy. We always enjoyed political debates around the dinner table, and this was just the decade for that. If you had the nerve to bring up an issue, it would be discussed, debated, and tossed about. My brothers took me on about feminism, and I countered by pointing out their controlling, chauvinistic ways. Dad was part of the National Guard, and during the late 1960s, when I lived with him while attending the University of California at Berkeley, we would have terrific discussions about tear gas, Vietnam, protest, and peace. We can joke about it now, but our discussions were heated and serious at the time. We could be pretty contentious, but it was all done within the framework of love and closeness. We never walked away angry. In fact, these discussions kept us connected to each other.

My two grandmothers were strong, present women in the world, in their communities, and in their churches. The idea of "being of service" grew to be part of our identity. It is imprinted on me. I never sit still for long without hearing the "call of the day," to be of service. I started going to the South Berkeley Community Church with my grandmother when I was very small, then was pulled by my aunt into Christian Science until I was twelve. I was very devoted, but the material world was too compelling for my mind to govern. As a teenager, I became a Methodist, along with my mother and grandmother, and I went to that church until my mid-twenties. Although I stopped going to church for a while, I was later confirmed as an Episcopalian. My spiritual self continues to reach and search and expand.

After attending six different elementary schools, I finally graduated from Berkeley High in 1963. I worked full time during the day and attended night school at Oakland City College. Eventually I earned enough credits and money so that I could transfer to UC Berkeley as a sophomore. I lived with my father and stepmother and became a full-time student. At this crossroads, I found maturity and love. I had a chance to reframe my sense of family and cement my social foundations. I was respected as an adult, yet I got to be a sibling again with my brothers and to enjoy the comforts of home. From this early, rich life in a safe and loving, if demanding, world, I took with me into adulthood wonderful images of what women could become.

I was a student at the University of California at Berkeley during the university's most politically significant years, 1968 to 1973. It was a time of revolution, black power, feminism, war, and the National Guard. With all the slack that being a full-time student allowed me, I went looking for a place to lend a hand, and found Y-House, home of the University YWCA. I wanted to expand my experience of community service, and started out by offering to tutor young children in a program that supplemented the newly introduced Head Start program.

The Y provided a way to be faithful to my own sense of priorities, and also a campus nesting place. From the midst of thousands of Berkeley students, I could walk through the front door of the YWCA and be welcomed by people who knew and cared about me. It was a quiet place to study if I needed a retreat, a place where I could keep a toothbrush, take a nap, and return refreshed to the big campus. (I went back recently for an eight-week class, and the Y continues to thrive, swarming with students who use the building in all the ways that I did.) At Y-House, I met Anne Kern, who was the executive director, and we became immediate friends, a close relationship that lasted as long as she lived. Meeting her was a definite juncture in my life. Anne became my mentor, supporter, and great adherent. She encouraged me to notice the important issues of the day, to live a big life, and to recognize my talents as a leader. Anne was sweet, wise, and strong. She became a guiding light for me, a woman who had lasting, deep, spiritual and professional impact.

Although I thought of the Y at that time as a sisterhood of volunteers, and not as a Christian student movement, our YWCA community could not help but be animated by the teeming activism at nearby Sather Gate, on the south side of campus. I had gone to meetings of the Black Student Union, but the unrelenting sexism of the male leadership gave me no home there. I had just begun my second round of tutorials with the kids when Anne asked me to consider running for president of the Y-House Student Cabinet. We had a powerful group of bright, capable women and a strong campus presence, and I agreed to be their leader. It was my first exposure to a mix of color and talent in women who were committed to social change—political, social, and historical. I had little notion of what such leadership would entail, but I was well aware of the group as a powerful political force. This was my beginning. During that year, there were two student strikes on campus. I was torn between the principles of the strike and my limited time and budget. We met our teachers in their homes and in church basements to avoid crossing the picket lines.

With less than a year as Student Cabinet president under my belt, I flew out of California for the first time, to St. Charles, Missouri, to represent our group at the YWCA's National Student Assembly in spring 1969. I didn't know anything beforehand about the National Student Assembly, and I did not think of myself as a leader. I was shocked when other women responded to my directness and simplicity on difficult issues. The assembly gave me a sense of how scary and powerful groups can be, and how they can project both great and terrible things onto their leaders—especially young, female, and black leaders.

Although I had not set out to become a national leader, I came home the newly elected chair of the National Student YWCA. I was stunned at the commitment needed to keep my focus on the whole group and on the mission and intent of the agenda. My confusion grew, but so did my understanding. Then, as now, I saw the task of leadership as keeping the peace and moving forward together. It was thrilling to be part of a group that brought together the unusual wisdom and diverse insights of students from across the country. I was getting a much broader picture of the great changes that were occurring in our culture and among our peoples.

My year as national chairwoman was a busy and enriching time. I was treated as an executive by the national staff, with one person assigned particularly to me to help with our work. I was still a full-time student at Berkeley, but I would fly in and out of New York twice a month. The summer of the National YWCA convention, I was working on a research project in San Diego, and I commuted between my small studio apartment there to Berkeley and New York.

During that year I also traveled abroad, to Ibadan, Nigeria, and Grata Farada, Italy, for two international student conferences, meeting people who were grappling with similar issues—justice, racism, economic equality, and access to our political system. It was my first experience of the global village, and I was really naive. Nine of us went from the United States to Nigeria right on the heels of the Nigerian civil war, a terrifying time in their history—and in mine. Hostility over class, color, and economics rose between the Africans and the U.S. black people, and between the women my color— a steaming café au lait—and the African women who had not been diluted by slaveowner or white ally blood. It took me months to recover from that trip, and not only from the dysentery I got there. I went to Nigeria little different from a white missionary, but I returned one of the converted. I learned from them and gained an experience of international, nonparochial views.

There were six of us in the American contingent to the Italian conference, and we were interviewed by *International Forum* magazine. I recall putting out political views that I'm not sure I'd have the courage to risk publishing now. I can remember feeling propelled by a momentum to create social change and work for justice that I continue to cultivate in young women today.

Working with the National YWCA and Student Assembly was exciting and effective. We had to plan out everything thoroughly in order to accomplish our broad agenda. Meetings were contentious, which was the style of that period, but we somehow always returned together to the table. Leadership development was my major objective, and I was determined to encourage nonwhite students into leadership positions just as I had been nurtured. I continued to reintroduce race-related issues, and we also did preliminary work on abortion rights, a central women's issue at that time. We were continually weaving the issues brought by representatives from local communities into the national agenda.

By May of 1970 I was in New York full time, planning for the Y's National Convention, to be held in Houston. One of the big events preceding the convention was a preconference meeting of YWCA black women. Five hundred black women attended, more than I had ever seen together in one room in my life. We caucused, and we met as one. In one of the large meetings, I gave a speech on neocolonialism, which I sent along to a friend, saying, "Don't distribute it, but can you believe I wrote this?" The speech ended, "and in the name of Malcolm, Martin, and Jesus. . . . " I wouldn't dare do anything like that now. This was a turning point for me on the subject of change. I was being exposed to a view of the world so broad that I allowed myself to embrace an openness to new ways of thinking. I would give nearly anything to go back and watch that time all over again, to see those in-your-face powerful women responding to the distinct call of the times. I thought we could just stop the war; I thought we could bring about peace; I thought we could come to mutual understanding; and I thought we women could bring this about in a way no one else could. The sky was the limit. I had come up in a childhood that had not frightened me away from expecting good from human beings and a world that helped us grow.

After my term as national chair was up, Anne Kern invited me to become a part-time staff member of the University Y while I finished up my studies at UC Berkeley. It was then that we organized the Black Women's Unit, a grassroots project modeled after the Black Women's Network that we had created at the YWCA National Convention in Houston. Under the direction of program coordinator Juanita Pappillion, we established a series of weekly support groups that ran for two years. Black women students met together in several groups to deal with issues they chose, mostly coming to grips with the major stressors: relationships with black men, education, politics, and self-identity. The support groups were very successful, a precursor to the women's self-help groups that are still so vital and crucial to our development thirty years later.

What we didn't talk about was the brokenness we felt from betrayals in our personal relationships—mistrust, lack of commitment to self and to family, residues of the ways we and those closest to us had internalized racism and sexism. We met on Wednesday and Thursday nights for the better part of two years, and though we made considerable strides in our support of one another in getting our educations and getting launched into adulthood, there were a few, even so, who never connected, whom we could not reach. Most of us did not have a sense of being grounded—some craved love that they should have received as young children but did not.

Relationships were everything, then and now. Women saw themselves, not men, as keepers of the relationships they were in, and they looked for ways to make the bonds solid—by losing weight, clearing complexions, opening the heart, being flexible and more patient. I was fed up with making these demands upon myself to keep a man. I wanted a partnership. I was in the minority then, and may remain so, but I've persisted in having high expectations of those to whom I choose to open my heart.

I have always liked being around women who challenge the way I see the world, or who nudge me from the unexamined comfort I seek with family and friends. A number of women in the National YWCA had enormous influence on me. Francie Kendall, whom I first met at the National Assembly, has been a friend for thirty years now. As a southern white woman, she confronted my prejudices in a big way. When I first met her, there was no way I was going to sit next to, sleep in the same room with, think about, respond to, or be within ten feet of a white woman with a southern accent. I came to admire Francie and her sister white southerners and developed an off-the-charts respect. We were thrown together enough that I had to look at her, to look at them, as unique individuals.

Another of the Y women who made a big difference to me at the time I was the student leader was Lillas Barnes, a longtime National Board member who was a seventy-five-year-old spinster. She was the epitome of the wealthy white lady. She always wore a hat and gloves and carried a handbag and was as cute as could be, with a little something off: a slightly skewed hat or a little bit of slip showing. Before every large student gathering, Lillas would send me a corsage that I was to wear as the students' leader. Prior to the 1970 convention, we had a string of meetings: the black women's conference, three days of student meetings, and a morning with the national student committee. By the time the conference arrived, I was wiped out. I couldn't imagine continuing on for another week. Lillas sent me an orchid to wear to the conference opening, and when I walked into the auditorium, there was a standing ovation, a truly uplifting moment. Lillas gave me inspiration to persist and a symbol to remind me to stick to the task.

My beloved brother Gerald's losing battle with AIDS was another crossroads for me. Gerald and I had been extremely close as children. He was a creative genius, a free spirit who grasped life with open hands, and who loved me. After his death, at the tender age of thirty-five, I deepened my commitment to the health field, where I've dwelt ever since. I worked for a while at the AIDS Health Project with the University of California at San Francisco, and I spent time with a major California foundation, funding health-related projects, but I really found my place when I took the helm of the Women's Health Collaborative in California in 1995. The Collaborative was my conceptual dream, given form, substance, and funding, and the courage to lead.

At one of our early convenings, we decided that for the women of color to be able to develop our relationships with one another, we could benefit from spending caucus time separate from the white women of the Collaborative. So many feelings about this came up that I found myself giving the same talk I had given in Houston twenty-five years earlier, when we had decided to bring the black women together for our own gathering. (This time, though, I left Malcolm, Martin, and Jesus out of it.) I felt I had come full circle. I was able to create a place where I could bring together smart, powerful, caring women, across racial and ethnic differences to nurture and show their strengths.

Even though I assemble major leaders in women's health in California through the Collaborative and guide their work together, and even though we instituted a program that systematically trains young women to become leaders in their communities, I have never consciously thought of myself as a leader. I think we often confuse leadership with empowerment, and my interest is in fortifying people so that they can become resources for themselves and their communities. This cuts across all sorts of gender and race issues for me. And even though my work for the past seven years has been organizing women to come up with creative perspectives and goals to better women's health, I still don't think of myself as a "feminist." Perhaps the word is too loaded now. I have struggled to maintain myself apart from these labels, to work across all boundaries and accept no limits, and manage the differences. Of course I see myself and other women as fully human, and that is what feminism is, yet I continue to feel corralled if I attach myself to some category.

The YWCA introduced me to a much bigger life than I could ever have dreamed of when I was a girl, even as "Herself." Along the way I married and had a lovely daughter, now graduated from college. I am a good mother, but one child was right for me. I have always honored women's reproductive dominion over their bodies. I want all women, but particularly younger women and girls, to have access to the same types of exposure and experiences and quality of life that I was able to have.

To have this, we must continue to build the foundations and structures of community that bring people together at the most basic level. We have to begin at home. I can't imagine being uninspired. I can't imagine being useless, or not having a sophisticated political sense about how I feel and think. Through my experiences as a student leader in the Y, I learned how to caucus with people, to solicit their thinking and to use resources and ideas to create change with others. It's easy to react to situations, and to know what is right from what is wrong, but the challenge for us is to direct our thoughts toward making things happen. Getting angry about events is a far cry from thinking about possible interventions, about how to organize a group, about how to improve conditions, and about how to give back for all that we have been given.

I believe relationships are everything—social, political, personal, work alliances. Without being in relationship "to" we do not have the power to change, move, develop, and grow. We become lost in a self-centered spiral.

The YWCA provided a pathway for my personal journey so that sexism, racism, self-doubt, and self-analysis would not bog me down.

The YWCA gave me a network of teachers always in conversation with one another and community, taking on difficult political and social issues with great force. I learned from that great body of women to be a conversation starter, an effective leader, and to find courage in my heart and head to live with meaningful determination in the world.

CHAPTER 15

Frances E. Kendall

Generally, when I talk about my work with the National Student YWCA, I use words like "changed my life" or "I'll never be the same," but I don't often stop to feel what that experience really was internally. Perhaps because it was too confusing and too painful and too joyful all at the same time. Perhaps because it was so tied up with my relationship with my family. And perhaps because it was then that I intentionally rejected many of the perspectives and behaviors that my southern culture and family held. I chose the National Student YWCA as my family because the women there cared for me and loved the person I was becoming in ways that my blood family could not. These women nurtured and challenged me to live the values that grew to be central to me during that time and have shaped my life's work.

I was born in 1947 and grew up in legally segregated Waco, Texas. My life as an upper-middle-class white child was not terribly unusual for the time, except that my father had died when I was four years old so my family configuration was not what was viewed as normal. Raised in an extremely patriotic, conservative, Texas Republican family, I was explicitly taught many lessons: America is the greatest country in the world and it is un-American to question anything it does; the race and class systems in the United States make good sense and should be defended at any cost; white people are better than black people—well, really black people are something less than human and so don't deserve the consideration that white people do; and segregation is God's way of designing the world. I fervently believed that the United States was "the land of the free and the home of the brave" and that everything I had been taught was right.

Then, for grades nine through twelve, I went to National Cathedral School, an Episcopal girls' school in Washington, D.C., and the lens through which I viewed life changed dramatically. I was in class with black girls who were smarter than I was and whose families were wealthier than mine. Lynda Bird and Lucy Baines, Lyndon and Lady Bird Johnson's daughters, went to Cathedral, as did girls who had been sent away to school because their parents' civil rights activity in the Deep South made it physically dangerous for them to remain at home. The perspectives of people around me were now entirely different. I heard weekly sermons at the National Cathedral on social ills in the country and particularly in the South. I was told that, to be truly Christian, I had to fight for social and racial justice, precisely the opposite of what I had been taught in my Episcopal church in Waco. I no longer knew where to place my allegiances. I was coming to understand that much of what I had been taught by my family and culture was not true, but I wasn't quite sure what or whom to believe. I began to feel torn between the beliefs my family had instilled and what I was seeing with my own eyes. The clash of opinions and values that was going on in the country was happening inside me as well.

My visits at home were rife with verbal violence. By that time my mother and I had had many fights about why she hadn't stood up to the racism in our family. I struggled to understand how it was possible that the person who was supposed to be my model, my closest connection to the world, who was so set on teaching me about the "right" and "tasteful" jewelry, clothing, and Christmas decorations, didn't seem to know the difference between right and wrong. Or, if she knew, she hadn't stood up to those around her. I was besieged by hideous racist jokes from my brothers-in-law and male cousins. The more I fought back, of course, the greater pleasure they took in recounting the stories. While the women usually didn't tell the jokes, they didn't stop them, either. Our family was spoken of as upstanding leaders in the community, and yet I knew they were also old members of the Ku Klux Klan. They had joined in the 1920s, my mother told me, "to protect their women and children." How could I trust a mother who seemed to me such a coward? What did it say about me that this was the blood from which I had come? Rationalization based on "historical context" was, and still usually is, worth nothing on the open market of my heart. And how could I love a country where such injustice was part of daily life? If I couldn't believe what I heard in "My Country 'Tis of Thee," what did I have to believe in? (I remember singing, "land where my father died," instead of "land where our fathers died," because he had.) It was in that state of disillusion and confusion that I went to college and became involved in the Y.

I walked into the University of Denver Campus YMCA-YWCA in September 1965, about a week after I arrived at college. I went there because I had seen a flyer about a program on tutoring "inner-city" black children in Chicago. I thought it might be an activity that would be of use to others and help me shed some of my white shame and guilt. (Also I knew about tutoring because some of my "cool" classmates at Cathedral had worked with poor black children at the Northwest Settlement House while I was feeding old and sick people at the Washington Home for the Incurables.) The Y was in the basement of a nondescript red-brick dormitory. The office was painted that shade of institutional pea-green that had been surplus after World War II. The chairs, tables, and desks looked as though they had been discarded by other offices or by students who needed to get rid of overstuffed furniture. The walls were covered with political posters—pictures of Martin Luther King, Rosa Parks, and Cesar Chavez, and the now-famous one of Malcolm X holding an assault rifle and looking out of a curtained window, with the words "By any means necessary" at the bottom. There were announcements of upcoming programs and meetings, all copied on a mimeograph machine, the likes of which don't exist anymore. The woman who spoke to us about tutoring was Sherry Miller, a white woman who had grown up on a ranch in Big Horn, Montana. She was filled with life and exuberance and stories about her summer in inner-city Chicago, including one in which her father, a tall lanky cowboy who'd never been out of the state of Montana, donned his best jeans and cowboy hat and took the bus to Chicago to meet a kid Sherry wanted her family to adopt. I was hooked.

I spent the next four years in and out of that office. The staff and students became my friends, the student president, Margi Duncombe, my roommate. Some, like Margi and Sherry, grew to be life-long friends. I adopted, and was adopted by, Sherry's family, and they are still the only parents I have ever met that I would have chosen, had I been able to. My first couple of years in the National Student YWCA were spent working locally and regionally. I quickly became an officer in the organization—people there were thrilled with any new warm body that showed up and was willing to work. We hosted programs about the ways that black and Latino people were being treated in Denver. We registered people to vote. We painted houses in poor neighborhoods, and we set up a tutoring program for poor children of color. We organized and participated in boycotts supporting migrant farmworkers—I haven't bought grapes and iceberg lettuce since that time, nor will I drink Coors beer because of their historically racist treatment of Chicano workers. We visited other campus Ys throughout the region—Kansas, Nebraska, Colorado—looking at their programs and organizing their communities with them.

My happiest times were spent at regional meetings, singing, dancing, and building relationships with people who were different from me, talking about changing the world and acting silly. Within an hour's time we could go from organizing a boycott against Safeway for selling nonunion grapes and lettuce to having a watermelon seed–spitting contest. At one particular meeting I remember skipping down the streets of Estes Park, Colorado, holding hands with Ann Duncan, a dark-skinned student from Panama. I called her "n——" and she called me "honky." Our friendship was naive and important, at least to me. I think I believed that if I had a black friend I couldn't really be like my family. It was a time.

But it wasn't always comfortable, and sometimes it was horribly painful. At one point during my freshman year I remember standing in my college dorm room, looking out at the mountains to the west of Denver and realizing at a deep level that the foundation I had built out of trusting and loving my mother and family and my country—I used to love singing all those patriotic songs—was crumbling. I had a card on my wall drawn by Sister Corita, an Immaculate Heart nun, with a quotation from Camus, "I should like to be able to love my country and still love justice," and it seemed clear at that moment that to do both was simply not possible. The cracks in the relationship with my family that had started appearing while I was at Cathedral widened and deepened, while my sense of despair in wondering where I would go if I emotionally left home lessened. I was discovering that there were people in the world who found my growing determination to work on racism hopeful.

In December of my sophomore year, 1966, I went to my first national meeting—the National Student Assembly of the YWCA. NSAY was held in Chicago between Christmas and New Year's. I left Waco, flew to Chicago, took a taxi to a big hotel, and walked into a whole new world. There were women students attending from colleges and universities across the country, and there were women—professional staff—who had chosen to make careers of working for social justice. That meeting is something of a blur to me because I got very sick with bronchitis and, for the only time in my life, had to call a hotel doctor. But evidently I participated sufficiently to be elected to the National Student Committee (NSCY), a group that met three or four times a year in New York City. Work on racism began in earnest for me as women students of color challenged the white women either to get serious about working on our own racism or they would leave the organization. I don't think I had any idea what working on my own racism meant, but I knew it was serious. The racial divide that existed outside the meetings was present inside as well. Of course. But I think it was a shock to many well-meaning white women—both students and professionals—to have our actions and our motivations questioned. The amazing thing that I witnessed was that, rather than getting huffy and defensive, the majority of the professional staff rolled up their collective sleeves and went to work. It was not simple and it was not everybody, but the message was clear: this is a path that the National Student YWCA must follow.

At roughly the same time, organizational challenges were facing the Y as well. Working with students in the late 1960s was significantly different from working with students in the 1950s. The times and the issues were changing. If the Student YWCA was to continue to be relevant to the times, it was going to have to question at a deep level what it was supposed to do as an organization. In response to requests from the Student YWCA, the National Board established a two-year Commission on New Directions. Its task was to "think radically on where we are and where we are called to be." The commission was made up of students, members of the national staff, and the National Board. We were charged with changing the Student YWCA at its roots in order to respond to the needs of the students of the 1960s. It is almost impossible for me to imagine a national organization in 2002 asking its student members to participate in tearing itself apart and rebuilding so that it might be a better instrument of change. In fact, my experience over the last twenty years is that most organizations have hunkered down rather than rising up to meet those asking for change.

A year and a half later, in the summer of 1968, a new organizational structure was presented by the commission at the National Student Committee of the YWCA; among its suggestions were the establishment of a Black Affairs Committee and task forces on white racism, middle-class economic power, and communication networks. Students at that meeting were clear that the work on racial justice at the national level must move beyond rhetoric to concrete action. The "Plan of Action for Middle-Class Economic Power," for example, had two objectives for using the Student YWCA's economic power to "end poverty and oppression": "to participate in organized boycotts of those target organizations which have been chosen by peace and racial justice groups because of their contributions to aims and goals antithetical to those of the Student YWCA" and "to purchase from and support institutions owned and controlled by people in ghetto [*sic*] and low income communities" (*Interact*, no. 7, October 1968).

The work that was occurring in the Student YWCA and the context of the civil rights movement also pushed the National Board to make changes in how it presented itself to the world. In 1970 the National Convention of the YWCA adopted the One Imperative, to thrust its collective power toward the "elimination of racism, wherever it exists and by any means necessary." Students who were representatives on the National Board, along with other key members, worked long and hard to move the board to take such a stand. At the last minute, some members at the convention tried to change the wording to "by any means possible." Black women rose as a group and threatened to leave the organization if that change was made, and "by any means necessary" remained.

At the age of twenty-one, not only was I learning that it is possible to change organizations from the inside, I was also seeing that it was possible, through economic power, for groups to use outside pressure to bring about change in the world. Following the lead of the Methodist Board of Missions, for example, which divested itself of investments in companies that supported the South African government, the National Student Committee decided that perhaps we could help push schools that had Student YWCAs to do the same. I volunteered to create a model for divesting and set to work. My challenge was to create a process to investigate university investments that could be understood by people who knew little about the ins and outs of university systems and who were not financially savvy. My assumption was that, by being knowledgeable about how a specific university invested its money, students at that institution would be better able to change the ways their tuition money was used. "A Model for Investigating University Financial Investments" was my first independent venture into understanding how systems change. It was prompted by what I was learning as a member of the National Student Committee in 1968–1969, and I have continued to study systems change and to teach others how systems work ever since. The model proved useful and was distributed by an arm of the United Nations to students around the world.

Within the National Student YWCA there was a belief that it was important to know what was going on politically in all corners of the world and a sense that we could and must have an impact on those events. We understood that making lasting political and organizational change requires deep understanding of what is happening, so we created study groups as part of the National Student Committee. I remember particularly the reports from the South Africa and Latin America groups and how well informed I felt about what was going on in those regions. I don't know that I have since been so clear about the dynamics in Latin America. It was probably in that time that it became obvious to me how essential it is to know the history of a country, not just the present, because the past informs the present and future in powerful ways. We involved ourselves in stopping the war in Vietnam, as did many other organizations. We also worked with the University Christian Movement in its work on white racism, with the North American Committee on Latin America (NACLA) on uprooting dictatorships in Latin American countries, and with antiapartheid groups in South Africa. Our objective was to be as informed about situations around the world as possible and to develop models to influence change.

The National Student Committee was also involved in creating antiracism pilot programs for campus Ys. At both Duke University and Oberlin College, Student YWCAs did significant work to address institutionalized racism on campus, involving students, faculty, and administrators. In some ways these pilots were an extension of the antiracism discussions and training we were regularly engaged in. Sally Timmel, Nancy Richardson, and Sunny Robinson, three white women, created a series of workshops based on materials Sally had created and that would be compiled to form "White on White: A Handbook for Groups Working against Racism." The workbook, printed in 1970, was intentionally designed to aid white people in examining our own racism. The following excerpt from the Preface gives a sense of the tone and the intent of the handbook.

> Racism in America is a white problem. It is woven into our institutions and our culture. We must all recognize how we benefit by racism and are caught in its web. Whites can and must change! Change themselves, their institutions, and their culture.
>
> As we begin to use this book, designed to help us come to terms with racism, we must recognize that a book, a set of discussions, does not eliminate racism. It is only when we have transformed the total fabric of our lives that we will have eliminated racism and created a truly pluralistic society. But we must begin somewhere and beginning with ourselves and the institutions in which we find ourselves is now clearly called for.
>
> We need help to look at ourselves. We need help to understand how we as a people through history have used others for our own ends. We need help to look, without fear, at the meaning of our own lives. We need help to understand that our own worth and power is not lost in a just distribution of power. The emotional weight that racism produces in whites blinds us from a vision of the fundamental changes we must work for and which will, in fact, free us all.

Racism and white privilege were part of my everyday conversation. I read constantly, never able to get enough information. And I began my personal exploration about what it meant to be white and southern that lasted for more than ten years. I was moved, and sometimes pushed, along in that excavation by my cherished friends—my family of choice—in the Y.

There were several formal events that addressed institutional racism, whiteness, and white privilege. Two in particular stand out in my memory. One was a large convocation held in New York City. It was organized by the National YWCA Center for Racial Justice, and the National Student Committee was invited to participate. What seems remarkable today, but did not seem odd at all at the time, was that hundreds of white women came together for a day to work specifically on their racism and their privilege. I was in workshops with Dorothy Height, the woman who has led the National Council of Negro Women for many years and who was the first director of the Center for Racial Justice, with Dorothy Gray, a wonderful professor at Queens College, and with Lilace Reid Barnes, whose grandfather had started Lake Forest College—an incredible woman whose every comment was filled with wisdom. I spent significant time with both Dorothy and Lilace because they were two of the National YWCA board members who served on the National Student Committee.

The second event I remember particularly was a three-day training on "Third World Leadership and Monitoring" that was held at a summer camp in northern Wisconsin in October 1972. The sleeping quarters had no wooden walls—just screens. It was incredibly cold. The meeting was led by Reginald Wilson, Patricia Bidol, Robert Terry, and Barbara Mays, each of whom had done nationally significant antiracism work. The concept of people of color "monitoring" the actions of white people was one that has really stuck with me. Inherent in it is a shift in the power dynamic—one of the definitions of "monitoring" in the *Random House Unabridged Dictionary* (second edition, 1993) is "to watch closely for purposes of control, surveillance, etc."—with the oppressed assessing the actions of the oppressor. Once we began to notice racism, Barbara Mays told us, we could never *not* see it again. We had bought a one-way ticket. Her idea, so descriptive of my work in the Y, is central in my life. In fact, it was reflected in the dedication of the first edition of my first book, *Diversity in the Classroom* (New York: Teachers College Press, 1983): "This book is dedicated to the women of the National student YWCA and the National YWCA. It was with them that I joined 'the struggle for peace and justice, freedom and dignity for all people' (YWCA Purpose, 1970). My life has never been the same and I am immensely grateful."

It is difficult now to describe the environment then in the YWCA and in the nation, much less what the YWCA did for me. Comradeship, working with people who believe strongly in the same issues, can probably be found in most organizations. But our goal was not to be friends, though life-long friendships surely grew. We struggled together, bringing all of our differences with us, toward "p.j.f. and d.," as we referred to the Y's Purpose. We were clear that together we could change the world, or at least the institutions to which we were connected, and that there was no other choice that could be made except to do it—regardless of the effort.

The Y provided a place to unpack and deconstruct—to take the lessons I had been taught about what was right and what was wrong, what was important and what was trivial, and rethink them, and to do that with the help, support, and pushing of people who were involved in the same struggle. Each of us had different questions to ask. Mine were centered primarily around issues of race, family, country and loyalty, and what it meant to be Christian—the easy ones.

*I*n regard to race, I had been taught that things were as they were supposed to be, and that, as white people, we only had what we deserved, and so there was no reason to feel guilty about my family's socioeconomic status or the benefits given to us because of our skin color. My family had been in the cotton business for decades; the manual labor on which the company's success was built was done by African Americans. Yet I was taught that black people were not as smart, good, worthy. They weren't "people like us" and therefore didn't deserve the same treatment or opportunities. Black people were there to serve us. It was their job to care for us as we went about our lives. In one hand I held these messages; in the other I carried my experiences of people like Dorothy Height and Valerie Russell. Miss Height, a true giant in the fight for civil rights, ran the National YWCA Center for Racial Justice. I was regularly in her presence, hearing her speak and watching her work. Val worked with the Student Y as the editor of its newsletter, *Interact*. I am still able to recall instantly her deeply resonant voice, her wisdom, and her laughter. We sang freedom songs deep into more nights than I could count; they gave us hope and nourished our souls. Daily I grew in the knowledge that I had not been taught the truth. What I had been taught was "right" was in direct opposition to what I saw and experienced.

I was extremely confused about what "family" was. I had been born into a family that was fine, upstanding, Christian—one filled with civic leaders. Yet I felt shame rather than pride about my history. On the one hand, I remember being crystal clear about my intentions and the path I was compelled to follow. It was for me, as for many others, a moral imperative. On the other hand, I was bewildered and heart-sickened by my family's response to racial struggles and to my participation in them. How was it possible that those who were supposed to love me most, to be closest to me, felt so alien? Not only were they different, but, to me, they were morally wrong. I constantly questioned myself: if I had come from them, was I one of them? At some level I feared that, "come the revolution," I wouldn't have the guts to stand where I so vociferously said I would, that all my work to be different from my family would dissolve, that they had instilled their values too early for me to change. In spite of my fears, I pushed on, learning more about myself as a white person, asking harder and harder questions, being expected by my "family of choice" to see the world differently than I had been raised to. As I made choices to separate myself from my family, I moved toward the Y, finding acceptance there precisely because of the person I was becoming rather than in spite of it.

My mother continued not to understand my life in and love of the Y, and it was always a point of dissension. I almost always chose the Y instead of Waco and her. Because of all that I was learning about what was happening in this nation, in the war in Vietnam, in the nation's role in supporting murderous regimes and training their soldiers for Latin American civil wars, the explosions during conversations at home never stopped. I felt great disdain for and anger toward my immediate family—my mother, my two older sisters, and the men they married. My mother died of cancer in June 1969, two months before I graduated from college. I was at the annual summer NSCY meeting when my sister called to say my mother was dying. The differences were never truly resolved between us, though about six months before she died she told me that I was the one she was least worried about and that she knew I would be fine in life. I'm sure she was confused as well. Her youngest daughter, whom she had had to raise on her own, openly disparaged the things that made sense to her—the family was wrong, the church was wrong, the South was wrong, and her daughter wouldn't make her debut or join a sorority unless blacks and Jews could be included. It probably made little sense to her.

I also struggled greatly with what it meant to be American, as many others did between 1966 and 1974. It was obvious that my country was not what it said it was—the land of opportunity in which anyone of any color, class, or gender could be anything she or he worked hard enough to be. What was not clear to me was how to participate in pushing the country to live up to its patriotic rhetoric when raising questions caused me to be seen as un-American and disloyal. Now, at age fifty-four, I'm not particularly invested in appearing patriotic. But in my mid- to late twenties, I felt betrayed by three institutions that were central to my life—my family, my country, and my church. I had relied on all three to tell the whole truth, and each had pretended to be something it wasn't. There were many times when I felt that the "ground of my being," one of the theologian Paul Tillich's most famous phrases, was being shaken.

The Y shaped my spiritual beliefs in many ways—those that were obvious at the time and those that were more subtle but have continued to guide what I believe and how I act as I get older. Because there was a great deal of open dialogue about whether to keep the "C"—for Christian—in the name during the years in which I was most intensely involved with the National Student YWCA, I focused on what it meant to be Christian, as an individual and as an organization. What did it say about us if we defined ourselves as a "Christian" group? Did it really express who and what we were? Did it exclude people who weren't Christian but were committed to social justice? And how did calling myself "Christian" affect the ways in which I would live my life? What I and we came to was that if we considered ourselves Christian, we had no alternative but to involve ourselves in addressing social problems, working for the common good as opposed to what is profitable for us individually. I still believe that.

The tenets that "seeped in" to my worldview were less immediately clear. They were gathered informally over time, and most of them grew out of poems, quotations, random comments that resonated with what I was learning about life. They came from meetings, communications, interactions, and relationships that were connected to the Y. These thoughts were reflected in the myriad cards that were push-pinned all over my apartments as I moved from Denver to New York City to North Carolina for graduate school: "To everything there is a season" (Ecclesiastes). "Look, love is all there is and that's enough" (the Beatles). "No noble, well grown tree ever disowned its dark roots, for it grows not only upwards but downwards as well" (Carl Jung). "I would rather die on the highways of Alabama than make a butchery of my conscience" (Martin Luther King, Jr.). "Sisterhood is blooming— Springtime will never be the same" (Anonymous). "Choose life, only that and always and at whatever risk" (Sister Helen Kelly). "for all that has been, thanks! for all that will be, Yes!" (e. e. cummings).

Even when I was in college in Denver, as my mother had frequently pointed out, I spent a great deal of time in New York City at the National

YWCA headquarters at 600 Lexington Avenue. The building was a wonderful old one—gray stone, lots of marble, huge chandeliers, grand ballrooms—and the National Student Y had its offices on one of the upper floors. Arriving there was like coming home. Lots of hugs and warm welcomes, particularly from my friend Valerie Russell. Often when I first walked into her office during a visit she would say, "Mothers, hide your sons! Here she comes!" and laugh with joy. Her voice could be loud and booming or quiet and gentle, but it was always wonderfully resonant. Val preached as she talked and as she sang, about rights and wrongs, about love, about peace. She sang folk songs—about the four little girls who were killed in the bombing of the black church in Birmingham, about "Bring me a rose in the wintertime, when they're hard to find." She frequently led us in prayers that were always focused on justice and social change. She was wise and powerful and playful and, at the same time, humble.

Val was one of my greatest gifts from the Y, the abundance of role models with whose presence I was blessed. I watched white women like Fran Jaynes, Dorothy Gray, and Jane Wells speaking up about race, putting themselves at risk of losing the respect of friends and family. They were examples for me of white women who were willing to look at white racism and our complicity in it. Lilace Reid Barnes was committed to the growth of young women. Time and again she underscored the necessity of taking risks, believing what Martin Luther King, Jr., said about there being "cosmic companionship" in the struggle for righteousness. Eula Redenbaugh, Elizabeth Jackson, and Theodora Ninesteel were tireless in their commitment to justice. The women of color, some of whom were professional staff and others who were student leaders, like Renetia Martin and Margarita Mendoza de Sugiyama, were willing to give me a chance to do and be something different, despite my white skin and Texas accent. As Renetia has said in my presence many times since, "I never believed I would trust someone who looked and sounded like her." And always there was Val. And Miss Height.

My experiences with the Y fed my head and my heart. We believed that a better, more just world was possible, even if it meant tearing down the institutions to which we were connected, either from the inside or the outside, and rebuilding. This rebuilding part is essential: the goal was not destruction but social change—it was about re-creating in order to move ahead and to make whole. And that's what it was about for me personally as well. My search has always been for wholeness—whether I described it as "being the best me I could possibly be" or re-membering and re-collecting. The belief that change is possible has continued to be interwoven throughout my life's work. I have devoted my career and life to doing antiracism work and work on white privilege. I am an organizational change consultant, focusing on social justice issues, working primarily with colleges and universities and with senior decision makers who are attempting to create a climate that is hospitable to all people there.

The Y was truly the turning point in my life and offered an environment in which to grow. The issue of race was front and center. It *was* the issue on which we worked. It is difficult to describe what it felt like to be white and southern and coming of age during the civil rights era. There is not the public turmoil now that then moved so many people to reflection and action. While racism continues unabated, Americans' responses are very different. The YWCA's position, however, is still reflected in its mission statement, which you can read today on its website: "The Association will thrust its collective power toward the elimination of racism wherever it exists and by any means necessary."

CHAPTER 16

Margarita Mendoza
de Sugiyama

I was born into a migratory farmworker family in Yakima, Washington, in 1949, the second oldest of eleven children. I was a part of a huge extended Mexican family system that was pretty raucous and worked the fields. Everyone used to refer to my grandparents' place as "God's Little Acre" because it had horses and chickens and cows and goats and a huge garden. My mom and dad moved into a little house that was built right next to my grandparents', and I always felt a part of that place. My grandmother was kind of the crew boss for all the grandchildren and the little kids. When we were out in the fields, she was the one who came behind us and cleaned up the rows that we were working on, whether it be strawberries or potatoes or beets.

Somehow, a critical Good Chicana attribute got lost on me, because I was never submissive. I was never willing to shut up if I thought I was right, and I always had the support of my mother and my grandmother. They were the two people who had the greatest influence on me. They would protect me even when I was fairly outrageous. Now, in middle age, I still aspire to be like my mother. Despite her incredibly difficult life, she had such serenity and a kindness about her. She was always out there rescuing people who needed love and caring. My grandmother was also one of those who cared for the community. She was known as a *curandera*, a healer, a spiritual doctor, a counselor. Her mother-in-law, my great-grandmother, whose name was Teresita Valdez, was also a *curandera*. She was the one who led my family from Colorado to Washington. She had five sons, and during the Depression they heard there were jobs in the state of Washington. So the whole community, the barrio that they lived in, came to Washington to look for work. When they got to the Yakima River—this is the story my grandmother told us—

they had no money and no food. So my great-grandmother led the people to kneel down along the river and pray, and then the men left to go look for work. My grandfather and his brothers went to the home of one of the big farmers in the Yakima area—Mr. Mackaleer—and asked for work. Mackaleer not only gave them jobs, but gave them money and some food so that they could go back and feed the rest of the people. It's one of those miracle stories.

Our background is Catholic. Wherever we went, if there was a Catholic church, we went to church. There are certain holidays that are very central to the Mexican family. One of them is called El Dia de los Muertos, which is translated "The Day of the Dead." It falls around All Saints' Day. It's the day that you celebrate the life of the people in your family who have passed away. You keep an altar in your home that has pictures of the people who have passed away. During El Dia de los Muertos, you decorate the altar and place food on it—special food like tamales. It's a big celebration of their lives with music and dancing and storytelling. I know so much about my great-grandmother, though I never met her, because of these celebrations.

It was a shock when my family left this community, yet I see that as the first step on the road that ultimately led me to college. My dad joined the army in order to pay off a huge medical debt incurred after my sister was born prematurely. For quite a while he was stationed in Yakima, but then he was transferred to Fort Lewis in Tacoma, Washington. Our family—two sisters, myself, and four younger brothers—all moved to Tacoma. For the first time, we did not live in a community that was predominantly Mexican or Chicano. Our neighborhood was all white, and my high school of 2,500 had only seven students of color.

My dad worked hard to make sure that we went to a Catholic school, because he felt it was important that we have a religious education. He was also a traditional Mexican man who expected his daughters to finish high school and get married in the church. By contrast, he wanted his sons to go on to college after high school. After we moved to Tacoma, my grandmother would come every summer and bring along young Mexican guys, because she was concerned that my sister and I would not meet nice Catholic Mexican boys to marry. Unfortunately, that wasn't my dream, and this caused a lot of conflict between me and my dad.

What really changed the direction of my life was the opportunity to participate in Project Overcome, an experimental project that was later known as Upward Bound, designed to open up the possibility of higher education to high school students of color. The pilot project, at Western Washington State College in Bellingham, Washington, right on the border of Canada, sent out recruiters to high schools across the state. When they hit my school, the first seven students interviewed were, of course, the seven students of color. That very summer my dad left for Vietnam.

In Upward Bound, I was, once again, the only Mexican, the only Chicana, in the group. But I learned that there really was a place for me in higher education. At Western, for the first time, I had teachers who were truly interested in me. To my surprise, I found out I was good at analyzing poetry and essays. I learned that I actually could do mathematics. In addition, I became much more politically conscious. In high school, I had been aware of the pride of farmworkers, and I admired people like Cesar Chavez and especially Delores Huerta. I really identified with Huerta, a strong woman who was making a difference in the lives of her people, my people, our people. Then when I went to Upward Bound as a high school senior, I met people who could teach me what I yearned to know about the movement in its broadest sense. We had the opportunity to learn as much as we wanted about racism and sexism. I had lots of interest because it fit my temperament, my passion for justice, and my willingness to argue for what I believed in. I read more that summer than I had read the whole four years I was in high school. It was empowering.

Upward Bound opened a whole new vista for me in terms of race and ethnicity as well. I was rooted in the Mexican community and knew a lot about Native Americans, especially the Yakima because of where my parents grew up. Then I met my husband, who is Japanese American and a Buddhist, then working on his master's degree in mathematics. We had a mutual friend, Sister Antoinette—we called her Toni—and the three of us used to play tennis and have lunch together. My husband and I had a testy relationship at the beginning, but because we were together all the time, we eventually did become friends. Getting to know my husband, his family, and their life experience opened another door to things I had known nothing about before. As a result I was completely changed.

To go off alone to an Upward Bound program was a very foreign experience. For the first time I could look at my life in my huge family in Tacoma and in Yakima with some degree of analytical distance. In farmworker families, you really aren't an individual, you are a part of the whole; you survive because every person contributes. It made me angry to see the effects of racism and sexism within my culture and on my culture. There is just such great injustice when people who work in the fields can't even afford to buy the produce that they harvest. My admiration for people like Delores Huerta and Cesar Chavez grew even greater. After that summer experience, however, I saw myself more as an individual, and I began to make life choices that were completely different from the ones my family and culture assumed I would make: I married a Japanese man and went off to college.

When my husband started a doctoral program at Washington State University in Pullman, I set out to finish my undergraduate degree. I was an activist right away and helped to found the Chicano student association. But the most active group on campus addressing the issues of apartheid in South Africa and the grape and lettuce boycotts in support of the farmworkers was the YWCA. At Washington State University, the YWCA was multiethnic and definitely the most formidable group on campus addressing issues of racism and sexism. I assumed, however, that because I was a Catholic woman of color I shouldn't be there. Although there was a YWCA in Yakima where I grew up, it was never a place where my family felt welcome, because the people there were white and, most important, they were Protestant. The Y was not a place for Catholics. On campus, however, I ran into a woman I had grown up with, Judy Fortier, who was a member of the YWCA and who kept after me to go with her. At that point in my life I really didn't like white people, because of what they represented. When Judy finally dragged me up to the YWCA, I found that the executive director was not only Caucasian, but the wife of a rancher, a farmer. This woman—whom I assumed I would hate—turned out to be the major influence in my life, the person who enabled me to let go of the anger and the hatred I felt and learn to deal with people as individuals—one on one. She ignored all my prickliness; she ignored all that anger; and she was there to work with me. She wanted us to be partners in addressing farmworker issues, with me being the contact with the Chicano student group on campus. When I learned about the YWCA's imperative to thrust our collective power toward the elimination of racism wherever it exists and by any means necessary, I joined. I became a card-carrying member of the national movement because I wanted to be a part of any movement that had that imperative. In fact, ever since 1970 I have belonged to a YWCA, and sometimes more than one at the same time, both as a community member and as a student.

In retrospect, I see that Elaine Zachariason, executive director of the YWCA at Washington State University, was the greatest influence in radicalizing young women on that campus around the social issues of racism and sexism and homophobia. She had us dealing with issues of oppression, and in an active way, doing something about them, not just intellectualizing. I liked that, because all my life I've been a doer more than a talker. Elaine helped me to see that my leadership could go beyond the scope of my campus, that I really could be a national leader dealing with the issues of racism and sexism and the issues of my people. She sent me to my first national meeting, part of a series of seminars sponsored by the National YWCA called "The Web of Racism." The focus of that meeting in Portland was "The Web of Racism and the Role of Women." There I met people of great stature, women of color who were central to the leadership of the National YWCA.

The second national meeting I attended was in Cleveland on the topic, "The Web of Racism and Higher Education." During the seminar, the Y's National Student Assembly and the National Student Council also met, and I was elected the National Student chairwoman. This was when I began to think of myself as a leader, because other people referred to me that way. I had always thought of myself as someone who had a passion about things and was a damned good organizer. I was articulate. I could out-talk anybody. Those skills, in that national, all female context, made me a leader.

Long before I became a leader or held an elected position, I had been consciously dealing with women's issues. In my family experience, women are central to the life of the family, but leadership is really the role of the male head of the family. I was aware of the inequities in high school when my dad was so willing and so open about supporting my brothers in going to college, but not us daughters. All he thought we should do is graduate from high school, get married in the church, and have a good family. In fact, my sister did not finish high school, but got married when she was sixteen to a nice Catholic boy, a Mexican Catholic boy. Yet all the time she was dating him, she couldn't go anywhere without taking my oldest brother with her. It was pretty clear who was running the show, and I didn't like it. In the beginning, I did not think of it in a feminist way as much as I thought of it as a matter of control, of who had the power. But once I started reading in Upward Bound, I read everything that applied to me, and because I was a woman I read a lot of feminist literature.

The YWCA was so attractive because I saw women who were so strong in their passions about issues like apartheid and the farmworkers' struggle, and I thought, wow, these are the folks that I want to work with and be with. Most of them were white, but by and large there were always women of color also involved in that organization. Johnetta Cole was one of my instructors at Washington State University. She was on the faculty; she was the first head of the black studies program. Of course, we all just loved her. She was articulate and funny and passionate. She was Elaine Zachariason's best friend. Just by association, my feelings about Elaine changed as soon as I got these little tidbits. Central to Johnetta's work was her focus on the role of women as carriers of the culture. Not only did she address issues of oppression in relation to race, but she always talked about the sisterhood and Latinas and black women and her relationship with Elaine. Just watching her and listening to her made a difference in my life. Women's issues, not racism, were actually the first issues that I addressed in a formal, constructive way.

When I was elected the National Student chairwoman, I automatically became an ex-officio vice president of the National Board of the YWCA. At that time, there were 120 women on this board and we were moving in some high-powered company. For example, Eleanor Holmes Norton, a leading African American civil rights lawyer, came to train the board members who were going to work with university officials in writing affirmative action plans. It was like moving into another world, however. Before our first meeting, someone had called me and asked if I would serve tea. Well, there I was in my usual outfit: hair falling to my butt, a red bandana that you wear when you work in the fields to hold your hair away from your face, and an amulet of the rising phoenix, the United Farm Workers' symbol, that we had made to raise money for the Chicano student group. That's how I served tea. And here was this board of women wearing white gloves and pillbox hats, and of course lots of gold jewelry and diamonds. It just shocked me! This serving tea business was in honor of the women who began the YWCA. One of those women happened to be the mother of Mary Rockefeller and her sister. We had all the Rockefeller brothers there, too. These were people I had seen on television, all these Republican guys, and I was asked to serve them tea. Nobody would come get tea from me until Rocky—Nelson Rockefeller—came up and got tea, and then David came up. They were very cordial people. Then the ladies started coming. My nametag said "Margarita Mendoza de Sugiyama." All the other name tags said, "Mrs. David Rockefeller" or "Mrs. William Jenet." So they would call me Margarita, and being the little shit that I was, I would say, "Oh, okay, Bill, and Calvin, and David." And they'd protest, "Oh, no, no, no. My name is Mary," or "My name is Betty." I said, "Well, that's not what your nametag says." By the end of the first day, every woman on the board had written her own name on her nametag. After that, at our very next meeting, they had their own names printed on the nametags. The roster of the board members' names had "Mrs. Betty (William) Jenet." We were all calling each other by our first names then.

This wealth of women role models and mentors was just incredible. I would find myself at national meetings in New York City with women who were trustees of Vassar or members of the New York City Board of Education. There was this wonderful Texas woman, Johnny Marie Grimes, who was the superintendent of public instruction for the state of Texas. She was 6' 2" in her stocking feet, and I'm 4' 10". We looked like Mutt and Jeff. She wowed me every day by being so down to earth, a real person. Other women there were just like my mom—earth women, like Betty Jenet, Lilace Reid Barnes—women who were so kind and loving and accepting. They coached me; they mentored me.

I went back home to Pullman and told Elaine about all these amazing women and what I was learning. Of course Elaine had set me up for this. She had been active in the southern civil rights movement, working in voter registration and marching on Washington. She was one who went where her conscience compelled her to go, and she instilled that in all of us. She is the one who taught us that the YWCA was a place where we could follow our conscience without censure, and that we could gain skills and knowledge by being with older women, younger women, women from all over the United States, who bring their own life experiences to the issues of oppression. She taught us that we could deal simultaneously with issues of racism and sexism as a single issue, without having to choose.

Just about anyplace we went outside of the YWCA, we were told we had to choose. Shortly after I was elected the National Student chairwoman for the YWCA, there was a meeting of the Washington State Chicano Higher Education Educators. I went with other Chicano students and participated in the meeting. Of course all the elected leaders were men. They took me aside and told me, "We think it's not in the best interest of our community for you to be associated as a leader with the YWCA. Will you resign?" They were trying to dictate, to tell me that they thought I should work with my own community. I didn't take very well to that. In fact, it made me angry. Who were they to tell me anything? The need for us to work with our own people was brought up in the meeting. Only one woman stood up and spoke on my behalf, and she was also associated with the YWCA. She pointed out the role that Dorothy Height played in furthering the concerns of the black community, not only in her leadership role with the YWCA, but in the National Council of Negro Women as well. She tried to make the point that we needed to be everywhere, not cloistered in only our groups. I was really angry. At least I kept my head so that I didn't swear at these men, but I did stand up and talk about the leadership that I had provided and continued to provide in the Chicano community in the state of Washington, in the student movement, and with my family. I hoped that they would use the opportunity of my being an officer in the YWCA to further whatever interests we had that were national in scope. It was a very, very quiet ride back from Yakima to Pullman. It was just silent. The woman who spoke on my behalf was the daughter of one of the Chicano faculty at Washington State University. After we got back, her father yelled at her and read her the riot act. I couldn't even talk to these people, because I knew if I did we'd say things that would irreparably damage our relationship. So I just stayed away. That's when the YWCA became my primary focus and involvement. Attending the Women of Color meeting, being involved in the national conventions of the Y, and willingly seeking election to be one of the twelve representatives to the World Council of the YWCA made it clear where my direction needed to be, and that was with women of color in a place where I could deal with racism and sexism as a single issue.

My first job after I graduated and got my degree was as the director of the Upward Bound program at Washington State University. In just ten years I had moved from being an Upward Bound student to the directorship of an Upward Bound program. My job as director was to get in my car and go to the Yakima Valley to recruit Mexican and Native American students so that they would have opportunities to learn and get some skills, and to support them to stay in high school and graduate. It was an experience of déjà vu.

Since then, all my jobs have focused on issues of equity and justice. People pay me to do what I did for years as a volunteer in the YWCA and in my communities. That is an extraordinary gift, to be able to have a vocation that also represents my avocation. I pinch myself and say, "People pay me to do this!" But I got there through the nurturing and support of so many women, and a few key men, especially my husband. His encouragement, his support, and his belief in the things that have been important to me made it possible for me to to look for the kind of jobs that enable me to do my heart work for money.

When I think about younger women today, I realize we have to do what our mentors and coaches did as well. Those of us who have been gifted by other women need to give those gifts back. That involves providing options for women, so that they see that there are many ways of doing things, and that they can do them in the style that is comfortable for them. We can provide many more models of leadership, many more opportunities for learning than the traditional leadership training that is provided to young men and to the women who have forced their way into these training environments. I think that all women need to be affirmed and validated for the gifts that they have. Mentoring is an incremental process in which you accept people where they are, affirm that which they have confidence in, and by doing so enable them to challenge themselves, to stretch in places where they are not as comfortable. I had a wonderful opportunity to do that for almost twenty years in higher education. But it's also done in our churches, it's done in our communities, it's done where we work, and it just means taking the time and being intentional about finding those women who have a hunger, a spark, a fire, that will multiply the success and progress that we make where we are.

The opportunities for younger women today are numerous, but they are not so obvious as they were when we were young. Before, with all the demonstrations and with all the overt organizational activity that was going on, there were many more opportunities visible. But that was a different time. Everybody was joining and participating. When any three people gathered in any place, there were bound to be ten more who joined just out of curiosity. That's not the case now. Now, I think we have to be much more intentional about building programs for coaching and mentoring that lift up where those opportunities are for women. In the current economic situation, the focus is, How do I survive? How do I do my work and do it in a way that can sustain myself and my family? I'm a living example that you can do both. You can sustain your family, you can live a very integrated life by finding that job that truly makes it possible for you to continue to pursue your passions and your ideals and make a difference, make a contribution to the whole, whether it be your organization or community.

I felt that recently when I served as the mistress of ceremonies for the Washington State Governor's Diversity Celebration. What I was celebrating was my life. I was celebrating people coming together, making progress on issues that were central to all of us. Standing there with Governor Lowry and having my director from Labor and Industries be a recipient of an award lifted up the congruity in my life. That was some celebration. My two sisters, a brother, a sister-in-law, a brother-in-law, my ten-year-old twin niece and nephew were there leading the song "We Are Family." This is an old song that's been used in a lot of peace group activities. The words to the song are: "We are family, we are too close not to let it be/we are sister, we are brother, we are a coat of many colors/we are one." That was the closing song for this event. Because we were transitioning to a new administration in the state, my comment, both as an introduction and as a closing, was that we have been involved in a joyful struggle. The struggle in this case had been to pull together what we knew we must do for affirmative action and what we desired to do in our ideals for diversity for our state throughout our agencies and our schools, our higher education institutions. That has been the struggle. The joy has been the relationships we've developed with each other. And that will go on.

NOTES ON CONTRIBUTORS

CHARLOTTE BUNCH, Executive Director of the Center for Women's Global Leadership at Rutgers University, is a Distinguished Professor in the Women's and Gender Studies Department. The author of numerous essays and editor of nine anthologies, she was inducted into the National Women's Hall of Fame in 1996 and received the White House Eleanor Roosevelt Award for Human Rights in 1999.

SARA M. EVANS has taught women's history since 1976 at the University of Minnesota, where she is now a Distinguished McKnight University Professor. She is the author of several books, including *Personal Politics: The Roots of Women's Liberation in the Civil Rights Movement and the New Left* (1979), *Born for Liberty: A History of Women in America* (1989), and *Tidal Wave: How Women Changed America at Century's End* (2003).

REV. JAN GRIESINGER is a sixty-year-old lesbian feminist from Athens, Ohio. She cofounded and lives at the Susan B. Anthony Memorial UnRest Home Women's Land Trust, a feminist education center, women's campground, and intentional community. Griesinger was ordained to ministry in the United Church of Christ in 1970 and is the Director of United Campus Ministry at Ohio University. She is also the National Coordinator of CLOUT, Christian Lesbians OUT.

ALICE HAGEMAN is an ordained minister in the Presbyterian Church (USA) and an attorney. Currently she is a parish associate at a Presbyterian church in South Boston and a U.S. Trustee for the World Student Christian Federation.

Since moving to Boston in 1971 she has practiced law in a community-based practice in Roxbury and taught at Harvard Divinity School, where she helped initiate the Women and Religion Program. She is the editor of *Religion in Cuba Today: A New Church in a New Society* and *Sexist Religion and Women in the Church: No More Silence!*

RUTH M. HARRIS was for more than thirty years executive staff of the United Methodist Board of Global Ministries in international program areas such as university world, urban-rural poor people's movements, development and planning, and global justice. An ecumenical Christian active in National Council of Churches committees, she has had especially strong solidarity ties with Philippine human rights movements and the WSCF Women's Commission. She remains actively involved as a resident of Pilgrim Place retirement community, Claremont, California.

JILL HULTIN is an organizational consultant whose primary focus has been improving the quality of health and mental health services to underserved populations. She has helped create and sustain a number of not-for-profit organizations, and is active on the board of Coro, a national leadership organization. Filmmaking is still her passion, and she continues to look for good stories.

TAMELA HULTMAN is a founder of AllAfrica Global Media, an African ICT (information and communications technology) group. Partnering with over one hundred African media organizations, AllAfrica produces the websites allAfrica.com and sustainableAfrica.org and operates the Charlayne Hunter-Gault Fellowship for African Journalists. Dr. Hultman was the founding director of the Center for Africa and the Media at Duke University and has reported, edited, and produced for national and international media, including the *New York Times*, the *Washington Post*, CNN, National Public Radio, and the BBC.

FRANCES E. KENDALL has continued to work in the ways that she learned from her mentors and leaders in the National Student YWCA—for the last twenty-five years she has consulted to colleges and universities across the country on organizational change for social justice, institutional racism, and white privilege. The second edition of her book *Diversity in the Classroom* was published in 1996, and she is currently working on a book on white privilege. She lives in the San Francisco Bay Area.

RENETIA MARTIN is the Director of the Women's Health Collaborative, a state-wide partnership of women representing California's diverse communities, working to improve access to quality health care for low-income and women of color. Renetia is a licensed clinical social worker and has worked for more than twenty-five years in health care for underserved communities. She is a published author and a frequent keynote speaker on nonprofit leadership and continues to work with the Berkeley YWCA. She would like to thank Jane Zones for helping her write down such tender thoughts about a period so potent in her life and for being such a good friend.

SHEILA MCCURDY is a United Methodist pastor currently serving a church in Baltimore County, Maryland. She and her congregation are working to develop a multicultural ministry. She is a former national president of the Methodist Federation for Social Action.

MARGARITA MENDOZA DE SUGIYAMA is Director of Consumer Services in the Washington State Attorney General's office. She has worked in public service for more than a quarter century in Washington State and Idaho supporting five governors, a college president, and four department directors. Margarita's lifelong personal and professional goals have focused on creating greater access to educational opportunities and governmental services for underserved populations. Born in Yakima, Washington, to a farmworker family, Margarita is the second oldest of eleven children.

ELEANOR SCOTT MEYERS is a retired theological educator and former president of the Pacific School of Religion. Earlier she was on the faculty at Union Theological Seminary in New York City. She is an author of children's literature and looks forward to pursuing this new passion for writing and illustrating books for young people.

ELMIRA KENDRICKS NAZOMBE is Program Director of the Center for Global Women's Leadership at Rutgers University, where she works on leadership development and human rights education. She has worked over the years for many different church and social justice organizations on issues of racial and economic justice.

REBECCA OWEN was a clinical psychologist for more than two decades in New York City, serving those afflicted with drug addiction and AIDS as well as survivors of sexual abuse and war. She came to New York seeking refuge from the South, where as a college student she was arrested at a sit-in at a segregated lunch counter in her native Virginia. As a young mother she fought for affordable child care for the poor and worked in staff positions related to the student Christian movement. Rebecca Owen died on July 19, 2002.

JEANNE AUDREY POWERS is a retired United Methodist clergywoman, now living in Minneapolis. For twenty-eight years, she lived in New York City and worked on the national staff of her denomination in its ecumenical office. She serves on a number of national boards, including those of Garrett-Evangelical Seminary, the Re-Imagining Community, the United Methodist Reconciling Congregations Program, and the Center for Lesbian and Gay Studies in Religion and Ministry of the Pacific School of Religion.

NANCY RICHARDSON is Associate Dean for Ministry at Harvard Divinity School. She is ordained in the United Church of Christ. Her professional work has been in campus and urban ministry, community organizing, theological education, and antiracism work.

LETTY M. RUSSELL is Professor of Theology Emerita at Yale Divinity School in New Haven, Connecticut. Ordained as a Presbyterian minister in 1958, she was a pastor in the East Harlem Protestant Parish in New York City for many years. She is an advocate for women in the ecumenical movement, having worked with the World Council of Churches, WARC, and the World YWCA. She chaired the International Connections Committee of the American Academy of Religion from 1993 to 1996.

INDEX

abolition movement, 2
abortion, 197–198, 219, 222
ACT, 153
Africa: Christian Citizenship Seminars
on, 33–35, 91; Frontier Intern
program in, 98–102, 154–155; study/
travel seminar in, 148–149
African American students: discrimina-
tion against, 90, 163; Duke protests,
226, 230, 234–235; in sit-in
movement, 17, 75–76, 89–90; SVM
recruitment of, 16; in Wesley
Foundation, 88–89, 90–91; at WSCF
Denver conference, 71; in YWCA, 8,
245
Africa News Service, 102, 155
African National Congress, 154
Alinsky, Saul, 115, 161
AllAfrica Global Media, 155–156
Altizer, Thomas, 56
American Friends Service Committee,
52
American Youth Hostels (AYH), 47–49
Angola, 33–34, 57, 91
antiwar movement, 1, 7–8, 116, 129,
216–217; campus demonstrations,
216–217; campus ministry and, 62–
63, 231; civil disobedience and
arrest, 193–194; Committee of
Returned Volunteers, 13, 183–184;

draft resistance sit-in, 193-194;
Fellowship of Reconciliation, 97-98;
Mobilization against the War, 231-
232; Vietnam Summer, 193
Arce, Sergio, 182, 187
Are You Running with Me, Jesus?
(Boyd), 57
Argentina, WSCF Assembly in, 36–37,
95, 108
Association Chrétian des Étudiants
(ACE), 178
Athens (Ohio): Ecumenical Student
Conferences in, 5, 6, 15, 16–17, 29,
59, 74, 89, 107–108, 126, 179;
quadrennial conferences in, 5, 15–
16, 90, 93–94, 126, 133
Auden, W.H., 190
Austin, Alice, 136–137

Baez, Joan, 152, 232
Baillie, John, 57
Baker, Ella, 227
Barnes, Lillas Reid, 246, 256, 260, 268
Barrosso, Carmen, 181, 187
Barth, Karl, 178
Bates, Searle, 178
Beaumont, Geoffrey, 58
Beecher, Lyman, 84
Benedict, Bobbie, 124
Bennett, John, 178

Bentley, Mary Edith, 77, 80
Bevel, Jim, 96
Beyond God the Father (Daly), 218
Bible Speaks to You, The (Brown), 56
Bidol, Patricia, 256
Biko, Steve, 154
Billings, Peggy, 3, 39, 41, 128, 130
black colleges: in Methodist Student
    Movement, 161; YWCA conferences
    at, 228-229
black power movement, 8, 62, 117
black students. *See* African American
    students
Blake, Eugene Carson, 41
Bonhoeffer, Dietrich, 4, 7, 70, 78, 81,
    89
Boraine, Alex, 154
Borges, Jorge Luis, 109
Boston-Cambridge Ministries in Higher
    Education, 235
Boston University School of Theology
    (BUSTH), 52–53, 235
Boyd, Malcolm, 57
Boyte, Harry, 153
Braden, Carl, 79
Brancel, Fred, 34, 57
Brandenburg, Art, 125
Brazil, 37–38, 95–96, 109–110
Brown, Amy Porter, 39
Brown, H. Rap, 151
Brown, Robert McAfee, 56
Brown v. Board of Education, 140, 227
Bunch, Charlotte, 9, 10, 122–139,
    201, 206, 271; in antiwar move-
    ment, 129; with Center for
    Women's Global Leadership, 14,
    103, 122; in community organiz-
    ing, 131; early influences on, 122–
    124; at Ecumenical Student
    Conference, 126; at Institute for
    Policy Studies, 133–134, 136; in
    Japan, 127; in Methodist Student
    Movement, 124–125, 126–127,
    144; in Selma march, 12, 41, 96,
    112, 128; sexual identity of, 138–
    139; in University Christian

Movement, 13, 117, 131–133, 137,
    150; in women's liberation
    movement, 14, 134–135, 136; at
    World Council of Churches'
    Geneva conference, 130–132; on
    WSCF Executive Committee, 135,
    138; at WSCF General Assembly,
    135; in YWCA, 124, 129, 146, 231

Caldwell, Doris, 20, 26
Camara, Dom Helder, 37–38, 95
Campbell, Dennis, 144
campus ministry, 4; activities of, 206–
    207; antiwar movement and, 62–63,
    231; Ecumenical Foundation for
    Higher Education, 183, 185;
    subversive, 229-230; United
    Ministries in Higher Education, 189,
    220; women's conferences, 199;
    women's organizations, 199, 201,
    206, 221; WSCF Women's Project
    and, 198-206. *See also* Wesley
    Foundation
Campus Ministry Women, 201–205, 221
Camus, Albert, 4, 174, 252
Canadian Student Christian Movement,
    203
Cantate Domine, 58
Caribbean Student Christian Movement,
    168-169
Carper, Elsie, 77
Carstens, Ken, 94
Carter, Jimmy, 188
Carter, Sydney, 58
Castro, Fidel, 182
Catholic Campus Ministry Association,
    205
Center for Women's Global Leadership,
    14, 102–103, 122
Chavez, Cesar, 264
Cheney, James, 61
China, 20–26, 72
Chipenda, Eva, 155
Chipenda, Jose, 91, 100, 101, 155
Christian Citizenship Seminars, 7, 33–
    36, 60, 91, 108

Peace Corps, 99, 168, 179; Committee of Returned Volunteers, 13, 183–184
Peking Language School, 22
Peking National University, 22–23
Phillips, J.B., 56
Poppendieck, Jan, 130, 144
Powers, Jeanne Audrey, 3–4, 10, 13, 45–65, 94, 274; campus ministry of, 53–59, 62–64, 229; in Danforth Graduate Program, 49-50; early influences on, 45–47; hosteling trip of, 45–47; with Methodist Student Movement, 53, 57, 59–63; ordination of, 53; in seminary, 50–53; sexual identity of, 3–4, 64–65
pray-ins, 12
Presbyterian Church: Frontier Intern program and, 38, 39, 99, 153, 177, 179; study/travel seminar and, 148
Presence magazine, 101
Prestwood, Charles, 162, 164
Preuss, Robert, 185
Princeton Theological Seminary, 50–53
Process '67, 133
Proudfoot, Wayne, 33, 94
Purdue MYF conference, 68

Quoist, Michel, 57

Ramparts, 184
Randolph Macon Woman's College, 30, 70, 71, 74, 75, 80
Reagan, Ronald, 188
Red Bird Mission, 60
Redenbaugh, Eula, 260
Religion in Cuba Today, 187
Response magazine, 31
Rhodes, Lynn, 199
Richards, Joan, 101
Richardson, Gloria, 151
Richardson, Nancy, 3, 10, 12, 151, 226–236, 274; antiracism work of, 233–235, 255; in antiwar movement, 231–232; early influences on, 226–227; racism, experience of, 227–228; in seminary, 229-230; theological

education posts of, 235-236; University Christian Movement and, 232; in women's liberation movement, 231; with YWCA, 150, 226, 230, 233
Rigg, Margaret "Peg", 3, 37, 92, 95, 108, 109
Rinker, Charles, 41, 91, 94, 96, 112, 126, 131, 161
Rinker, Lori, 91, 131
Robinson, David, 129
Robinson, John, 56
Robinson, Sunny, 255
Rockefeller, Nelson, 267
Roe v. Wade, 219, 222
Roosevelt, Eleanor, 27, 28–29, 81
Russell, Letty M., 177, 183, 189, 237–239, 274
Russell, Valerie, 3, 8, 10, 233, 237–239, 257
Rust College, 60

safe houses, 220
St. Paul Wesley Foundation, 53–55, 60
Sale, Nell, 137
Sartre, Jean-Paul, 4
Scarritt College, 19–20, 74
Schaull, Richard, 15–16
Schmemann, Alexander, 107–108, 192
Schomberg, Steve, 133
Schomer, Elsie and Howard, 98
school desegregation, 212
Schwerner, Michael, 61
Scott, Anne, 130
Seattle Coalition Task Force on Women and Religion, 199
Secular City, The (Cox), 56
Seeger, Pete, 152, 232
Selma march, 12, 39–43, 44, 61, 96–97, 112-114, 128, 163–165
"separate spheres" ideology, 3
settlement house movement, 2
Sexist Religion and Women in the Church: No More Silence (Hageman), 13, 189
Seymour, Betty Jean, 227, 228–229
Shaull, Richard, 135